About the Editors

Bill Cooke is director of the MA programme in Development Administration and Management at the Institute for Development Policy and Management, University of Manchester. He teaches change management, organizational behaviour and development management, researches into the history of development and management, and works internationally as a consultant. He began his career in the public sector, and was a partner in a management consultancy in Britain before becoming an academic in 1992.

Uma Kothari is a lecturer in Social Development at the Institute for Development Policy and Management, University of Manchester. She has carried out research and consultancy work in various parts of the world including India, Mauritius and Egypt. She is currently co-director of a DfID-funded project, Social Development: Systems for Co-ordinated Poverty Eradication, and co-researcher on a project on migrant workers and Export Processing Zones.

About this Book

A timely critique of the participation discourse and exposé of the seductive arts of official incorporation. Essential reading for all those studying and practising international development as well as social policy nearer home. *Geoff Wood, Professor of International Development and Director of the Institute for International Policy Analysis at the University of Bath*

This volume unmasks the moral tyranny imposed through the language of participation which has come to dominate the discourse of 'devspeak'. In exploring participatory practices from several points of view – social psychology, sociology of management, Goffman's analysis of social performance, Foucauldian analysis of discourses and their power – it shows how radical and democratic language may be co-opted with the aim of bringing people's views and expectations into line with the plans devised, with their participation, by their betters. Makes a vital contribution to the sociology of development. *Gavin Williams, University of Oxford*

Contents

Boxes, Tables and Figures

Boxes

Tables

Figure

Acknowledgements

First, we would like to thank those directly involved in the production of this book. The contributors not only kept their nerve and agreed to contribute to a book that challenges a prevailing orthodoxy, but by and large kept to agreed deadlines, no mean achievement these days. Our editor at Zed, Robert Molteno, has been of great support, and Karen Hunt here at the Institute for Development Policy and Management (IDPM), University of Manchester, helped considerably in the production of the manuscript. We would also like to thank IDPM as a collective for making it easy for us to set up the conference that preceded this book, and all the contributors to, and participants in, that conference. Phil Woodhouse of IDPM was also involved at that stage, and his help then and subsequently is gratefully acknowledged.

A number of people, working in NGOs, in bilateral and multilateral agencies, in universities and as 'beneficiaries' of participatory development processes, have contacted us while this book has been in production to make suggestions and to voice their support. This encouragement, often given in confidence, has been invaluable to us, affirming that this book is needed. We would also like to thank our students at IDPM, particularly, but by no means solely, those on the MA Development Administration and Management and the MA Social Policy and Social Development programmes, who, on the basis of their personal and professional experiences of participatory development, have been more than willing to challenge both the participatory orthodoxy and our critiques of it. The seriousness of their engagement with us, and their underlying interest in what the book is saying, helped us sustain the enthusiasm needed to produce this volume.

We would like to thank Francesca Gains and Tim Edensor for their love and support and for their insightful comments on drafts of our chapters.

Finally, we would like to thank the 'participants' in the workshops and other participatory processes in which we have been involved. In particular, our gratitude is due to those awkward participants who have made our role as 'facilitators' uncomfortable, by asking difficult questions, by challenging the process, by refusing to go along with consensus, by questioning our legitimacy as facilitators, or just by remaining silent.

An earlier version of Frances Cleaver's Chapter 3 appeared as 'Paradoxes of participation: questioning participatory approaches to development' in *Journal of International Development*, Vol. 11, No. 4, 1999. Copyright John Wiley and Sons Limited. Reproduced with permission.

List of Contributors

Frances Cleaver is a senior lecturer at the Development and Project Planning Centre, University of Bradford, specializing in gender and water projects, and social capital and participatory projects.

Paul Francis is a social anthropologist and senior lecturer at the School of Development Studies, University of East Anglia.

John Hailey is deputy director of Oxford Brookes University Business School, and was a founder of the Oxford-based International NGO Training and Research Centre (INTRAC).

Pandurang Hegde has worked with the Chipko-Appiko movement for the past two decades to protect the tropical forests of Western Ghats, in southern India, and currently works on the sustainable use of tropical forests.

Heiko Henkel was educated in Germany, Denmark and the UK before going to Princeton, where he is presently a doctoral candidate researching in Turkey.

Nicholas Hildyard has been working on environment and development issues since the 1970s. He currently works with the Corner House, a UK-based research and solidarity group.

Giles Mohan is a senior research fellow in the Department of Geography at the University of Portsmouth. His research concerns the likelihood of local interventions producing sustainable development.

David Mosse teaches anthropology at the School of Oriental and African Studies, University of London, and has worked as a researcher and consultant on participatory rural development in India.

Somasekhare Reddy works with local communities on the consolidation and adaptation of village institutions to manage communal natural resources, and is a research fellow of the Institute of Management in Bangalore.

Roderick Stirrat is a reader in Social Anthropology at the University of Sussex, specializing in the anthropology of religion and the anthropology of development.

Harry Taylor is a lecturer in Human Resources at the Institute for Development Policy and Management, specializing in the application of HRM concepts in the Third World.

Paul Wolvekamp has been an affiliate of the Amsterdam-based organization Both Ends for nearly ten years. His main interest is the recognition of the priorities of local people in environmental management and 'development'.

Abbreviations

AKRSP	Aga Khan Rural Support Programme
AR	Action Research
BA	Beneficiary Assessment
BAIF	Bhartiya Agro-Industries Foundation
BRAC	Bangladesh Rural Advancement Committee
DfID	Department of International Development
EA	Environmental Assessment
EIP	Employee Involvement and Participation
FSR	Farming Systems Research
IDPM	Institute for Development Policy and Management
ITK	Indigenous Technical Knowledge
HRM	Human Resource Management
JFM	Joint Forest Management
JFPM	Joint Forest Planning and Management
KFD	Karnataka State Forest Department
KRIBP	Kribhco Indo-British Farming Project
NGO	non-governmental organization
ODA	Overseas Development Administration
PAR	Participatory Action Research
PLA	Participatory Learning Analysis
PRA	Participatory Rural Appraisal
RRA	Rapid Rural Appraisal
SA	Social Assessment
SWC	soil and water conservation
VFC	Village Forest Committee

TO JAY, KIM AND KITTY

1

The Case for Participation as Tyranny

Bill Cooke and Uma Kothari

The Purpose of this Book

This book follows on from a conference with the same title held at the Institute for Development Policy and Management at the University of Manchester, organized by the two editors of this book and our colleague Phil Woodhouse. At a very basic level the impetus for the conference came from our growing discomfort at the dissonance between a number of conversations we had been having, which we were aware were also taking place elsewhere, and the received wisdom about the overwhelming benefits of participation in development.

These private conversations were with other participatory practitioners and with 'participants', and with people outside or on the margins of development and Development Studies. The conversations with practitioners and participants were often characterized by a mildly humorous cynicism, with which tales were told of participatory processes undertaken ritualistically, which had turned out to be manipulative, or which had in fact harmed those who were supposed to be empowered. The conversations with disciplinary outsiders, on the other hand, were typified by an irritation, at times bordering on anger, at the way in which a conceptually isolationist participatory development establishment had chosen to ignore the challenges posed by their particular understandings and analyses of participatory orthodoxy.

Despite our participation in these conversations we found ourselves, in our roles as workers in the development industry, more often than not promoting and perpetuating the received wisdom. Of course, as academics, we claimed that our work was informed by a critical understanding of participatory development. However, the criticisms we raised were often at the level of problems of technique, or about how the practitioner should operate. We did not do justice to the scale or depth of the criticisms and concerns being voiced privately, nor could we see, in the practice of participatory development, many others doing so (although there have been, as we note below, admirable exceptions). We came to realize that the very difference between private and public accounts of participatory development was in itself cause for concern.

Our primary aim with this book is to provide a set of more rigorous and critical insights into the participatory development discourse than has hitherto been the case, through a conceptual and ideological examination of its theory, methods and practices. There are four reasons for doing this through a book. First, we wanted to provide a stimulus that would help the conversations mentioned above develop as arguments in terms of depth and rigour. Second, we wanted these arguments to be put on the record. This is not just because they are of value in their own right, but because for all the rhetoric of 'handing over the stick', authority and the ability to have one's position taken seriously in participatory development appear to be closely related to the power to publish. Third, we wanted to provide an arena where the hitherto marginalized voices of practitioners and of those outside the orthodoxy could assemble and, it was hoped, in (metaphorically) speaking together, increase their chances of being heard. Fourth, while we knew that the chapters in the book reflected a diversity of authorial experiences and perspectives, we suspected that alongside this diversity and difference common themes would emerge. We wanted to demonstrate the different strands of the critique and at the same time show the ways in which together they provide a serious and fundamental challenge to participatory approaches and demand at best their rethinking, if not their abandonment.

This introduction will map out, on a chapter by chapter basis, how this diversity of perspectives on participation challenges the participatory development orthodoxy. It will also identify what for us, as editors, are the common and mutually reinforcing themes among the chapters (recognizing that there are others that other contributors and readers will identify). But before we do this, however, we want to explain – and justify – our use of the word 'tyranny' in the title. Building on this explanation we then want to acknowledge that the orthodoxy is not without its own reflexive self-criticism. This is, however, limited in scale and scope, and serves, perhaps unintentionally, to pre-empt more profound critique, as the contrast with the subsequent summary of the individual chapters demonstrates.

Why Tyranny?

Our choice of title was, in part, a sharp reaction to the humorous, almost light-hearted way in which we expressed our unease with participatory approaches to development. This, we came to feel, was serving as a release valve that enabled us, and perhaps other practitioners too, to articulate and share worries about participatory development, and at the same time minimize their significance. That we behaved in this way reflected, perhaps, a tacit anxiety about the consequences of having to challenge a set of practices to which the major development institutions, powerful individuals within them, and perhaps most importantly, people who are good friends of ours, are committed. These potential consequences may of course have been fantasized (we hope so), but it is with some trepidation, reinforced by supportive colleagues who nevertheless advised that we 'be careful', that we now publish this book.

Perhaps our title seems incongruous with this supposed uneasiness, and no doubt we might be accused of letting the irritation and anger we mentioned get the better of us. We are certainly aware that 'Participation: The New Tyranny?' has not endeared us to some in the development world. However, the term 'tyranny' is both necessary and accurate. It is necessary because the manner in which participation has been critiqued, and the language with which this has been done, has clearly thus far failed to affect, qualitatively or quantitatively, the apparently inexorable spread of participation in development. Clearly argued and quite profound analyses, exemplified in the work of Stirrat (1997) or Mosse (1994, 1996) have largely been ignored and have had little or no apparent impact on mainstream discourse and practice. We felt it necessary, therefore, to use language that would be harder to ignore. The accusation that has been levelled – that our use of the word tyranny is attention-seeking – is therefore not without truth. The attention we seek, though, is for the concerns that first led to the conference being set up, and for the arguments set out in the following chapters.

However, although reactions to our initial conference, supportive and otherwise, suggest that our choice of title worked in this respect, it was not used solely to get attention, nor is it simply rhetorical. The term 'tyranny' is also accurate. The arguments presented in this book collectively confirm that tyranny is both a real and a potential consequence of participatory development, counter-intuitive and contrary to its rhetoric of empowerment though this may be. Our choice of the word was influenced by Simon Bell's 1994 article 'Methods and Mindsets: Towards an Understanding of the

Tyranny of Methodology'. While Bell's focus was the transfer of methodologies in development practice generally, he did argue as a case in point (drawing on the work of a contributor to this volume, David Mosse) that rapid and participatory rural appraisals: 'are only as untyrannical ... as the context and the scientist [i.e. the practitioner] are prepared to be, and perhaps more meaningfully are able to be, given the limitations of their own culturally based view of their own methods' (Bell 1994: 332).

The second part of this quote hints at a premise that is central to this book. This is that participatory development's tyrannical potential is systemic, and not merely a matter of how the practitioner operates or the specificities of the techniques and tools employed. We wanted to move away from the methodological revisionism that characterizes the limited self-reflexivity within participatory development and to address more directly how the discourse itself, and not just the practice, embodies the potential for an unjustified exercise of power.

This brings us to what we mean by tyranny. In the *Collins English Dictionary* (1979: 1645), a tyrant is, among other things, 'a person who governs oppressively, unjustly, and arbitrarily ... anything that exercises tyrannical influence ... a ruler whose authority lacked the sanction of law or custom; usurper'; and tyranny 'government by a tyrant or tyrants; despotism ... similarly oppressive and unjust government by more than one person ... arbitrary, unreasonable, or despotic behaviour or use of authority ... any harsh discipline or oppression ... government by a usurper'. In sum, then, tyranny is the illegitimate and/or unjust exercise of power; this book is about how participatory development facilitates this.

The Limits of Internal Critiques

A number of the chapters in this book contain their own accounts of the spread of participatory development. Those of David Mosse (Chapter 2), Frances Cleaver (Chapter 3) and Bill Cooke (Chapter 7), for example, are derived from participatory development's accounts of itself; Paul Francis takes the case of a single institutional setting, the World Bank (Chapter 5); and Heiko Henkel and Roderick Stirrat (Chapter 11) and to a lesser extent John Hailey (Chapter 6) propose a genealogy and a history of participatory development that challenge the orthodox account. Given that this ground is covered, from a number of angles, in subsequent chapters, our consideration of the internal critiques of participatory development and the orthodox history here is brief, and serves to locate the arguments presented in the following chapters.

Participatory development is conventionally represented as emerging out of the recognition of the shortcomings of top-down development approaches. The ineffectiveness of externally imposed and expert-oriented forms of research and planning became increasingly evident in the 1980s, when major donors and development organizations began to adopt participatory research and planning methods. Particularly influential in this trend was the work of Robert Chambers (1983, 1992, 1994a, b, c, 1997), which built from an interest in participatory rural development, and an advocacy of Participatory Rural Appraisal (PRA) to participatory development more generally.

The ostensible aim of participatory approaches to development was to make 'people' central to development by encouraging beneficiary involvement in interventions that affect them and over which they previously had limited control or influence. Thus, 'the broad aim of participatory development is to increase the involvement of socially and economically marginalized peoples in decision-making over their own lives' (Guijt 1998: 1). Similarly, the World Bank (1994) saw participation as a process through which stakeholders influence and share control over development initiatives, decisions and resources that affect their lives. This recognition and support for greater involvement of 'local' people's perspectives, knowledge, priorities and skills presented an alternative to donor-driven and outsider-led development and was rapidly and widely adopted by individuals and organizations. Participatory approaches to development, then, are justified in terms of sustainability, relevance and empowerment.

There have recently been a number of reviews and critiques of populist participatory approaches (Bastian and Bastian 1996; Mosse 1994; Nelson and Wright 1995; IIED 1995). These take two main forms: those that focus on the technical limitations of the approach and stress the need for a re-examination of the methodological tools used, for example in PRA, and those that pay more attention to the theoretical, political and conceptual limitations of participation.

From within the orthodoxy, there is an espousal of ongoing 'self-critical epistemological awareness', which for Chambers (1997: 32) is an essential component of participatory ideology and practice. As McGee (forthcoming) suggests, 'this generates an ongoing dialogue between practitioners on the quality, validity and ethics of what they are doing, which is intended to guard against slipping standards, poor practice, abuse or exploitation of the people involved'. Such continual reflexivity and self-critique by the practitioner do not represent a critique of participatory methodology *per se*, however, but are seen more as intrinsic facets of the approach itself. In this way, the methodological and practical problems of the approach are supposed to be recognized, highlighted and subsequently addressed. Participatory approaches are presented as flexible and continuously evolving in the light of problems of application and adapting to specific contexts. This, it is claimed, has led to significant methodological adjustments being made to the approach, encouraged by the continual need for introspection.

These critiques focus primarily on definitional differences and debates over the objectives of participation, i.e. whether it is a means or an end, and the applicability and appropriateness of the techniques and tools used (see Nelson and Wright 1995). There are other critiques of participation, particularly focusing on PRA, which, rather than demanding greater reflexivity *per se*, require that it be cognizant of issues of diversity and differentiation. In their book *The Myth of Community* Guijt and Shah (1998) question the use of the term 'community' in PRA discourse, arguing that simplistic understandings of 'communities' see them as homogeneous, static and harmonious units within which people share common interests and needs. This articulation of the notion of 'community', they argue, conceals power relations within 'communities' and further masks biases in interests and needs based on, for example, age, class, caste, ethnicity, religion and gender. Andrea Cornwall also encourages practitioners to question their assumptions about gender differences in particular societies and to find out what categories of difference are appropriate and relevant to people and, more specifically, what it means to be a man or a woman in a given context (Cornwall 1998).

Further concerns and reflections of participatory techniques were highlighted in a special issue of *PLA Notes* on 'Critical Reflections from Practice' (IIED 1995). The editorial suggests that:

> We have come full circle. PRA started as a critical response to the inadequacy of existing research and planning processes. Yet many of the concerns discussed here focus precisely on the inadequacy of local participation in the process ... By reflecting critically on what we do, we can learn from our mistakes and move forward. (Guijt and Cornwall 1995: 7)

Much of the analysis presented in this issue of *PLA Notes* takes us to what might be seen as the border between the orthodoxy and more critical positions. So do some of the more infrequent conceptual and political challenges to the approach, which demonstrate how participation can result in political co-option, and can require contributions from participants in the form of labour, cash or kind and thus transfer some of the project costs on to beneficiaries, and those who challenge the rhetoric of participation, arguing that it masks continued centralization in the name of decentralization (see Biggs and Smith 1998; Mosse 1994; Stirrat 1997).

We recognize, therefore, that distinguishing where critiques from within the orthodoxy end, and critiques of that orthodoxy *per se* begin, is difficult. Furthermore, not only is the boundary blurred, but we should be wary of the dichotomous thinking to which Henkel and Stirrat alert us in Chapter 11, which masks nuance, difference within, and exchanges between, the categories of ideas. It is certainly the case, and we are proud of the fact, that the contributions in this volume do not present a unified and singular challenge to participation. Opinions diverge, for example, on what fundamental flaws there are, the implications they have, and/or the extent to which they require a total revisioning of participatory development; to lump the contributors to this volume together as opposed to participation would be mistaken stereotyping.

However, we are also clear as editors that our objective for this volume as a whole is not simply to rehearse the methodological limitations of participation that have been addressed elsewhere. Indeed, for us the time has come to ask whether the constant methodological revisionism to which some of us have contributed (e.g. Cooke 1998), has obscured the more fundamental problems within the discourse, and whether internal critiques have served to legitimize the participatory project rather than present it with a real challenge. The aim here, therefore, is to move beyond an identification of technocratic limitations of, and adjustments to, the methodology to more fundamental critiques of the discourse of participation, and to recognize that some of these do emerge out of technocratic concerns. The question that stands out, however, is how many such concerns need to be raised before participatory development itself comes to be seen as the real problem? Essentially, our problem at this stage of the development of participatory approaches and their application lies not with the methodology and the techniques but with the politics of the discourse, and, as Henkel and Stirrat's final chapter states, with what participatory development does as much as what it does not do.

What the Book Says

Early on, when we were organizing the conference, three particular sets of tyrannies were identified. First was what we called 'the tyranny of decision-making and control', where we asked in the conference flyer 'Do participatory facilitators override existing legitimate decision-making processes?' Second was 'the tyranny of the group' – where the question posed was 'Do group dynamics lead to participatory decisions that reinforce the interests of the already powerful?' Third, we raised the issue of the 'tyranny of method', asking 'Have participatory methods driven out others which have advantages participation cannot provide?' As we will go on to see, between them, the chapters in this book suggest that the answer to each of these questions is, or can be in some circumstances, 'Yes'. In this book, however, the first two of these questions are more strongly addressed, or at least more explicitly stated than the last, although John Hailey's Chapter 6 does explore how, and suggests reasons as to why, some NGOs have avoided the tyranny of the method. Together, however, the chapters show just how methodologically parochial the participatory development discourse is.

David Mosse in Chapter 2 challenges the populist assumption that attention to 'local knowledge' through participatory learning will redefine the relationship between local communities and development organizations. Using project-based illustrations, he shows that 'local knowledge', far from determining planning processes and outcomes, is often structured by them. For example, what in one case was expressed as a 'local need' was actually shaped by local perceptions of what the agency in question could legitimately and realistically be expected to deliver. Indeed, 'participatory planning' may, more accurately, be viewed as the acquisition and manipulation of a new 'planning knowledge' rather than the incorporation of 'people's knowledge' by projects.

Mosse then shows how participatory ideals are often operationally constrained by institutional contexts that require formal and informal bureaucratic goals to be met. Participation nevertheless remains important as part of a project as a 'system of representations'. As such, ideas of participation are oriented towards concerns that are external to project locations. These representations do not necessarily speak directly to local practice and provide little by way of guidance on project implementation, but they are important in negotiating relationships with donors, and more widely in underpinning positions within development policy debates.

In Chapter 3 Frances Cleaver also makes use of case studies, here in relation to water resource usage. The chapter begins by questioning 'the heroic claims made for development', and by presenting the case for understanding the role of social structure and of individual agency in shaping participation. Participatory development, Cleaver suggests, tends to conflate social structures with institutions, most commonly conceptualized as organizations, not least because such institutions apparently make social structures 'legible'. However, participatory development bureaucracies have preferences for institutional arrangements that may not correspond with those of 'participants'. Problems identified include an espousal of the importance of informal institutions while actual concentration is on the formal; the varying forms of participation that different institutional types require; the questionable assumptions about 'community' upon which participatory institution-building is based; and the tendency towards foundationalism about local communities.

The chapter goes on to consider the inadequacy of participatory approaches' models of individual agency and the links between these and social structures. The argument presented here is that understandings of the motivations of individuals to participate, or not, are vague, and simplistic assumptions are made about the rationality inherent in participating, and the irresponsibility of not doing so. Furthermore, participatory approaches fail to recognize how the different, changing and multiple identities of individuals impact upon their choices about whether and how to participate, and overlook the potential links between inclusion in participatory processes and subordination.

Chapter 4, by Nicholas Hildyard, Pandurang Hegde, Paul Wolvekamp and Somasekhare Reddy, examines, in light of the increasing fashion for participatory forest management, conflicts over the meanings of 'participation' and 'forests'. It begins by suggesting that the failure by donors to implement policies on participation is institutionally deep-seated and structural, and that through participatory development grassroots organizations are in danger of becoming 'the human software through which investments can be made with least local opposition'. It then shows that while participatory forest management arose from institutional and political pressures resulting from popular unrest about the commercial exploitation of forests and local people's exclusion from forest resources, it nevertheless served to maintain that exploitation and exclusion. The chapter demonstrates the further marginalization, loss of livelihoods and increased hardship of already disadvantaged groups as the result of a participatory Joint Forest Management project in which the chapter authors were involved as local activists or staff of Northern-based solidarity groups. The authors conclude by arguing that unless participatory processes take into account the relative bargaining power of so-called stakeholders they are in danger of merely providing opportunities for the more powerful.

In Chapter 5 Paul Francis begins by summarizing the three main approaches to participation employed by the World Bank – Beneficiary Assessment, Social Analysis and PRA – before going on to focus on the last of these. Initially the chapter sets out PRA's methodological and epistemological bases before questioning the relationship between 'the community' and 'the professional', suggesting *inter alia* that the importance of charismatic specialists, who claim a moral position combined with an inner-directedness and the symbolism of 'reversal', recalls the role of the shaman. Francis suggests that PRA is a rite of communion, the performance of which 'enacts an exorcism, of sorts, of the phantoms of "conventional" development practice', and analyses the *World Bank Participation Sourcebook* as 'part self-improvement manual and part mythical text'. At the same time, though, the reductionist simplifications of PRA techniques are noted. Next, Francis considers the uptake of participatory approaches at the Bank within the context of the new emphasis on 'the social' in terms of process, consultation and partnership. He argues that underlying structural determinants of well-being are given little attention and that this is reinforced by the individualist nature of PRA, and the absence of any real alternative vision of development leaves it vulnerable to opportunism and co-option.

In Chapter 6 John Hailey draws on a range of ideas to question the formulaic approaches to participatory decision-making promoted and even imposed by donors and other development actors. These include Hoftstede's work on cross-cultural management, a Foucauldian analysis of power and the discourse of participation, and a recognition of the Cold War uses of community participation. Hailey begins by reviewing recent research into the development and growth of successful South Asian NGOs that suggested that NGO success resulted from the understandings of, and responses to, the needs of the local communities with which they worked. However, the research showed that this closeness to communities arose not from the application of the well-known formulaic approaches to participation – indeed, they were conspicuous by their absence. Rather, as case examples in the chapter illustrate, success was achieved by a long-term effort by NGO leaders to build close personal relationships with individuals and groups in the communities with which they worked, and with NGO staff. The chapter then offers three explanations for the absence of formulaic approaches to participation. The first is that they have real operational limitations, the second is that they are culturally inappropriate, and the third is that their history and the reality of their practice indicate that they might (legitimately) be seen as a means of imposing external control.

In Chapter 7 Bill Cooke uses four concepts from social psychology (risky shift, the Abilene paradox, groupthink and coercive persuasion) to demonstrate how individuals' thoughts, feelings and behaviours are influenced by the presence – real, imagined or implied – of others. These concepts suggest that problems can arise as a consequence of the face-to-face interactions that are a defining feature of participatory development. Taken together the four concepts suggest that participatory processes can lead people to take, first, collective decisions that are more risky than those they would have taken individually (i.e. risky shift). Second, they can lead to people taking a decision that participants have second-guessed is what everyone else wants, when the opposite is the case (the Abilene paradox). Third, particular dynamics, the symptoms of which include a belief in the inherent morality of what is being done, self-censorship, and the existence of 'mindguards', can lead to evidently wrong decisions, which can be harmful to 'outgroup' members (groupthink). Fourth, the manipulation of group processes can lead to malign changes in ideological beliefs, or consciousness (coercive persuasion). All four challenge participatory development's claims for effectiveness and empowerment, and suggest a disciplinary bias that permits the use of a technology on the world's poor without the safeguards that the rich would expect.

In Chapter 8 Harry Taylor challenges Robert Chambers' positive spin on the parallels between participatory development and participatory management. Taylor argues that participation in both cases is part of a wider attempt to influence power relations between elite groups and the less powerful – be they individual project beneficiaries or the employees of organizations in the developed world. He makes his case by first drawing parallels between project beneficiaries and employees within organizations in terms of their relative dependency and powerlessness. Moving on to consider arguments for participation from mainstream management, he suggests that even on its own terms doubts about its feasibility and desirability exist. From a more critical management perspective he then draws on Foucauldian and labour process critiques, which suggest that participation is always constrained, and hides and at the same time perpetuates certain sets of power relations. Taylor rounds off his chapter by suggesting why there is a disillusionment with participation in both development and management arenas, and by speculating on the prospects for 'genuine' participation.

In Chapter 9 Uma Kothari challenges the truth claims made by participatory development. Like Harry Taylor and John Hailey she proposes a Foucauldian approach to the understanding of power, as something which circulates, rather than as something divided between those who have it and those who do not. This latter dichotomous approach typifies participatory development, and leads to practices based in conventional stratifications of power. These serve both to conceal daily oppressions in people's lives that run through every aspect of everyday life and to ensure that participants remain the subject of development surveillance. Although PRA seeks to reveal the realities of this everyday life, paradoxically its public nature means that the more participatory it is, the more the power structure of the local community will be masked. The chapter continues by exploring how participatory research 'cleans up' local knowledge through mapping and codification, and marginalizes that which might challenge the status quo or is messy or unmanageable. The chapter concludes by drawing on the work of Goffman to consider how the ritual practices of PRA actually serve to subvert it, by producing front stage performances that conceal both the 'real' reality of the back stage, and come to be taken for that reality.

In Chapter 10 Giles Mohan has two major aims. The first is to critique participatory practices, in particular the ways in which local knowledge is supposedly produced as a reversal of 'top-down' approaches. This critique is made using the ideas associated with postcolonial studies, and argues that a subtle Eurocentrism pervades the interventions of non-local development workers. By supposedly focusing on the personal and the local as the sites of empowerment and knowledge, participatory approaches minimize the importance of the other places where power and knowledge are located, for example with 'us' in the Western development community, and with the state. The chapter then addresses its second aim, which is to explore the possibility of moving beyond these pitfalls, weaving theoretical observations with a discussion of the work of Village Aid. Mohan calls for a radicalized hybridity, beyond bounded notions of self/other and insider/outsider; and a scaling up of local interventions, linking them to the complex processes of democratization, anti-imperialism and feminism.

Heiko Henkel and Roderick Stirrat's Chapter 11 takes an anthropological approach. They are concerned with the practices, ideas and cosmologies of those who plan and practise 'development projects'. They begin by looking at genealogies of participation, which they identify as being primarily religious, noting that participation was a moral imperative of the Reformation, and tracing this imperative through nineteenth-century British nonconformism to the founding of British development NGOs. The chapter, like Chapter 5, then considers participation as a religious experience, but sees different parallels, particularly in the reversal of binary oppositions that characterize both the work of Robert Chambers and Christian traditions of 'the World turned upside down'. Henkel and Stirrat go on to address the notion of 'empowerment', which they claim may not be as liberating as the new orthodoxy suggests. The question that should be asked, they argue, is not how much people are empowered, but for what. Their own answer to this question is that participatory approaches shape individual identities, 'empowering' participants 'to take part in the modern sector of developing societies'. This empowerment is therefore tantamount, in Foucauldian terms, to subjection.

Is Tyranny Inevitable?

Notwithstanding the critiques in this book, and its title, we would resist being labelled anti-participation. There are acts and processes of participation that we cannot oppose. Some of these, such as sharing knowledge and negotiating power relations, may be part of everyday life; others, such as political activism or engagement in social movements, are about challenges to day-to-day and structural (for want of a better word) oppressions and injustices within societies. But it is also the case that acts and processes of participation described in the same way – sharing knowledge, negotiating power relationships, political activism and so on – can both conceal and reinforce oppressions and injustices in their various manifestations. The chapters in this book demonstrate how this can happen with participatory development, and we have already argued that this is a systemic problem. The question that remains, though, is this: is participatory development inevitably tyrannical?

At the beginning of this Introduction we suggested that previous criticisms of participatory approaches to development have focused primarily on technical limitations of the method and/or on the workings of the practitioner. We did not feel that the depth of concerns being articulated privately were reflected in these earlier discussions and so our initial aim in putting together this volume was to provide a space within which more conceptual and ideological examinations of the theory, method and practices of participatory development could take place. From the vantage point afforded to us as editors, which readers will share having read the book, we are now able to see the way the arguments highlighted in the individual chapters in this volume appear as a whole, and thus what sort of challenge they present to participatory development.

In the individual chapters there are of course divergences in perspectives and differences in the focus; the danger in looking for common themes is that these are lost. However, those that do emerge suggest that there are more overarching and fundamental problems with participatory approaches to development than those reflected in earlier critiques. Without giving too much away, and not in any order of priority, those that are most apparent to us are the naivety of assumptions about the authenticity of motivations and behaviour in participatory processes; how the language of empowerment masks a real concern for managerialist effectiveness; the quasi-religious associations of participatory rhetoric and practice; and how an emphasis on the micro level of intervention can obscure, and indeed sustain, broader macro-level inequalities and injustice.

Taken together, these themes (and there are others, which readers may identify) point to what for us is the fundamental concern. It becomes clear from a reading of the chapters in this book that the proponents of participatory development have generally been naive about the complexities of power and power relations. This is the case not only 'on the ground' between 'facilitators' and 'participants', between 'participants' and more widely between 'donors' and 'beneficiaries', but also historically and discursively in the construction of what constitutes knowledge and social norms. While analyses of power in participation are not new, what is evident here is that there are multiple and diverse ways in which this power is expressed; furthermore, articulations of power are very often less visible, being as they are embedded in social and cultural practices. Thus this book identifies a more nuanced set of understandings of the workings of power as being necessary, in order to uncover its varied and subtle manifestations in the very discourse of participation.

The genealogies and histories of development in general, and participatory practices in particular, that are found in some of these chapters further explicate how a misunderstanding of power underpins much of the participatory discourse. This identification of the (mis)interpretations of how and where power is expressed within participation compels us to reconsider the notion of empowerment, and the claims to empowerment made by many participatory practitioners. Since an understanding of the concept of 'empowerment' is based on particular realizations of its root concept, 'power', and since this, as some of the chapters in this book argue, has been simplified in the theory and practice of participation, the meanings ascribed to the condition of empowerment and the claims made for its attainment for those who have been marginalized must also be subjected to further scrutiny.

This confirms, for us, that we were right to discuss participation in terms of its tyrannical potential, remembering that tyranny is precisely about the illegitimate and/or unjust uses of power. The question that we will not answer here, however, is whether this potential can be overcome. What we do suggest, however, is a starting point for those who might try to redeem it. This is to build in a more sophisticated and genuinely reflexive understanding of power and its manifestations and dynamics. Written into this understanding must be a recognition that participatory development does not have a reified existence 'out there', but is constructed by a cadre of development professionals, be they academics, practitioners or policy-makers, whose ability to create and sustain this discourse is indicative of the power they possess. This must be accompanied by an acknowledgement that questions such as 'Whose reality counts?' (Chambers 1997), which suggest that there are contrasting versions of reality, mask the extent to which these development professionals, in their applications of the ideas of participatory development, are actually still engaged in the construction of a particular reality – one that at root is amenable to, and justifies, their existence and intervention within it.

What we are calling for as a first step, therefore, is a genuine and rigorous reflexivity, one that acknowledges the processes and consequences of these constructions. This means going beyond the evident narrowness (verging on narcissism) of the existing self-acclaimed 'self-critical epistemological awareness' (Chambers 1997: 32) to draw on a deeper and more wide-ranging set of analyses than has hitherto been the case. This book has provided some of these analyses and, we hope, initiated this reflexivity. Ironically, though, authentic reflexivity requires a level of open-mindedness that accepts that participatory development may inevitably be tyrannical, and a preparedness to abandon it if this is the case. Thus any meaningful attempt to save participatory development requires a sincere acceptance of the possibility that it should not be saved.

2

'People's Knowledge', Participation and Patronage: Operations and Representations in Rural Development

David Mosse

Introduction

An important principle of participatory development is the incorporation of local people's knowledge into programme planning. In some circles this is now the dominant understanding of participation, particularly where techniques of participatory learning and planning (PRA/PLA) are taken as defining features of 'participation' in development. Clearly the meaning of 'participation' is not confined to 'people's knowledge' and planning, but it is an important element.

Firmly embedded in the literature on PRA and participation is the supposition that the articulation of people's knowledge can transform top-down bureaucratic planning systems. Chambers, for instance, posits PRA as a key instrument in challenging the institutionally produced ignorance of development professional 'uppers', which not only denies the realities of 'lowers' but imposes its own uniform, simplified (and wrong) realities on them.

> The essence of PRA is changes and reversals – of role, behaviour, relationship and learning. Outsiders do not dominate and lecture; they facilitate, sit down, listen and learn ... they do not transfer technology; they share methods which local people can use for their own appraisal, analysis, planning action, monitoring and evaluation. (Chambers 1997: 103)

Deferring to local knowledge provides the key to the reversal of hierarchies of power in development planning; PRA reduces dominance and is empowering to the poorest. It stands, in Chambers' view, as a major counterbalance to the power of dominant development discourses. PRA, Chambers (1997) argues, 'draws on, resonates with, and contributes to' a wider new paradigm in which positivist, reductionist, mechanistic, standardized-package, top-down models and development blueprints are rejected, and in which 'multiple, local and individual realities are recognized, accepted, enhanced and celebrated' (ibid.: 188).

With a few project-based illustrations, this chapter will question the potential that a PRA-based focus on 'people's knowledge' has to provide a radical challenge to existing power structures, professional positions and knowledge systems. It will indicate ways in which, on the contrary, participatory approaches have proved compatible with top-down planning systems, and have not necessarily heralded changes in prevailing institutional practices of development. The possibility of transformation is not denied, but the need to examine the social practices of 'local knowledge' production is emphasized, especially given the growing popularity of PRA-based planning and its spread from NGOs into public sector development bureaucracies. The critical point is that what is taken as 'people's knowledge' is itself constructed in the context of planning and reflects the social relationships that planning systems entail. As Long and Villareal point out, knowledge must be looked at relationally, that is, as a product of social relationships and not as a fixed commodity (1994).

Participation and Bureaucratic Planning

'Participation' no longer has the radical connotations it once had (e.g. in the radical popular movements of the 1960s). More prominent in present-day discourse are such pragmatic policy interests as 'greater productivity at lower cost', efficient mechanisms for service delivery, or reduced recurrent and maintenance costs (Rahnema 1992: 117). Under the influence of both international donors and domestic policy shifts towards local resource management and cost recovery, participatory planning techniques are now incorporated into the routines of public sector implementation agencies. Here, however, they place new demands on resources, imply a significant departure from normal procedures and decision-making systems, and/or are implemented in the field by people who may as yet have little to gain from the new accountabilities they signify. In short, there are often strong disincentives to adopting participatory approaches. Indeed, in India participatory approaches are still mostly pursued where external agency funding is available to cover the perceived additional risks. It is the optimistic belief of 'agrarian populists' (Bebbington 1994: 205) (and the intention of several development programmes) that exposure to participatory experiences and 'rural people's knowledge' will effect change in values, attitudes and behaviours in authoritarian bureaucracies (ibid.: 207). In this chapter, I look at the accommodation that 'participatory planning' makes with organizational practices, and the way in which organizations seek to secure the benefits (financial, political and symbolic) but avoid the costs of 'participation'.

Any useful discussion on the meaning of 'participation' requires a context, and here this is provided by the experience of the Kribhco Indo-British Farming Project (KRIBP), a donor-funded programme of a large public sector organization in India, which is managed by a special unit combining features of both NGO and government systems. This project is not selected because it, in particular, illustrates problems and constraints in participatory planning. On the contrary, the project is one of very few that has given explicit attention to the processes and dilemmas involved in implementing participatory approaches, and has sought constantly to engage in critical reflection on practice and to modify its planning approach and strategy in the light of experience.[1] Nevertheless, many of these dilemmas come from the need to weld a donor policy interest in 'participation' onto existing organizational interests and processes.

KRIBP (described in detail elsewhere, see Jones et al. 1994; Mosse 1994) is a participatory farming systems development project situated in the Bhil tribal region of western India (the border areas of Gujarat, Rajasthan and Madhya Pradesh states). The project strategy, oriented towards the goal of improving the livelihoods of poor farming families, involves generating location-specific natural resources development plans through a PRA-based process,[2] organized locally by a team of field-based Community Organizers. In principle, local problems are identified and prioritized by villagers, workable solutions found (a joint process) and implementation regimes agreed and negotiated between project staff and members of communities.

Programme activities cover a range of farming system areas: crop trials and community seed multiplication, agro-forestry and 'wasteland' development, horticulture, soil and water conservation, minor irrigation, livestock development, and credit management for input supply. As far as possible these interventions are low-cost, involve minimal subsidies and/or encourage cost-recovery. Planning such activities requires a high degree of commitment on the part of women and men from villages, and the sustainability of benefits beyond the life of the project depends upon continued management of local resources, and access to external capital and state development programmes through village-based groups (e.g. irrigation groups, credit management groups). In terms of most 'scales of participation', the project has a fairly high (or deep) level of participation: it aims for an intense relationship with farmers at early stages in decision-making (Biggs 1989; Farrington and Bebbington 1993).

The project, benefiting from uncommon clarity in its participatory planning methodology (Mosse et al. forthcoming), nevertheless faced some characteristic problems in putting this into practice. These throw light on the way in which what is read or presented as 'local knowledge' (such as community needs, interests, priorities and plans) is a construct of the planning context, behind which is concealed a complex micro-politics of knowledge production and use. I will briefly comment on four aspects of this: first, the shaping of knowledge by local relations of power; second, the expression of outsider agendas as 'local knowledge'; third, local collusion in the planning consensus; and finally the direct manipulation of 'people's planning' by project agents.

Knowledge and local relations of power 'Local knowledge' reflects local power. PRA events have become a crucial medium through which local perspectives are identified and expressed. But as I have argued elsewhere (Mosse 1994), in KRIBP (as in other contexts) these events can be seen as producing a rather peculiar type of knowledge, strongly shaped by local relations of power, authority and gender (e.g. women being constrained in their expression of opinions). While 'local knowledge' is highly differentiated in terms of who produces it and in terms of different ways of knowing (see also Hobart 1993), it is precisely these relevant differences that are concealed in planning PRAs. What make PRAs especially subject to the effects of dominance and muting is their character as *public* events – events taking place in the presence of local authority or outsiders and directed towards community action. But it is not only the 'public' nature of participatory planning that makes it political, but also its 'open-endedness'. When definitions of need, programme activity and 'target group' are open, much is at stake in controlling these. As Christoplos, writing on rural development in Vietnam, says: '[B]y leaving open the definition of the poor farmer, the most significant variable in the planning process, participatory projects become tools for various actors (even the poor themselves) in the political arena' (1995: 2).

Outsider agendas as 'local knowledge' Project actors are not passive facilitators of local knowledge production and planning. They shape and direct these processes. At the most basic level, project staff 'own' the research tools, choose the topics, record the information, and abstract and summarize according to project criteria of relevance. Given project–villager power relations, it is not greatly surprising that what was recorded in village PRAs reflected (and endorsed) a broad project analysis, for example, that the long-term loss of soil fertility (along with deforestation) was a major cause of declining agricultural productivity in the area. More generally, PRAs 'did not reveal an alternative to the official view of poverty ... but served to further legitimize (the official) discourse with farmer testimonies' (Christoplos 1995: 17–18, commenting on PRA analyses in the Mekoing Delta, Vietnam).[3] In fact, farmers' practical interest in soil erosion arose from the more urgent need for off-season wage labour, which project works offered. Subsequent research on rural livelihoods in the project gave a more central place to wage labour, as well as indebtedness, relationships of dependence and the advanced sale of migrant labour (Mosse et al. forthcoming), while more detailed ethnographic research indicates considerable farmer investment in soil and water conservation (SWC) in the region, leading to an increase in fertility and intensification of cultivation with population increases (Sjoblom 1999). Had other issues such as credit or wage labour been given a more central place in the early analysis of livelihoods (unclothed in 'farming system' concerns), some rather different interventions might have been conceived. The prior emphasis on declining soil fertility is, of course, unsurprising in a farming project integrated into the national goal of increasing the productivity of hitherto neglected rainfed areas (Jones et al. 1995).

Projects clearly influence the way in which people construct their 'needs'. Not all the information recorded in PRAs will register as legitimate 'needs' and so influence technology preferences or programme decisions. In KRIBP villages, for example, the matrix ranking of tree species was used in initial PRAs to identify a wide range of species and multiple uses for them.[4] The focus of discussion was on the actual *uses* of trees. When, however (in 1993), village-level nurseries were being established and farmers (women and men) were asked about their needs, and which species should be raised in the nurseries, a far more limited range of options was considered. Indeed, there was an overwhelming preference (reflected in the nurseries raised) for one particular species – eucalyptus.[5] There was a significant gap between patterns of usage (reflected in PRAs) and the expressed needs (or desires) that ultimately influenced decisions. Actual uses were even reinterpreted in terms of needs expressed in the light of project deliverables. Some villagers, for example, expressed a strong preference for eucalyptus as timber for housing when, in fact, they had little or no experience of using the species for this purpose. It happened that the village nursery programme was sponsored by the State Forest Department, which was perceived as strongly favouring eucalyptus (which was indeed the most commonly planted tree under 'social forestry' locally). Villager 'needs' were significantly shaped by perceptions of what the agency was able to deliver.[6] The expressed need for eucalyptus was, like the desire for soil and water conservation, in effect a low-risk community strategy for securing known benefits in the short term (trees or wages) that might have been jeopardized by some more complex and differentiated statement of preferences.[7] Farmers used a wide range of trees and were well aware of soil erosion effects, but these ideas *about* livelihood constraints would not be the same as those employed *for* action involving change with external agents. The latter take account of technology *availability*, and perceptions about which demands are likely to be considered *legitimate* (i.e. compatible with given project objectives). Following a KRIBP-organized visit to the local Krishi Vigyan Kendra (agriculture science centre), for example, some village women prioritized the planting of subabul and lemon, species to which they were exposed during the visit. Important and valuable though these innovations are, they may not be those that arise first from the more descriptive understanding of women's livelihoods.

Local collusion in the planning consensus Clearly needs are socially constructed (Pottier 1992) and 'local knowledge' shaped both by locally dominant groups and by project interests. 'Insider' and 'outsider' are inseparable in what would more correctly be referred to as 'planning knowledge' rather than 'people's knowledge'. Arguably, through participatory learning, it is farmers who acquire new 'planning knowledge' and learn how to manipulate it, rather than professionals who acquire local perspectives. This, then, is the third point, namely that people themselves actively concur in the process of problem definition and planning, manipulating authorized interpretations to serve their own interests. It was farmers, after all, who were able to use a consensus on the loss of soil fertility as the means to address the far more urgent requirement for paid employment and to secure delivery of more certain benefits of wage labour in the short term. Local power hierarchies intersect with project priorities as a multitude of local perspectives and interests struggle to find a place within the authorizing framework of the project. While expression of 'illegitimate' interests gets suppressed, some individuals or groups have the skill or authority to present personal interests in more generally valid terms, others do not.

Over time and through negotiation, project staff *and* villagers (in the first instance only men of influence, but later a wider cross-section of people) collude in translating idiosyncratic local interests (such as in wage labour, wells, pumps, housing support and loans) into demands that can be read as legitimate. Both benefit. Villagers gain sanction for activities in their neighbourhoods, and field staff, by delivering desirable goods and schemes and wage labour, win support from locals who agree to 'participate', attend meetings, train as volunteers, host visitors, save and make contributions, do things for the poor, and in other ways validate both the wider project and staff performance within it. This planning process, driven by a shared interest in producing a plan for concrete action, invariably suppresses difference in favour of consensus, and prioritizes action over detailed design. Staff who try to be *too participatory*, spend too much time investigating 'real needs' or women's needs rather than delivering schemes, are soon seen as under-performing by both project and community.

Of course, these planning negotiations are not between equals. Whatever the rhetoric, the reality is that people participate in agency programmes and not the other way round. In relation to its tribal villagers, the KRIBP project was clearly the most powerful player. Moreover, it is project outsiders who need and use 'local knowledge' about livelihoods, often to bargain with villagers, to challenge claims on the project, to reject as well as accept villager proposals, to negotiate subsidy levels, savings, cost recovery, and resource-sharing arrangements, and to allocate labour benefits or gender roles on project works. In this sense, 'local knowledge' is part of the project's exercise of power in *constraining* as well as enabling 'self-determined change'. The polarity set up between extractive and participatory modes of learning obscures the fact that, once produced, information will be used in various ways in a project system, including to privilege certain subordinate perspectives within communities. People's knowledge is also used to advance and legitimize the project's own development agenda, or even to negotiate its participatory approach with other stakeholders such as funders, technical consultants, senior management.[8] The fact that 'PRA-type' information has been set as a new scientific standard by donor and other agencies does not, in itself, democratize power in programme decision-making. Participatory approaches and methods also serve to represent external interests *as* local needs, dominant interests *as* community concerns, and so forth.

Manipulation of 'people's planning' 'Rural people's knowledge' (including, for example, analysis of problems, needs and plans) is collaboratively produced in the context of planning. As 'planning knowledge' it is a rather unusual type of knowledge with some specific characteristics: it is strongly shaped by dominant interests and agency objectives/analyses; it is conditioned by perceptions of project deliverables and the desire for concrete benefits in the short term;[9] it is consensual and obscures diverging interests both within villages and between the village and project (simplifying and rationalizing local livelihood needs to ensure consistency with project-defined models); it closely matches and supports programme priorities; and it involves bargaining and negotiation between agency staff and villagers but ultimately is a collaborative product, concealing both villager and project manoeuvres. 'People's knowledge' is undoubtedly a powerful normative construct that serves to conceal the complex nature of information production in 'participatory' planning, especially the role of outsiders.

The final point here is that, not infrequently, programme decisions take place with little reference to locally produced knowledge at all. PRA charts and diagrams provide attractive wall decorations, making public statements about participatory intentions, legitimizing decisions already made – in other words symbolizing good decision-making without influencing it. Even where considerable effort is directed towards the involvement of local people and their knowledge in planning, there are compelling reasons why locally generated plans do not provide the basis for programme choices. Quite apart from problems surrounding the use of 'people's knowledge' in planning systems, programme decisions are usually influenced by other interests altogether. The simplistic assumption that better access to local perspectives (even supposing this is unproblematic) will ensure that programme decisions are more participatory is, perhaps, only too obviously blind to the institutional realities of rural development.

For one thing, a new project such as KRIBP has its own needs. First, the project had to work out an acceptable compromise with villagers (in practice, key village leaders), a compromise between their hopes and expectations and project objectives, as a basis for continuing to work in the area. At a local level KRIBP project field staff (like others; see Arce and Long 1992) initially found that the acceptability of their presence in villages was largely based upon benefits they could, or promised to, deliver. They therefore felt constrained to initiate activities and programmes as a way of meeting new social obligations, demonstrating their influence and retaining their status as educated experts. Indeed, early programme choices were often shaped by the pragmatic need to manage villager petitioning while securing a social position locally. This may have been exaggerated by competition with peers working in other villages or by a perception that concrete actions would be rewarded over knowledge-building.[10]

Second, priorities are influenced by a project's wider institutional setting and its need to maintain relationships with local government, senior management, research institutions or donor advisers, with distinct development agendas that require the introduction of a stream of frequently flawed or inappropriate schemes such as the promotion of new winter crops, grain banks, farm machinery, mushroom cultivation, women's handicraft and drip irrigation, all presented as 'local needs'. More generally programme action is shaped by the project's engagement in wider coalitions contending for influence within national or international policy arenas (cf. Biggs 1995a, b). A project such as KRIBP may, in fact, participate in several coalitions pursuing different objectives – for example, agricultural production, environmental protection, poverty reduction and gender equality.

Third, choices and programme delivery are constrained by organizational systems and procedures (for example, budgeting time-frames, procedures for approval, sanctioning, fund disbursement and procurement). New concepts of 'process' have not obviated these institutionally grounded needs. Project managers still face other pressures to get things done, and other measures of efficiency than those provided by measures of participation. There are pressures for a local planning system to be sensitive to organizational realities as well as to villagers' livelihood constraints, and fieldworkers working under pressure to 'keep up momentum', to meet expenditure targets and to maximize quantifiable achievements may find themselves giving priority to familiar, conventional programmes over innovative initiatives where approval may be uncertain or delayed. There is therefore often a tendency for project works to cluster around a fixed set of standard interventions, limiting the potential creativity of participatory problem-solving.

Fieldworkers develop their own operational interpretation of both villager needs and project goals, and their own strategies of intervention, which are sensitive to the managerial and institutional environment as well as the village contexts in which they work.[11] Moreover, as villagers shape their needs and priorities to match the project's schemes and administrative realities, validating imposed schemes with local knowledge and requesting only what is most easily delivered, the project's institutional interests become built into community perspectives and project decisions become perfectly 'participatory'. So, if projects end up ventriloquizing villagers' needs it is not only, or primarily, because artful and risk-averse villagers ask for what they think they will get. It is also because development agencies are able to project their own various institutional needs onto rural communities. In short, through project systems of participatory planning, 'local knowledge', far from modifying project models, is articulated and structured by them.

In certain institutional contexts, 'participatory' processes can produce not diverse and locally varied development programmes, but strong convergence into a fixed set – crop varieties, soil and water conservation measures, agro-forestry and a range of *ad hoc* welfare programmes, in the case of KRIBP. Indeed there are inherent disincentives (among staff and villagers) to exploring or developing complexity and a preference for deep and reinforcing grooves. Far from being continually challenged, prevailing preconceptions are confirmed, options narrowed, information flows into a project restricted, in a system that is increasingly controllable and closed. The danger, of course, is that a participatory project that has diverged away from analysing problems will have limited impact, miss opportunities, or, at worst, by mis-specifying the problem, contribute to an aggravation of poverty or environmental decline (see Starkloff 1996).

This shift from an open, exploratory system towards a closed one is not to be understood as intentional. It is the side-effect of institutional factors that are unlikely to be perceived by project actors themselves, by their supporting bureaucracies, or even by external observers. Ironically, it is often when the expressed needs of client villagers most perfectly 'mirror' organizational systems, when programmes have become most impervious to variable local needs and new perspectives, that they begin to be acclaimed for their participatory processes or the sophistication of their methods. Indeed, through the mirroring of project assumptions in local plans, a project can advertise its participatory achievements while retaining control over an increasingly standard set of project activities, reproduced through conservatism, convenience, and risk aversion on the part of both villagers and staff.

Over time, and through a Weberian process of routinization, the operational demands of a project such as KRIBP (i.e. timely implementation of high-quality programmes) can become divorced from its participatory methods and goals. These latter have invariably been established and promoted by donors, rather than implementing bureaucracies, and place enormous demands on existing procedures, or conflict with existing accountabilities (e.g. setting targets of quantitative achievements). Tensions between established and donor demands for 'participation' produce a characteristic 'dual logic' in projects. One logic, set out in donor project documents and 'logframes', gives emphasis to local-level integrated planning and local capacity-building. The emphasis is on participation and sustainability. The other is the operational logic of the project agency, which emphasizes upward accountability, proper use of funds, and the planning and delivery of quality programmes. The emphasis is on *delivery*.

In the following section I try to understand how this tension is resolved, but to do so requires the introduction of another distinction.

Operation and Representation

Running through this account of project action is a distinction between, on the one hand, the immediate operational concerns of project actors – efficient programme implementation, maximizing physical works (e.g. soil and water conservation bunds or trees planted), maintaining and extending networks of patronage – and, on the other, the validation of this activity in terms of the project's participatory development objectives.

The success of the KRIBP project from the point of view of donors, senior management and villager beneficiaries depended upon the timely delivery/implementation of development programmes. In practice, delivery mechanisms involved a reassertion of hierarchical modes of operation. The orientation of staff, backed by unofficial systems of rewards and punishments, ensured strong vertical control of programme activities and implementation schedules. Under pressure to get things done, project staff took on more of the organization of activities and villagers retreated from temporary planning/decision-making to the more familiar role of passive beneficiary, strategizing to maximize short-term benefits from wages and subsidies. Social hierarchies challenged in early planning became reasserted at implementation. For example, one KRIBP Community Organizer pointed out that when he began to pay wages for soil and water conservation work being implemented in villages, the honorary suffix to his name used by tribal villagers changed from *bhai* (brother) to *sahib* (sir). Handling money conferred power, and where male staff took on the role of wage payments, gender inequalities within the field team were also seen to be reinforced. Villagers became easily incorporated into programme work as low-status project employees, foremen, wage labourers, and above all as clients of the project and its field-level representatives, rather than as development partners making their own investment decisions. The KRIBP project developed a strong patronage relationship with villagers (mostly organized into savings/activity groups, cf. Mosse 1996), and used this to ensure the delivery of a high-quality programme of soil and water conservation, forestry, minor irrigation and other works, supported by timely inputs, quality technical support, as well as rigorous fund management practices that held the project accountable for donor grant money.

The success of the overall project, however, required not only the delivery of visible schemes with demonstrable livelihood impact, but also the achievement of wider participatory development objectives and the validation of a project model. In particular, this model established a link between better programmes and sustainable livelihood improvements, on the one hand, and 'people's participation' (i.e. participatory planning, and skills and capacity development), on the other. Project success demanded that programme activities be seen and understood as participatory, just as much as it depended upon timely delivery. Here, KRIBP was a project organizing itself not just as a system for the delivery of development benefits (an 'operational system'), but as a 'system of representations', a set of validating ideas about participation or people's knowledge, which needed to be maintained.

What I am suggesting, then, is that the participatory goals of the project should not be seen only or primarily as operational, as ways of doing things. Indeed, we have seen in relation to planning how un-implementable the ideals of 'participation' actually are, in that they contradict an organization's basic operating procedures (cf. Quarles van Ufford 1993: 143). Rather, participatory goals are 'official models' in Bourdieu's (1977) sense, maintained through practices and 'officializing strategies' that translate the ground-level operational and tactical concerns of a project into authorized categories (just as villagers themselves translate their concerns into the valid categories of the project). In this sense, participatory goals including ideas about 'people's knowledge' and 'participatory planning' are significantly (if not primarily) oriented upwards (or outwards) to legitimize action, to explain, justify, validate higher policy goals, or mobilize political support rather than downwards to orientate action. Let me exemplify this role of a participation discourse with reference to the KRIBP project.

In the project, the participatory development project model was established by the donor and formulated through consultants as a key strategy and a convincing argument to justify the investment of public money (cf. Wood 1998). The official project text first established the project area as one in need of 'participation' as much as in need of better agricultural technology; that is, an area remote and muted in relation to government services, agricultural inputs, institutional credit and markets, and dependent on exploitative intermediaries. Second, the text invoked a 'model of change'; that is, a simplified set of problem–solution linkages connecting activities and objectives, inputs and outputs in which participation was central. These established, for example, the relationship between farmer participation, widening cultivar choice and crop-yield increases; farmer-designed SWC and yield stability; farmers' organizations and access to institutional credit.

Throughout, the project was defined by a 'theory of participation', which asserted that persisting poverty and isolation, and inappropriate and unsustainable development programmes, were the consequence of 'top-down' planning and the non-involvement of farmers in the process of need identification and programme design. Correspondingly maximizing farmer participation (including the specific involvement of women) would result in better-designed, more effective and sustainable programmes. And, to quote the project document, '[T]he basic premise is that sustainable development can only be achieved by enhancing local self-reliance through institutional and community development' (ODA 1992: 6). The participation model was synthesized into the currently dominant project formulation model, the Logical Framework (or logframe), so as to convey to outside decision-makers the idea of manageability based upon the existence of logically and causally related activities and objectives, an ordered sequence of events, the functional integration of different components and institutional actors (donors, implementing agencies, field staff and villagers) within a single knowledge system (cf. Quarles van Ufford 1993: 139).

But donor policy ideas on participation were only partly and imperfectly written for internal coherence; they were also, *third*, part of a wider policy argument both within the donor agency and externally. For example, farmer participation in varietal selection and plant breeding (a core project idea) was explicitly a challenge to prevailing bureaucratic practice in the Indian agricultural research establishment. The emphasis on 'sustainability' through self-reliance and farmer control was intended both to restrain the dominance of technical agendas over social ones within donor and project agencies, and to de-legitimize prevailing welfare and patronage approaches within project agency; the participation and poverty focus was aimed at answering domestic public criticism of the donor aid programme from NGOs and media.

As Raymond Apthorpe points out, policy discourse aims to *persuade* rather than inform (Apthorpe 1997).[12] This project design and its emphasis on 'participation' was, like most others, a bid for political support, a site for institutional politics (including the conflicting agendas of donor advisers, between donor and project agency and project management and field staff) which, *pace* Ferguson (1994), can be as much about coalition-building in order to restrict bureaucratic and technical power as to extend it.

The project idea and 'participatory approach' were also a means to enrol different project stakeholders with other interests. While the 'participatory planning' and the project model advanced by the donor was the dominant rationalizing discourse of the project, and the terms of consensus-building, it was far from hegemonic. As a legitimizing idea, 'participation' is sufficiently ambiguous to allow many different readings, and several shadow or subordinate models – rationalities validating action from different points of view. Experience of 'participatory development' in India is testimony to the diverse agendas clothed in the language of 'participation': government agencies use 'participation' to reach expenditure targets through enrolling NGOs or community institutions in implementation; public works agencies view 'participation' as a means to reduce operations and maintenance costs; marketing agencies may see 'participation' as a means to enhance an organization's profile, or the 'seed' for future markets; while for NGOs participation may mean patronage and reputation-building.

The agency behind KRIBP was a leading national commercial organization involved in the production and marketing of agro-inputs. It had its own organizational interests, expressed directly in early drafts of the project text, and later more indirectly as a practical interpretation of the official participatory model. These interests included: advancing the profile of the organization to its farmer client base; establishing close linkage with government and its national goals; extending the organization's capacity as an agent of modern agriculture through client-service centres, soil testing and local input supply nodes; and exploiting commercial/marketing possibilities through land and resources development.

'Participation' as a project goal proved compatible with these institutional priorities in a number of ways. First, through the development of a package of field techniques, participatory planning could itself become a commodity (a formula) that could be 'marketed' – distributed with a corporate image. This was possible in particular because of a rising demand for 'participatory methods' (mostly PRA) by government agencies implementing a huge new national watershed development programme. For this reason 'participation' provided high-profile opportunities for agency reputation-building and establishing relationships with government.

Second, the emphasis on community participation enabled the project organization to extend its own client-focused networks of patronage in the region. Close agency–community relations, participatory needs assessments, and the employment of village volunteers all provided the means to achieve efficient delivery of project programmes to client villagers, and so to identify the organization with visible rural development success and an expanding range of programmes. Indeed, the identity and credibility of the project and its field staff locally (as well as the popular understanding of 'participation') became consolidated around its role as benefactor and patron, source of technology, inputs and subsidies, a role underlined by the high public profile the agency gave to its welfare activities. The evolution of a participatory strategy into a set of patron–client relationships is perhaps unsurprising in a region where tribal farmers have historically engaged with outsiders as clients, whether they are departmental employers (e.g. forest, public works department), labour contractors, traders, moneylenders, or development projects.

Third, participation provided a strong basis for defining programme success. As a normative framework and a set of field techniques, participation became embedded in project practices and monitoring. The record of village meetings, PRAs and trainings provided an unassailable quantitative record of the project's participatory performance. The ambiguity of participatory goals generated multiple criteria by which the project could claim success with authority, but which did not depend upon field-level verification. But most importantly the project's 'participation model' allowed project patronage and efficient programme delivery to be interpreted as people's involvement leading to 'sustainable development'. A landscape of well-laid-out soil and water conservation bunds, woodlots, wells and pumpsets and an expanding range of activities could be taken to demonstrate achievement of donor goals of 'people's participation'. Activities were successful because of people's participation, and successful programmes demonstrated farmer decision-making, capacity enhancement and control.

In this sense the idea of 'participation' can become a self-validating theory of the relationship between successful outputs (e.g. forestry and irrigation) and people's involvement. As such it could be viewed as a crucial tool for project management – not, however, to shape the implementation of programmes (since this is successfully achieved through field staff-operated networks of patronage), but to produce internal coherence and manage relationships 'upwards' with donors. By its second and third year the project management became increasingly oriented towards the management of the invisible internal contradiction between high-profile 'participation' on the one hand, and the 'strong control over programme delivery' and expanded patronage on the other. Now the key point is that the core validating project model established ideologically precisely the link between 'participatory processes' and efficient implementation, which was weakest in practice. Indeed, this is precisely why the core model was constantly repeated and invoked in meetings and workshops and during donor review visits. Through ritualized expression the model allowed an interpretation of events and landscapes (smartly bunded) that confirmed its presuppositions. As with many projects, donor review visits often served as occasions to explicate project assumptions, rather than to examine their practices in any detail. And a good deal of management, donor and consultant effort (for example, through monitoring and reviews, and project workshops) went into the re-articulation of the participatory project model. Not only reports, but video films and manuals reaffirmed the model, and by the third year, demonstration of the project's participatory approach had become *the* key project 'Purpose' (Revised Logframe 1995). Moreover, the project had developed a dissemination strategy and defined a 'Replication Programme' as a key 'Output' (including production of manuals, national/regional seminars/workshops, audiovisual productions, training for NGOs and GOs) on the now systematized 'Participatory Approach'.

The effectiveness of 'participation' as a validating theory can be judged by the rising international profile of this, and other, participatory projects, their invitation to contribute to national and international programmes, all of which underscore the participation model, and blur the distinction between the normative discourse of manuals and the descriptive world of the project.

However, models of participation are not immune to criticism. The mid-term evaluation of the project in 1995 refused to accept the central assumption of the model, that more participation meant better programmes. Indeed, the report criticized the project for having too much participation and too little impact, or rather criticized the project for displaying its concern with people's participation, but not being able to demonstrate its impact on rural livelihoods. This was the first indication of donor disenchantment with 'participation' and a re-evaluation of the benefits and cost-effectiveness of participation as against what was coined as the alternative 'investment' approach. The project response was to organize a series of detailed impact assessment studies involving both economic surveys and village case studies, which generated an unusually rich body of information on rural livelihoods and project impact.

These village studies demonstrated overwhelmingly that the project was perceived by villagers as having a significant, positive impact in virtually every field of activity (although not always the impact expected). What they did not do, however, was validate (or invalidate) the project's participatory model, or investigate the relationship between livelihood impact and project processes (they could not, for example, distinguish impacts from patronage and programme delivery from those of 'self-determined change'). Indeed the representational edifice of 'participation' remained intact.

And this really is the point. In most projects, 'participation' is a political value to which institutions will sign up for different reasons. But it remains a way of talking about rather than doing things. It is not a provable approach or methodology. Indeed, as a global policy value, participation has many different operational interpretations. This means that analytically fruitful avenues for future enquiry are not to be found in the normative honing of participation as a singular policy idea, or in the development of the perfect set of participatory techniques, but rather in the development of a grounded understanding of the relationship between policy ideas and development practices, paying more attention to the development projects, organizations and professionals that frame and control 'participation' (cf. Craig and Porter 1997). It is from this perspective that it is possible to see that there is an oblique relationship between the rationality of 'participation' policy and the world of practice; to see how projects and programmes shape as well as implement policy; how the language of participation is co-opted from below as much as imposed from above; how there is never a singular voice, or a harmonious consensus around projects; and how power in development is multi-centred, and practices indeterminate and adaptive. A theory of participation separate from analysis of the meaning of the concept in specific organizational practices would be impossible.

Conclusions

The first part of my argument can be summarized by saying that the popular 'PRA' assumption that learning and 'local knowledge' defines, or redefines, the relationship between local communities and development institutions needs to be reversed. It is often the case that the 'local knowledge' and 'village plans' produced through participatory planning are themselves shaped by pre-existing relationships – in the present case, by patronage-type relationships between a project organization and tribal villagers. Rather than project plans being shaped by 'indigenous knowledge', it is farmers who acquire and learn to manipulate new forms of 'planning knowledge'. In this way local knowledge becomes compatible with bureaucratic planning.

The second part of my argument looks at what ideas of participation *do* rather than at what they fail to do. 'Participation' can be seen primarily as a representation (or a theory) oriented towards concerns that are external to the project location. Such representations do not speak directly to local practice and provide little guide of implementation, but are important in negotiating relationships with donors, and part of wider development policy arguments. Participation as a set of development ideas or interpretative frameworks is sustained locally through its links to the wider policy process.

Models of participation and normative schemes are prevalent and powerful. In various forms, they provide the lenses through which we (project workers, consultants, academics) see and judge projects such as KRIBP as successes or failures. Laudatory or critical commentaries both draw attention to and endorse the same models of participatory development. In doing so, however, they privilege the model over project practices, first, obscuring the agency of project organizations and their staff, and second, producing ignorance of project impacts.

As the long-term 'social development' consultant to KRIBP, I myself held a strong external monitoring concern with participation, local autonomy, sustainability and project withdrawal, which challenged the project's operational emphasis on patronage and programme delivery, largess and local dependency. The problem is that such a normatively driven perspective obscured the agency of the development organization itself as a politically conscious, strategically operating marketing organization, and the particular institutional context and constraints that this provided for participatory development. In practice, it proved rather difficult to get the donor/consultant interpretation of participation in terms of local control, autonomy and villager capacity-building procedurally internalized in the project (in terms, for example, of targets, monitoring and staff rewards), even though it remained a key part of the project as represented. There are many reasons for this difficulty that cannot be gone into here, but some of them at least may be less surprising when we consider that the particular understanding of participation advocated was, in some quite fundamental ways, at odds with what was driving the project. After all, the project's reputation, the validation of its participatory approach, the performance of local field staff, indeed the core rationale of the project from the organization's point of view, were all based on its network of patronage and the delivery of an expanding range of programmes, increasingly through village 'volunteers' (*jankars*) who operated as the lower orders of the project delivery mechanism. This structure was not (easily) going to be replaced with a striving to independent capacities, local autonomy and the withdrawal of the project. Why would the organization want to rid itself of its best customers, and villagers take leave of a serviceable patron?

Furthermore, the privileging of participation models over project practices overlooks some significant impacts. For instance, a more pragmatic appraisal of project activities would be able to regard the project's achievements – such as new input lines for improved technology, new marketing possibilities, new avenues of patronage and the matching of local needs and the organization's own marketing strategy – as advantageous in a remote tribal area, rather than as a failure to meet the objectives of participation. The benefits of high-quality soil and water conservation, improved seed inputs, assisted seed distribution and storage, mediated links to national and international agricultural research agendas are highly significant. They may depend upon the permanent and expanding presence of the organization as a parastatal extension service – offering better technology and more affordable inputs rather than autonomy and independence to remote tribal villages. This may be a subversion of the currently dominant international development idea of 'farmer-managed development', but it is undoubtedly an operationally successful and institutionally supported version of participation.

Notes

1. It should be clearly understood that this is in no way a descriptive account of the KRIBP project. Experience from the earlier years of the project is selectively cited only to illustrate some more generally applicable points. The perspective I offer comes from my own experience working as a social development consultant to the project over several years. It remains a personal perspective, and the KRIBP project, its consultants and donor bear no responsibility for the views and opinions expressed here.

2. See an earlier paper (Mosse 1994) for discussion of the project's early experience with PRA, and the lessons learned.

3. The worry that rapid participatory research methods would, in practice, often perform a legitimizing function for decisions already taken was raised well over a decade ago in the early debate on RRA (Wood 1981).

4. In one women's group 37 species were ranked in relation to eight different uses.

5. Of course the earlier PRAs were not free of omission or selectivity. Fruit trees, for example, emerged as an important priority but were not mentioned during the initial tree matrix exercises (Bezkorowajnyj et al. 1994).

6. This relationship has changed over time, and correspondingly there has been a change in the proportion of eucalyptus seedlings raised. This has fallen over the years of the project.

7. There is of course no uniformity of needs. A strong bias towards eucalyptus might meet some people's needs, but not those of others. Some people have the power and authority to influence the collective decision in favour of options that better meet their particular needs (cf. Mosse 1994). Women, typically, lack this power, and in this case their unarticulated experience of burdensome labour and time devoted to the collection of fuel and fodder (for which eucalyptus is not a first choice) or the economic and nutritional importance of forest species and the collection of non-timber forest produce did not overly shape programme choices, even though they clearly featured in separate informal PRAs.

8. PRA information on the customary role of tribal women in decision-making about household finance, in livestock management, manuring and seed selection and management, for example, is necessary in arguing a case for their central role (as policy) in the project activities of credit, input supply or crop development that would otherwise by default come to be controlled by men.

9. In another example of project-related 'short-termism' Starkloff (1996) shows how participatory mechanisms generate support for 'coping mechanisms' rather than addressing underlying environmental problems.

10. The way in which gender relations ensure that women fieldworkers are placed at a distinct disadvantage in generating information from women and presenting this in terms of readily implementable programmes is properly the subject of a separate discussion.

11. Arce and Long (1992) examine in some detail the way in which a Mexican fieldworker (a *tecnico* or technical agronomist) devises his own strategies of intervention in both the village and official administrative arenas, which enable him to retain legitimacy in the eyes of both villagers and bureaucrats.

12. To persuade, consultants selectively draw on the testimony of other experts and officials, even future 'beneficiaries'.

3

Institutions, Agency and the Limitations of Participatory Approaches to Development

Frances Cleaver

Participation in Development Discourse

Heroic claims are made for participatory approaches to development. Participation of community members is assumed to contribute to enhanced efficiency and effectiveness of investment and to promote processes of democratization and empowerment. The conundrum of ensuring the sustainability of development interventions is assumed to be solvable by the proper involvement of beneficiaries in the supply and management of resources, services and facilities. There are even claims that participation constitutes a 'new paradigm' of development (Chambers 1997).

Despite such significant claims, there is little evidence of the long-term effectiveness of participation in materially improving the conditions of the most vulnerable people or as a strategy for social change. While the evidence for efficiency receives some support on a small scale, the evidence regarding empowerment and sustainability is more partial, tenuous and reliant on assertions of the rightness of the approach and process rather than convincing evidence of outcomes. Trenchant critiques of participation approaches to development exist (see Stiefel and Wolfe 1994; Biggs 1995), but these seem to have had little impact on development and policy discourses.

Participation has therefore become an act of faith in development, something we believe in and rarely question. This act of faith is based on three main tenets: that participation is intrinsically a 'good thing' (especially for the participants); that a focus on 'getting the techniques right' is the principal way of ensuring the success of such approaches; and that considerations of power and politics on the whole should be avoided as divisive and obstructive.

In questioning these it is not my intention, as some critics have suggested, to deny the usefulness of a people-centred orientation in development, or to dismiss all attempts at community-based development as well-meaning but ineffectual. Indeed, I am not a complete pessimist about such approaches; rather I see them as promising but inevitably messy and difficult, approximate and unpredictable in outcome. Subjecting them to rigorous critical analysis is as important as constantly asserting their benefits.

This chapter outlines some of the conceptual underpinnings of participatory approaches and illustrates how the translation of these into policy and practice is not necessarily consistent with the desired impacts. In illustrating these points I draw heavily on my research into collective action and the institutions that shape the management of common property resources (Cleaver 2000) and on my work on gender and water resource management (Cleaver 1998a).

Efficiency and empowerment The theorizing of participatory approaches is often dichotomized into means/ends classifications (Oakley et al. 1991; Nelson and Wright 1995). These distinguish between the efficiency arguments (participation as a tool for achieving better project outcomes) and equity and empowerment arguments (participation as a process that enhances the capacity of individuals to improve or change their own lives). The predominant discourses of development are practical and technical, concerned with project-dictated imperatives of efficiency, with visible, manageable manifestations of collective action. These, however, are commonly cloaked in the rhetoric of empowerment, which is implicitly assumed to have a greater moral value. Radical empowerment discourse (with its roots in Freirean philosophy) is associated with both individual *and* class action, with the transformation of structures of subordination through radical changes in law, property rights, the institutions of society. The model of 'participation' implied is of development practitioners working with poor people to struggle actively for change (Batliwala 1994). Such ideas, associated with structural change and with collective action facilitated by and in opposition to the state, are rather out of fashion in development, although within feminist scholarship and within the Latin American participatory tradition the debate continues (e.g. Fals-Borda 1998; Jackson and Pearson 1998). As 'empowerment' has become a buzzword in development, an essential objective of projects, its radical, challenging and transformatory edge has been lost. The concept of action has become individualized, empowerment depoliticized.

A number of problems arise in analysing empowerment within projects. It is often unclear exactly *who* is to be empowered – the individual, the 'community', or categories of people such as 'women', 'the poor' or the 'socially excluded'. The question of how such generalized categories of people might exercise agency is generally sidestepped. The mechanisms of such empowerment are either startlingly clear (i.e. empowerment of the individual through cash transactions in the market) or conveniently fuzzy (as in the assumed benefits to individuals of participation in management committees). The scope of and limitations on the empowering effects of any project are little explored; the attribution of causality and impact within the project alone problematic.

Participation, social capital and inclusion There is a need to conceptualize participatory approaches more broadly, for more complex analyses of the linkages between intervention, participation and empowerment (Moser and Sollis 1991). We need to better understand the non-project nature of people's lives, the complex livelihood interlinkages that make an impact in one area likely to be felt in others and the potential for unintended consequences arising from any intended intervention or act (Giddens 1984; Long 1992).

A move away from narrow project approaches may be seen in the current concern with the role of social capital in development. Ideas about overcoming the problem of social exclusion have linked concepts of community, democracy, the key role of non-governmental organizations, individual responsibility and citizenship. Concepts of participation are partly subsumed within this discourse. The concept of social inclusion emphasizes involvement in the structures and institutions of society – 'most fundamentally, the participatory and communicative structures, including new forms of social partnership through which a shared sense of the public good is created and debated' (IILS/UNDP 1997).

The tyranny of techniques Much debate about participatory approaches concerns the appropriate techniques for uncovering the 'realities' of poor people and ensuring their involvement in decision-making. Any cursory review of the literature on participation in development reveals a huge volume of work on techniques (PLA, PRA etc.). As the solution to locally based development they have the advantage of being tangible, practically achievable and fitting well with project approaches. This techniques-based participatory orthodoxy is increasingly being subjected to critical analysis (Mosse 1995; Goebbel 1998). Biggs (1995) suggests that such an approach to participation fails adequately to address issues of power and control of information and other resources and provides an inadequate framework for developing a critical reflective understanding of the deeper determinants of technical and social change. It is not my intention here to deal substantially with this debate except to point out that reviewing and improving participatory techniques cannot substitute for a more fundamental examination of the very concepts that inform such approaches, issues to which I now turn.

The place of structure and agency Some of the artificial dichotomies and critical paradoxes in current thinking about participation and development can be accommodated by analysing the recursive relationship between structure and agency. Considerable attempts have been made to understand the complexities, diversity and regularities of patterns of interaction between individuals and social structure; examples from social theory include Giddens (1984), Douglas (1987), Granovetter (1992) and in development studies include Long and Long (1992), Goetz (1996), etc. However, such critical reconceptualization and analysis have little impact on the development mainstream as articulated through policy and practice. Concepts of individual action underlying participatory approaches swings widely between 'rational choice' and 'social being' models. The former attributes individual behaviour to calculative self-interest, the latter to culture and social norms. Social structure is variously perceived as opportunity and constraint but little analysed; the linkages between the individual and the structures and institutions of the social world they inhabit are ill modelled. A convenient and tangible alternative is found in the ubiquitous focus on the *organizations* of collective action; *organizing the organizations* then becomes a central plank of participatory approaches to development.

It is in an attempt to highlight some of these issues and to illustrate the value of an analysis that considers the role of both social structure and of individual agency in shaping participation that the following discussion will be structured.

Institutionalism

Discourses of participation are strongly influenced by the new institutionalism, theories that suggest that institutions help to formalize mutual expectations of cooperative behaviour, allow the exercise of sanctions for non-cooperation and thereby reduce the costs of individual transactions. Social institutions are perceived as clever solutions to the problems of trust and malfeasance in economic life as they can make cheating and free-riding too costly an activity to engage in (Granovetter 1992). Institutions (mostly commonly conceptualized as *organizations*) are highly attractive to theorists, development policy-makers and practitioners as they help to render legible 'community', and codify the translation of individual into collective endeavour in a form that is visible, analysable and amenable to intervention and influence (Scott 1998).

In participatory approaches institutions are seen as particularly important. Associations, committees and contracts channel participation in predictable and recognizable ways, the aim of many development interventions apparently being to establish community structures that most clearly mirror bureaucratic structures. (A paradox, surely, when part of the justification for participatory approaches is that they avoid the shortcomings of development delivered by state bureaucracies?)

Ideas about social capital and civil society are also strongly institutionalist, although often vague. Visible, often formal, manifestations of association are attributed normative value, denoting initiative, responsibility, good citizenship and democratic engagement as well as allegedly facilitating vibrant economic activity (IILS/UNDP 1997; Putnam 1993).

Institutional inclusion, then, has become an integral strand of participatory approaches, a process that is assumed to ensure the more efficient delivery of development, the inculcation of desirable characteristics among participants (responsibility, ownership, cooperation, collective endeavour) and therefore empowerment. Exclusion from local institutions is considered undesirable, marginalizing, inefficient. Such institutional models of participation may be criticized on a number of grounds.

Formalization and functionalism There is a tendency in the development literature to recognize the importance of social and 'informal' institutions but nevertheless to concentrate on the analysis of 'formal' institutions (Uphoff 1992a, 1992b).[1] Here there is a concentration on contracts, committees and property rights as mechanisms for reducing transaction costs and institutionalizing cooperative interactions (Brett 1996; Folbre 1996). Formalized institutional arrangements are considered more likely to be robust and enduring than informal ones, and desirable characteristics include a clearly specified user group and boundaries, a system of clear rules and sanctions against offenders and public conflict resolution mechanisms (Ostrom 1990). Such a formalization of collective action, it is suggested, will clarify and make transparent local arrangements. Formalization is strongly linked to evolutionism in these models. A general progression from traditional (implicitly 'weak') forms of management to

Box 3.1 Local arrangements, 'project' perceptions: shallow well, Nyanguge Village, Magu District, Tanzania

This well had been dug in 1989 and served the sub-village of 120 households. When we arrived there were a number of young boys collecting water in containers which they tied to the back of bicycles.

This well contains salty water and so is only used in the mornings to collect water for domestic purposes other than drinking and cooking. Another well nearby in the same sub-village is opened in the afternoons for people to collect sweet water (it was locked when we visited). There are six caretakers for the two pumps (three men and three women) and they monitor the pumps by rota for two days at a time each.

After some years of intermittent breakages and disrepair community members decided, through their sub-villages, ratified at the village council, to establish a maintenance fund. In this sub-village households were required to pay Ts500 per year and an additional Ts200 every two months. The figures were decided upon at the village council after calculating the maximum amount it would cost to replace all 12 pumps in the village if they broke down. There are 720 households in the village so revenue collection is potentially high.

This money is collected by the caretakers, and households are given receipts. One caretaker interviewed said that he collected the money by visiting the households on a twice a week timetable and talking to the male head of household. Of course, the woman might have to influence her husband to pay up. If people refuse to pay then they are banned from taking water and the caretakers regulate this. The numbers of non payers are small but the community also decided to exempt old women from payment because they have few means.

Promotion staff from the HESAWA programme said that they were planning to return to this village in Phase 4 to mobilize them to set up the required Water User Groups to ensure sustainability. Without such Water User Groups sustainable local maintenance could not be ensured, and project objectives would not be achieved.

Source: Cleaver and Kaare 1998

modern (by implication 'strong') forms is considered desirable and is the focus of much 'institution building' in development (INTRAC 1998). Very influential here is Elinor Ostrom's concept of the possibility of 'crafting' institutions to render them more fit for the job in hand. Such crafting generally is seen to involve formalization in the interests of functional ends.

These models have been criticized for an over-simplistic evolutionism (Nelson 1995), and for a blindness to historical and social context. Evidence suggests more complex and fluid processes of institutional evolution, their ebb and flow according to circumstances (season, political intervention, need), the *ad hoc* use of different institutional arrangements as appropriate, not necessarily conforming to project activities. An organizational model of participation ignores the fact that many interactions between people also take place outside formal organizations, that the interactions of daily life may be more important in shaping cooperation than public negotiations. This I have illustrated regarding the use and management of water resources in Zimbabwe (Cleaver 1995, 2000). Despite the focus of development agencies on the promotion of community involvement through waterpoint committees I illustrate how the local institutions for the management of water and grazing land are deeply embedded in social relations. Management thus depends on the maintenance of a number of grey areas and ambiguity regarding rights of access, compliance with rules, on a continuous process of negotiation between all users, on the strong principle of conflict avoidance and on a large amount of decision-making taking place through the practical adaptation of customs, norms and the stimulus of everyday interactions.

This is not, of course, to suggest that formal institutions are irrelevant. In one project in Tanzania local management indeed took place through participation in 'formal' organizations, but not those specified by programme plans. This example illustrates how a narrow project focus on establishing new functional institutional mechanisms of participation (in this case Water User Groups) may obscure the actual activities being undertaken by community members through other well-established, familiar and locally adapted channels (see Box 3.1).

Organizations, participation and representation Organizational approaches to institutions contain two strong and conflicting ideas about individual participation. The focus on committee-like institutions is associated with participation through democratic representation and a concentration on the election/selection of committee members. Paradoxically,

Box 3.2 Participatory decision-making and representation

Two examples raise some relevant challenges to predominant concepts of participatory decision-making and representation.

For example, in one of my study villages in Zimbabwe committees (Waterpoint, Food for Work, Pre-School, Village Development) were established according to the requirements of governments and donor agencies. However, decision-making and debate rarely took place within committees; when it did it was hotly disputed and the decisions rarely complied with. Decision-making was considered valid only when all those (adults) potentially affected by it were present. This, of course, resulted in lengthy decision-making processes conducted at large meetings of the people. Discussions and ideas arising from these continued to be developed through people's daily interactions. Tellingly, records were kept at village level of such multipurpose 'meetings of the people', but not of the meetings of functional committees.

Reviewing a large water and sanitation programme in Tanzania, we noted the concern of project officers that at large village meetings there was a notable disparity between the number of men speaking and the number of women speaking, and the need to implement measures to ensure the greater participation of women. However, women themselves explained their participation differently. Our female informants suggested that they deputed one or two women, known for their eloquence, to speak for them. These were not formal representatives and might be decided upon during the course of the meeting, according to need. But in this way women felt they could have their voice heard and their priorities put forward in meetings most effectively. At a recent meeting villagers had debated how to spend a surplus of funds. Men were mostly in favour of buying beer and having a celebration. Women, however, insisted that the money go towards a new water source. And so it did. The triumph of water over beer illustrated, according to our female informants, the efficacy of their model of participation in decision-making.

Source: Cleaver and Kaare 1998

there is also a strong assumption (particularly in PLA approaches) that meaningful participation in public meetings is evidenced by individual (verbal) contributions. Such principles are not necessarily in concurrence with local norms and practices and an insistence on them may both exaggerate and disguise people's actual involvement (see Box 3.2).

How far do the participatory fora that we promote through development accommodate such complexities? There is a danger that unless they are taken into account the formal manifestations of community-based approaches to development become mere empty shells, with meaningful decision-making, interaction and collective action taking place elsewhere.

Socially embedded institutions are not necessarily 'better' than organizational ones, as they may uphold and reproduce locally specific configurations of inequity and exclusion. However, the mere setting up of formal organizations and the specification of their membership does not necessarily overcome exclusion, subordination or vulnerability. It does not do so because the wider structural factors that shape such conditions and relations are often left untouched. Codifying the rights of the vulnerable must surely involve far more wide-reaching measures than the requirement that they sit on committees, or individually speak at meetings.

Myths of community Ideas about local institutions are often based on problematic notions of community. The 'community' in participatory approaches to development is often seen as a 'natural' social entity characterized by solidaristic relations. It is assumed that these can be represented and channelled in simple organizational forms. Such assumptions are unsatisfactory for a number of reasons.

There is strong assumption in development that there is one identifiable community in any location and that there is a coterminosity between natural (resource), social and administrative boundaries. Development committees are therefore established as representative of 'the community'. The assumed self-evidence of 'community' persists in our participatory approaches despite considerable evidence of the overlapping, shifting and subjective nature of 'communities' and the permeability of boundaries (IASCP 1998). A concentration on boundaries highlights the need in development for clear administrative arrangements, more to do with the delivery of goods and facilities than a reflection of any social arrangement (see Box 3.3).

Participatory approaches stress solidarity within communities; processes of conflict, and negotiation, inclusion and exclusion are occasionally acknowledged but little investigated. The 'solidarity' models of community, upon which much development intervention is based, may acknowledge social stratification but nevertheless assume some underlying commonality of interest (Li 1996). For example, fieldworkers on a community-based water and sanitation programme in Tanzania were reluctant to publicly refer to, or even admit, socio-economic differences within the communities with which they worked. They had dropped wealth ranking from their PRA exercises, fearing that this highlighted difference and saw the public acknowledgement of difference as incompatible with the cooperation necessary for the smooth functioning of the project (Cleaver and Kaare 1998).

More realistically, we may see the community as the site of both solidarity and conflict, shifting alliances, power and social structures. Much

Box 3.3 Multiple communities, permeable boundaries

In research in Zimbabwe it became clear to me that the idea of an administratively defined community little reflected the wealth and complexity of local networks of resource use, decision-making and interaction. Thus while water resources were managed at water-point and at village level, decisions about grazing land involved a wider group of people from part of three villages. Cultural ceremonies such as rainmaking (surely an occasion for the reinforcing of community) also involved a wider and more diverse constituency than that of the village. Analysing the social networks within which my active and dynamic hostess was involved I was hard pressed to identify a single or even dominant 'community'; her life was lived through overlapping interactions between extended family (rural and urban), the physical locality, the wider cultural and resource-using locality, development-defined groups (for sewing, saving, vegetable growing), the church (a strong local and international 'community') and the school where she taught with its own networks of teachers, pupils and families. Moreover a historical review of her family fortunes during this century revealed the constantly shifting and changing nature of such networks as people were settled and (forcibly) resettled, as government introduced new administrative structures or reformed old ones, as shifting and growing populations created different patterns of natural resource use and as marriage and migration of family members changed the extended family network.

Source: Cleaver 1996

recent work on common property resource management recognizes the role of communities in managing internal conflicts (IASCP 1998), and various authors have illustrated the shifting, historically and socially located nature of community institutions, the power dimensions of public manifestations of collective action (Mosse 1997; Peters 1987; Goebel 1998).

Development practitioners excel in perpetuating the myth that communities are capable of anything, that all that is required is sufficient mobilization (through institutions) and the latent capacities of the community will be unleashed in the interests of development. The evidence does little to support such claims. Even where a community appears well motivated, dynamic and well organized, severe limitations are presented by an inadequacy of material resources, by the very real structural constraints that impede the functioning of community-based institutions (see Box 3.4).

Culture and foundationalism Contradictory ideas about the nature of

Box 3.4 The limits of participation

The people of Sando village in Nkayi district, Zimbabwe had built their own school, established a variety of income-generating clubs, had high levels of associational activity. They were in every sense a creative community, admired by district officials and neighbours for their self-reliance and resilience. And yet they were unable to ensure the functioning of their borehole or to secure adequate alternative water supplies; a problem partially explained by their location (deep in the forest remote from the district offices, in an area where the water table is over 100m below ground), their lack of political influence (a small population) their low incomes and the restrictions on government's ability to finance new facilities. While they had established a fund for the purchase of a windmill pump, set up a system of collection of money from households and defined those exempt from payment (newly-weds), they were unable to raise a sufficient sum to secure their new pump. Several years after initiating the Windmill Fund they still lacked adequate water supplies and were forced to travel 10km to use a borehole in another village.

Source: Cleaver 1996

'culture' feature prominently in development discourses about community and participation. Culture is variously perceived as a constraint (for example, restricting the participation of women in development activities), the 'glue' that keeps the community together (the supposed 'cultural' inheritance of solidarity and cooperation from some past golden age) and a resource to be tapped in development (in terms of using the 'authority' of 'traditional' leaders to legitimize development interventions).

Positive views of local culture (culture as community glue, a form of social capital) tend towards a profound foundationalism about local communities and their inhabitants (Sayer and Storper 1997). There are elements of this in the writings of Robert Chambers, where a moral value is attributed to the knowledge, attitudes and practices of 'the poor', the task of development being to release their potential to live these out. How, then, do we deal with situations where 'local culture' is oppressive to certain people, where appeals to 'tradition' run contrary to the modernizing impulses of development projects? Why do we see so little debate about these tensions in the development literature? Is it for fear of criticizing local practices and being seen as the professionals so roundly condemned in Chambers' work? Are we not in danger of swinging from one untenable position (we know best) to an equally untenable and damaging one (they know best)?

Model of Individuals

Participatory approaches can further be criticized for their inadequate model of individual action and the links between this and social structure. Despite the strong assumption of the links between individual participation and responsibility, there is little recognition of the varying livelihoods, motivations and impacts of development on individuals over time. Indeed, project approaches that focus strongly on institutions as a development tool often see people as 'inputs', as the 'human resource' (see, for example, Khan and Begum 1997). Social difference is recognized through the categorization of people into general occupational or social roles: 'women', 'farmers', 'leaders' and 'the poor'.

Paradoxically, models of individual motivation and action in participatory approaches swing between the under- and over-socialized (Granovetter 1992). The concept of the 'rational economic man' is so deeply embedded in development thinking that its influence is strongly felt even where development efforts are concerned with activities that are not directly productive – with community, social action, citizenship. However, there is often a simultaneous and rather vague assumption of the 'social being' whose better nature can be drawn upon in the interests of community and development. In both abstractions the complex positions of real individuals and real groups are lost.

Incentives, rationality and participation While the participatory literature is often rather vague on the incentives that will persuade people to participate, it is infected by the pervasive functionalism and economism of development thinking. It is assumed that people will find it in their rational interests to participate, due to the assurance of benefits to ensue (particularly in relation to 'productive' projects) or, to a much lesser extent, because they perceive this as socially responsible and in the interests of community development as a whole (particularly in relation to public goods projects). Interestingly, many policy approaches make significant efforts to link participation with social responsibility, to characterize non-participation as irresponsible, and at the same time to define benefits which may in fact be long-term, cumulative and community-wide rather than of immediate advantage to the individual. Such positions are well illustrated in the literature on women's participation in water projects, on the advantages of time savings to be obtained through improved supplies and the supposed economic benefits to individual women of paying for water (see Cleaver and Lomas 1996 for a critique).

In explaining motivations to participate, social norms are seen to occupy a secondary place to economic rationality; social relations and participation are seen ultimately to serve the ends of economic development. Such perceptions allow little place for personal psychological motivations, for the needs of individuals for recognition, respect or purpose, which may be independent of other material benefits. Accounts of the involvement of young men in community activities in Zimbabwe and St Vincent illustrate this point (Cleaver 1998b; Jobes 1998). Nor are the complexities of long-term and diffuse relationships of reciprocity occurring over lifetimes adequately recognized as shaping participation (Adams et al. 1997; Cleaver 2000).

The fragility of a conceptual model that directly relates individual motivation and participation to receipt of benefits can be illustrated with the following example. It is commonly asserted that women should participate more fully in the upgrading and management of water supplies as they are the primary carriers and users of domestic water. It is claimed that because of this role they have great incentives to participate and that the outcomes of such participation (greater sense of ownership and responsibility leading to improved supplies) will directly benefit them. However, analysis of actual water use and decision-making leads us to question such assumptions. Women in a position to do so (older, richer, senior women) commonly delegate water fetching to other women and men (relatives, poor neighbours, hired workers) and, significantly, to children. The water-user, decision-maker, manager and beneficiary are not always, then, manifest in one individual. Do children and young people participate in public decision-making about water supply improvement or management? Do those to whom water work is delegated have strong interests in reducing water-fetching times and improving supplies? Perhaps they supplement their livelihoods through water work, perhaps it is part of a complex web of reciprocal exchange upon which they depend. Are old women not to be included in participatory decision-making processes regarding water supply improvements because they no longer fetch the water directly themselves?

Located identities, differential costs and benefits Functional project approaches to participation little recognize that in examining motivation it is helpful to see a person positioned in multiple ways, with social relations conferred by *specific* social identities (Giddens 1984), and that, in Long's words, individuals are only ever partly enrolled in the projects of others (Long 1992).

According to Giddens the actions of human agents should be seen as a process rather than as an aggregate of separate intentions, reasons, motives and acts, and much of our day-to-day contact is not directly motivated. In querying the modelling of action as individual acts, Giddens draws attention to the difference between much routinized day-to-day activity, which forms part of 'practical consciousness', and that about which actors may be discursively conscious and can analyse and reflect upon. Crucial to such alternative interpretations is the role of agency in processing experience and shaping action, and the role of structure in both enabling and constraining such choices.

The individual in participatory approaches is usually defined in terms of the functional nature of the project. Little recognition is made of the changing social position of individuals over life courses, of the variable costs and benefits of differently placed people, of contending and complementary concerns with production and reproduction. Age, gender, class and individual agency may all shape people's willingness and ability to participate. For example, while poor young women with small children commonly find it difficult to participate publicly in development projects

Box 3.5 Differing strategies of participation and compliance

Two women in similar circumstances in the same village displayed very different practices in securing their livelihood needs. They both had husbands resident but not working, small children, poor land and no livestock:

Mrs CN participated in no community meetings, relying on her husband's very occasional attendance. She contributed to no development projects. She relied instead on kinship relations, waiting to borrow cattle for ploughing from wealthier relatives, asking for assistance from the extended family for school fees and even food during the drought months.

Mrs Z, on the other hand, facing similar problems, had become the representative of a local NGO (ORAP), the major advantage of this being that it built on traditional concepts of communal labour and assistance but organized them in new ways. Traditionally, if a person calls communal labour to work their fields the host must provide beer and food, a condition few poor people can meet. Under the ORAP arrangements, any member of the development group can call on others for assistance but without the requirement of providing refreshment.

Another example suggests that 'cheating' may be a viable strategy.

In Eguqeni village I observed Mrs PN persistently breaking community rules by using the communal water pump at closed times, apparently without incurring punishment, or even disapproval. When questioned villagers suggested that this was acceptable in her case as she had a large number of young children and lived far from the pump. In view of her labour constraints and spatial distance it would be difficult for her to collect sufficient water for her basic needs at the specified opening times, as, by the time she had carried one bucket home and returned for another, the pump would be closed again. Her reputation for hard work and her (distant) relationship through marriage to the pump chairman undoubtedly contributed to her ability to break the community rules without punishment.

Source: Cleaver 1996

due to their burden of productive and reproductive activities, some individuals find ways of doing so while others meet their needs in differing ways, as Box 3.5 illustrates.

Contrary to the ubiquitous optimistic assertions about the benefits of public participation, there are numerous documented examples of situations where individuals find it easier, more beneficial, or habitually familiar not to participate (Adams et al. 1997; Zwarteveen and Neupane 1996). Non-participation and non-compliance may be both a 'rational' strategy *and* an unconscious practice embedded in routine, social norms and the acceptance of the status quo. A fascinating study by Zwarteveen and Neupane of irrigation management in Nepal shows how some women, constrained by prevailing ideas about proper gender roles, saw it more beneficial *not to participate* in the irrigation association. Instead they secured their water partly through the participation of male members of their own household, through other kin and neighbour networks and partly through stealing and cheating. Their absence from the formal user association made it far easier for them to do this without detection or censure.

There have recently been several calls to recognize both the costs and benefits of participation for individuals (Mayoux 1995) and yet these are little pursued, the conventional wisdom being that participation is 'a good thing'. If we accept that costs and benefits fall differentially and are mediated and perceived by people in differing ways, where does this leave us, for example, in terms of policies that target the participation in development of 'the poor'? Also, how do we link the evaluation of such costs and benefits with a model of choice and voluntarism? It seems that where poor people are concerned their choices may be seriously limited, the scope for variation of action narrow. They may lack the resources for effective participation and yet remain vulnerable in their livelihood strategies based on kin and existing social structures. Participation in water supply projects, where water is scarce and it is difficult to procure enough for basic needs, is less a matter of choice (or an expression of agency), more a matter of necessity imposed by constraint.

Interpreting inclusion and exclusion The recursive relationship between structure and agency is illustrated by the variability of individual participation. A recognition that the public participation of individuals may be negotiated and mediated within households and communities and shaped by prevailing social norms and structures raises critical questions about the scope of personal agency and the power of structural constraint. In the example of women irrigators in Nepal outlined above, some women chose not to participate in the irrigators' association partly because they saw that in so doing they would be bound by rules that did not favour them. However, in drawing on ideas about the 'proper' role of women to justify their non-participation were they exercising agency or simply acquiescing to their structural gendered subordination, or both? Doubts among individuals about the merits of being included in development

Box 3.6 Inclusion and exclusion, participation and rights of access to water

In Nkayi District in Western Zimbabwe there were generally accepted principles by which access to water is managed.

A hierarchy of 'rightful' users is apparent at waterpoints; ranging from those immediately local residents with undisputed rights of use to more distant residents whose usage is considered conditional. 'Conditional' users negotiate access to waterpoints (often through kinship and appeals to custom) but remain vulnerable to exclusion. However, the deeply held idea that universal access to water is a right generally ensures that 'conditional' users can meet their water needs.

Access rights are further complicated by participatory development initiatives which emphasize the concept of 'ownership' of water sources, specifying that only those who have participated in implementation (through providing labour and materials) have earned the right to be considered owners. Participation in implementation is generally organized on the basis of residence close to the water point. Such differentiation between users has little impact until the dry season, or longer-term droughts when the general socially embedded principle of allowing all to draw water contracts. In drought months the rights of 'conditional users' contract severely; they have to wait until all others have collected water and often there is not sufficient available for them. Increasingly they are seen as *not* 'the rightful owners' of a particular water source. Often such people are poor, their residences spatially marginal and their ability to participate in community decision-making limited by their poverty. Participatory development efforts may thus reinforce the marginalization of poor and peripheral households.

Source: Cleaver 1996

projects from the point of view of preserving individual freedom are common, suggesting a sophisticated analysis among people of the structural instruments of their subordination and a blindness among development agencies to this (Long 1992; Scott 1985).

The participatory literature in development maintains oversimplified ideas about the beneficial nature to individuals of participation, overlooking the potential links between inclusion and possible subordination. We would do well to examine issues of empowerment and subordination more critically, recognizing that they are not necessarily diametrically opposed conditions (Jackson 1998) and seeking lessons from literature on participation and inclusion outside the development field (Willis 1977; Allen 1997; Croft and Beresford 1996). It is important to remember that 'community' may be used as a definition of exclusion as well as inclusion, that associating concepts of responsibility, ownership and social cohesion with local entities (which may draw on religious, ethnic, locational differences in definition) is not necessarily compatible with the universalizing of equality or with the rights of particular individuals. Exclusionary tendencies may be increased in locally based participatory development, as the example of changing ideas about access to water (Box 3.6) shows.

Conclusion: Reassessing Participatory Approaches

'Participation' in development activities has been translated into a managerial exercise based on 'toolboxes' of procedures and techniques. It has been turned away from its radical roots: we now talk of problem-solving through participation rather than problematization, critical engagement and class (Brown, n.d.). This limited approach to participation gives rise to a number of critical tensions or paradoxes. While we emphasize the desirability of empowerment, project approaches remain largely concerned with efficiency. While we recognize the importance of institutions, we focus attention only on the highly visible, formal, local organizations, overlooking the numerous communal activities that occur through daily interactions and socially embedded arrangements. A strong emphasis on the participation of individuals and their potential empowerment is not supported by convincing analyses of individual positions, of the variability of the costs and benefits of participation, of the opportunities and constraints experienced by potential participants. The time is ripe for a critical re-analysis of 'participatory approaches'.

Many claims about participation, most of which assert that it is a good thing, remain unproven. We need, then, a detailed collection of empirical evidence of the effects of participation, which, despite nearly two decades of the implementation of participatory approaches, is surprisingly lacking. The well-developed tools of PRA/PLA, which currently assume the desirability of participation and are commonly used as formulaic engagement activities in development projects, could effectively be adapted to investigate relations of power, to uncover the variability in people's perceptions of the costs and benefits of participation, the complexity of individuals' motivations.

Further empirical evidence and analysis is needed of whether and *how* the structures of participatory projects include/protect/secure the interests of poor people. What *exactly* are the linkages between the participation of poor individuals and the furthering of their social and economic good? Understanding this requires analyses of 'competent' communities and 'successful' participatory projects that focus on process, on power dynamics, on patterns of inclusion and exclusion. These could be built up through process documentation of the dynamics of conflict, consensus-building and decision-making within communities, not just the recording of project-related activities.

Understanding how participation can benefit the poor might also involve identifying the role of better, more responsive development agencies in promoting more effective and equitable forms of involvement (Jarman and Johnson 1997; Thompson 1995), or in offering state action to substitute or reinforce community participation where the costs of this are very high to the participants. Several studies now link meaningful societal change to state action prompted by popular political and social movements (for example, see Deere and Leon 1998), and we would do well to expand our focus away from the institutional nuts and bolts of development projects to consider the wider dynamics of economic and social change.

I have suggested in this chapter that we can further our understanding of participatory processes through an approach that takes into account the relationship between social structure and individual agency. In particular, we can use this to improve our understanding of the institutions of participation and the individuals involved.

A more dynamic vision is needed of 'institutions' and of 'community', one that incorporates social networks and recognizes dispersed and contingent power relations, the exclusionary as well as the inclusionary nature of participation. We need a much better understanding of local norms of decision-making and representation, of how these change and are negotiated, of how people may indirectly affect outcomes without direct participation.

It is also necessary to develop a more complex modelling of livelihood concerns over life courses, of the negotiated nature of participation and a more honest assessment of the costs and benefits to individuals of becoming involved in agency- and state-directed development processes. In order to do this we need to be able to analyse the resources that people need in order to be able to participate in development efforts, and to find ways of assessing which participatory approaches are low-cost and of high benefit to poor people.

In conclusion, I see the need for a radical reassessment of the desirability, practicality and efficacy of development efforts based on community participation. This involves rethinking not just the relationship between differently placed individuals and historically and spatially specific social structure, but also the role of individuals, households, communities, development agencies and the state.

Note

1. The terms 'formal' (modern, bureaucratic, organizational) and 'informal' (social, traditional) institutions are convenient but misleading. Traditional and social institutions may indeed be highly formalized, although not necessarily in the bureaucratic forms that we recognize. Much literature also exists in organizational studies about the informal dimensions of organizations. An alternative terminology might characterize institutions as 'organizational' and/or 'socially embedded', more nearly representing our actual usage of the terms. Obviously the two terms are not mutually exclusive; the dichotomy is a false one.

4

Pluralism, Participation and Power: Joint Forest Management in India

Nicholas Hildyard, Pandurang Hegde, Paul Wolvekamp and Somasekhare Reddy

Introduction

Participation, forests and environment all mean different things to different people and different interest groups. For some government departments and industry groups, the environment is principally what is around their economies; for local villagers, it is what is around their homes and livelihoods. For Forest Department officials, forests may be what pass across their desks; for villagers, they represent secure water supplies, the availability of fodder for animals, medicines for friends or family, places to play or sources of spiritual power. Similarly, 'participation' covers a spectrum of meanings: for many project managers, it may signal a means to cut costs, secure cheap labour or co-opt opposition; for marginalized groups, by contrast, it is a right – both a means to an end and an end in itself.

Understanding whose meanings do and do not prevail – and the processes by which this comes about – punctures much of the rhetoric of empowerment that accompanies current 'participatory' development projects: far from unsettling oppressive power relations, what passes for participation frequently serves to sustain and reinforce inequitable economic, political and social structures – to the detriment of marginalized groups.

This chapter looks at conflicts over the meaning of 'participation' and 'forests' in the context of the growing vogue for 'participatory forest management'. It begins by examining the wide gap between the experience of participation on the ground and the rhetoric of development agencies, such as the World Bank. The following section traces the rise of 'participatory forest management' in India and examines the institutional and political pressures that have made 'Joint Forest Management' an attractive response to widespread popular unrest over the commercial exploitation of forests and the exclusion of local people from forest resources. Next, the chapter focuses on one project, the Western Ghats Forestry Project, in which the authors have been variously involved, either as local activists or as staff of Northern-based solidarity groups. This sets out what participation has meant in practice for local villagers: who has benefited and who lost out, and how local people have used the project to further their own agendas, both positive and negative. The concluding section argues that a participation that fails to engage with the distribution and operations of power within local communities and the wider society in which they live is likely to offer little to marginalized groups.

Participation and Forest Management

Many popular movements, rooted in the day-to-day struggles of marginalized and oppressed groups, seek change through agrarian reform, local control over resources, the power to veto developments, a decisive say in all matters that affect livelihoods, and a politics that is committed to unsettling inequitable power relationships at all levels of society – not only between communities but within them. The search is generally not for 'alternatives' in the sense that Western environmentalists might use the term; rather it is often to rejuvenate what works, to combine traditional and new approaches and to develop strategies that meet local needs. For them the question is not how their environment should be managed but whose environment gets managed, by whom and in whose interest (*The Ecologist* 1993).

But while 'management', a buzzword now common in development literature, is not what grassroots organizations want more of, it is increasingly what is on offer. The preferred response of many planners, politicians, development practitioners, civil servants and heads of industry to environmental degradation lies in increasingly global forms of management. In contrast to commons-based movements – which place particular store by the virtues of receptivity, patience, open-endedness, and respect for the opinions of others – the managerial approach is instrumental and (inevitably) top-down.

Therefore, given the very different approaches to environmental degradation in general and to forests in particular, it is perhaps unsurprising that the growing enthusiasm among forestry departments the world over for participatory forms of forest management – and, increasingly, for participatory approaches that stress 'community-based resource management' – should arouse deep suspicions even within those movements that have made participation and community control of forests a central plank of their political agenda.

One reason for that suspicion is that few of the institutions that are now pushing for participation – a 'warmly persuasive word' which seems 'never to be used unfavourably' (Williams 1976: 76) – have a history of taking such participation seriously. Consider, for example, the World Bank, which is committed to the principle of participation in numerous policy documents. Its Forest Policy, for example, states that the 'Bank will stress new approaches to the management of protected areas that incorporate local people into protection, benefit sharing and planning and will highlight the need to consider the needs and welfare of forest-dwelling people' (World Bank 1994: 65). That policy, according to an internal 1994 *Implementation Review*, has been successfully implemented by Bank staff, the *Review* stating that the Bank:

> has responded to the mandate provided by the policy to focus its assistance on helping governments ... empower rural people to better conserve and manage all forests and 'incorporated into its work the need to involve stakeholders with interests in the forests'. (World Bank 1994: paras v and xi, Executive Summary)

The reality on the ground, however, is very different. As Larry Lohmann points out in a critique of the Bank's record on participation, written at the time of the Bank's *Implementation Review*:

> I have in front of me hundreds of pages of a Pre-Investment Study for a GEF project called The Conservation Forest Area Protection, Management and Development Project, which is a project in the pipeline for an important protected area in Thailand, and which is mentioned in the *Implementation Review*. These hundreds of pages are only part of the Study ... The project is slated for an area – the Thung Yai-Huai Kha Khaeng sanctuaries – inhabited by thousands of Karen people, who speak a language distinct from that of the Thai majority. The project calls for their eviction. Yet not one of these hundreds of pages of bureaucratic English has been translated in Thai, much less Karen: much less communicated to, much less discussed with, much less agreed to by the local Karen people in the sanctuary to be affected. This in spite of the fact that NGOs have requested Thai translations of all this material.
>
> The task manager of the GEF project I've referred to ... perhaps

> provided some insight into this novel concept of 'participation' and 'empowerment' when he told a Thai audience ... that the eviction of the Karen people of Thung Yai-Huai Kha Khaeng – a course of action which is, by the way, opposed by the chief of the Thung Yai sanctuary himself – would have to be carried out by means of 'the sword, the carrot and the stick'. (Lohmann 1994: 5–6)[1]

Lohmann's purpose in recounting the failure of 'participation' in Thung Yai-Huai Kha Khaeng is 'not to embarrass the task manager for his ignorance or for his contempt for his employer's policies' but rather 'to suggest that the failure to implement the Forest policy's clauses on participation is deep-seated and structural'. The sort of attitude and practice followed by [him] is 'not an isolated individual aberration'; it is 'embedded throughout the culture of the World Bank' (ibid.: 6). Indeed, judging from the Bank's 1997 *World Development Report*, such support as exists within the more influential quarters of the World Bank for participatory approaches appears to derive not from a concern for the democratic rights of local people but from a perception that participation helps to save on the 'transaction costs' of projects (World Bank 1997). This is not to say that there are no sympathetic individuals within these institutions; on the contrary. The reality is, however, that they have to operate within a framework which is often not sympathetic to their points of view and which blocks their intentions.

Not surprisingly, when development agencies, such as the World Bank, actively begin to pursue participatory programmes, those who have had past experience of Bank projects have good reason to be wary. What is the Bank up to? Why the sudden enthusiasm for consulting people? What is the Bank's game plan? In the main, the answers to those and other sceptical questions are either supplied by the Bank's own project documents (with their paternalistic emphasis on 'educating' local people into 'better practices') or by the cosmetic nature of participation in the vast majority of projects where participatory approaches have actually been implemented. Not only does consultation tend to be desultory, but even where meetings are held, the voices of local people rarely appear to be listened to. Local people become a ghostly presence within the planning process – visible, heard even, but ultimately only there because their involvement lends credibility and legitimacy to decisions that have already been made. Far from being a transformative process in which local people are able to exert control over decision-making, participation becomes a well-honed tool for engineering consent to projects and programmes whose framework has already been determined in advance – a means for top-down planning to be imposed from the bottom up. As a minister in a recently 'democratized' country recently commented on his ministry's use of participation: 'We decide what is to be done and we tell the people to do it' (Peters, P. 1996: 22) (see illustration in Box 4.1).

The call for local people to have a decisive say in the matters that affect their lives have been contained through the directed use of 'participatory' processes that are reworked to suit the ends of industry and other powerful groupings – notably that of increasing control over local people. Grassroots organizations thus become the human 'software' through which investments can be made with least local opposition. As Majid Rahnema, formerly of the UNDP, puts it: 'Participation is now simply perceived as one of the many "resources" needed to keep the economy alive. To participate is thus

Box 4.1 Resisting imposed participation?

The minister may well find that 'telling people what to do' does not always bring the desired effects. 'Stakeholders' at the receiving end of imposed participation are adept at defecting or otherwise subtly resisting the obligations placed on them. Even so, the sense of anger at being treated as passive know-nothings is acute. The Catholic Institute for International Relations, for example, recounts the outcome of one 'participatory' project in Southern India, which involved 19 village women being given a Bank loan to buy a dairy cow: 'The loans were guaranteed by a local development project and given on condition that the women attended a two-week training course in dairy management organized by the development project. To the project's staff, this seemed like a very sensible scheme. There was a large market for milk in a nearby city and the scheme appeared to have the support of the beneficiaries. But 90 per cent of the women didn't use the money to buy a dairy animal: some of them kept the money, some of them used it to retrieve mortgaged jewellery, one woman's husband gambled it. When questioned by the project's staff the women claimed that they had bought dairy animals and they showed a friend's or relative's animal to prove it. However, when the staff of the project performed a role-play of what happened in the villages where the women lived the effect was instantaneous: there was arguing and shouting, women admitting reduced to the act of partaking in the objectives of the economy and the societal arrangements related to it' (Rahnema 1990: 120).

Joint Forest Management

In India, JFM and its latest incarnation, JFPM (Joint Forest Planning and Management), has played an increasingly central role in forestry projects and programmes since the late 1980s. Its adoption by both central and state governments followed widespread protests against both the degradation of forests through industrial forestry and the exclusion of local people from forest resources.

Under the prompting of agencies such as the World Bank, the Indian government initially responded to this growing public unrest by initiating

that they had no cows, men laughing at wives and friends who had been exposed. But there were also accusations from the women that shocked the project staff: 'You did not ask us if we wanted dairy animals', 'I would rather have had a loan to start a tea business', 'I wanted to retrieve my mortgaged coconut trees' (CIIR 1995). Happily, in this instance, the outcome was not detrimental to those local people who were participating in the project, which, as CIIR points out, had broad local support (CIIR 1995). In many other projects, however, local people become effectively 'trapped' into projects whose ends may be far from beneficial to the majority of the local community. In some cases, participatory 'self-help' schemes or 'food-for-work' programmes have been used to secure cheap labour for infrastructure projects (Chambers 1995; Nelson and Wright 1995; Peters 1996); in others to soften the social and economic consequences of policies, such as structural adjustment programmes, which have exacerbated social and economic inequalities and eroded still further the position of poorer sections of the community. In still others, the nature of the participation and the design of the programmes have resulted in state and commercial interests extending their influence into villages and households - or in more subtle forms of control. For a discussion of one such project in the Philippines, which mainly served to institute sophisticated mechanisms to manage women, see St Clair 1995.

a series of social forestry programmes, the stated aim being to meet local needs for firewood and other forest products through the active participation of villagers in plantation forestry. Far from defusing the protests, however, the widespread take-over of communal lands for commercial plantations (chiefly environmentally damaging eucalyptus for the pulp and paper industry) rather than woodlots for villagers led to still further unrest, with villagers uprooting the eucalyptus.

However, as Dolly Arora, an Indian political commentator, points out, 'although successful experiments carried out in several local settings (undoubtedly) increased the openness of the state in adopting participatory approaches', the embracing of JFM by so many states in such a short space of time cannot be explained by this factor alone. Perhaps more to the point is the increased bargaining power achieved by local movements as a result of strategic alliances not only with sympathetic foresters but also with urban-based environmental groups and international NGOs.

> With powerful national or international NGOs entering the scene and extending support to local organizations of people to assert their rights on forest resources, the capacity of states to overlook the claims of people without worsening the crisis of their own legitimacy weakened considerably – it seemed better to relate to the programme of these organizations than to alienate them. (Arora 1994: 693)

Significantly, in Orissa and West Bengal, the two states that led the way in adopting JFM, the promulgation of formal provisions for participation only took place after numerous village groups had already taken matters into their own hands and set up organizations to protect local forests. In Orissa, for instance, 'a survey ... revealed that as many as 1,181 blocks of forest patches ranging from 9 to 1,000 hectares ... were already under the protection of adjoining villages at the time of the promotion of new JFM regulations' (ibid.: 694). Likewise, in West Bengal, 'a very large number of villages were already engaged in protection work when the JFM rules were promoted' (ibid.). In effect, 'people's participation and people's power preceded, rather than resulted from, policy change in these areas' (ibid.).

In a number of states, however, JFM came to India not so much as a result of domestic institutions responding to popular pressure as from international agencies doing so. In Karnataka, for example, people's movements were extremely active throughout the 1980s (and indeed for decades beforehand) in defending and regenerating forests: resistance to social forestry programmes in the state, funded by the World Bank and Britain's Overseas Development Administration (now Department of International

Development, DfID), were particularly widespread. While the Karnataka Forest Department (KFD) all but ignored the national shift towards JFM, however, it took the opportunity to cash in on national and international concerns over forest degradation by drawing up a funding proposal for an extensive tree-planting programme and submitting it to the Overseas Development Administration (ODA) for funding.

Entirely missing from the proposal was any element of people's participation. Instead, local people featured largely as a source of cheap labour for replanting schemes. Nevertheless, eager to redress the failures of the previous Social Forestry project, the ODA agreed to consider the project provided that people's participation and poverty alleviation were incorporated as central concerns. A series of workshops with the Karnataka State Forest Department (KFD) and local NGOs followed, as a result of which the project was substantially modified, although NGOs still expressed considerable concern, particularly over plans to divide the forest up into zones, with people being excluded from 'core' conservation areas, and over the weakness of measures to address social justice issues. Intense lobbying by NGOs, both in Karnataka and in Britain, forced the ODA to postpone signing the agreement and undertake a further appraisal. In April 1991, a final project document was drawn up by the KFD incorporating 'off-the-shelf' participation plans (largely based on proposals drawn up by UK forestry experts) that would bring Joint Forest Planning and Management to the Western Ghats. Subsequently, the UK government agreed to commit £24 million to the project. A condition of the ODA funding was that the Karnataka State Government should issue government orders facilitating JFPM in Karnataka. The orders, however, were issued only in April 1993 – a year after the start of the project – and JFPM was explicitly to focus on degraded forest areas: elsewhere, villagers would have no rights to participate in the decisions affecting forest use (Feeney 1998: 67).[2]

Village Forest Committees

The above project highlights many of the failings of JFM in general and JFPM in particular, and is worth considering in some detail. Its main aim, as laid down in the final project documents, is to enhance and improve the management capacity of the KFD, and in particular to enable it to respond to the conflicting demands from different users for access to the forest.

Villagers were encouraged to form Village Forest Committees (VFCs) with responsibility for conserving and restoring specified areas of forest and sharing the benefits (sales of timber from plantations, for example) with the Forest Department. However, VFCs have proved highly problematic. In many cases, particularly at the start of the project, the KFD proceeded with plantations even though no VFC had actually been formed. As Patricia Feeney of Oxfam reports, 'Although public meetings were held ... to tell the local community about the project and to listen nominally to their suggestions about planting, nurseries had already been raised and pits dug before any consultation occurred. Planting was pre-determined by the KFD' (Feeney 1998: 72). Where VFCs were formed, the meetings were often held at short notice at the convenience of the KFD, officials of which kept the minutes of meetings and managed the funds, leading to suspicions that the VFCs were little more than outreach arms of the KFD set up solely to satisfy the ODA's conditions of funding. Indeed, many VFCs appeared to exist on paper only.

Although supposed to ensure the participation of all sections of the village in deciding planting regimes, many VFCs are dominated by more powerful social groups and by men. In half the villages where VFCs had been formed by 1997, for example, many households are not members. In the majority of these cases, the non-members tend to be from the poorest families in the village. As Feeney notes:

> Non-membership not only excludes them from information about income deriving from plantations but it also excludes them from information about JFPM and the decision-making process. [Moreover] those villagers who become members acquire the responsibility and authority to compel the non-members to confirm to the VFC's decisions regarding areas of forest to be protected and to respect new rules about access to and use of forest produce. This can have a dramatic impact on the rights of the poorest villagers to collect non-timber forest products (NTFPs) on a day-to-day basis to meet their subsistence needs. The Karnataka Government Order fails to specify whether non-members continue to enjoy their customary rights and privileges in JFPM areas. Denial of such rights has serious equity implications and may become a future source of conflict. (Feeney 1998: 74)

In effect, the VFCs directly or indirectly reorder access to and rights over the environment, generally (though not exclusively) in favour of the landed elites who dominate the VFCs even in villages which have full membership (Saxena et al. 1997). As an ODA-sponsored independent review of the project, initiated in response to NGO lobbying, comments, such elite-dominated VFC leadership carries with it 'the very real danger that the wealthier members of the VFC may use JFPM as a means of gaining control over additional forest resources (thereby increasing their own political and economic power), while further reducing the access of marginalized groups who depend on forest resources to meet their basic needs' (ibid.: 205).

One reason for the dominance of elites on the VFCs is the old boy network that the KFD brings into play when initiating new VFCs. Generally, forest officers tend to contact those whom they consider to be the most important people in the village, who also happen, in many cases, to be those with whom they have had previous contact: sometimes a forest contractor, sometimes a former KFD official, or sometimes a relative of such a contact. Usually, it is these village bigwigs who wind up being the president of the VFC or becoming its members. Understandably, many are suspicious of the VFC's impartiality. A recent Oxfam appraisal of the project quotes a villager from Honnavar:

> What difference does this JFPM make? Our president has worked in the KFD for many years. Do you think he is any different from them? They suggested his name as the president. And we had to agree. It's not that they forced us but you know what will happen if we don't agree to what the KFD says. We have to live in this village for the rest of our lives. (Mitra 1997: 60)

Women, in particular low-caste women, have found their voices marginalized by the project, despite genuine efforts by the ODA to include participation of women. Originally, the Government Order, as laid down by the KFD, prescribed one representative to the VFC per household, which, as Patricia Feeney of Oxfam reports, 'had the effect of systematically excluding women from the VFCs and from active participation in JFPM' (Feeney 1998: 77). Subsequently, at the insistence of the ODA, the Order was amended to make 'spouses' automatic members of VFCs. Even so, this still leaves many marginalized women (and men) within households excluded –for example, single women and men, women whose partners have left them, second wives, and widowed elders.

Almost five years after the start of the project, many remained unaware of even the existence of VFCs, let alone their intentions. Although the ODA subsequently insisted that VFC management committees include at least two women, the places often go to higher-caste women who generally have little or no contact with poor and landless women. Where women attend the VFC meetings, they generally 'sit quietly and serve tea and snacks', while some 'fail to attend VFC meetings altogether because there is no discussion of problems affecting them' (ibid.). Even where such discussion does take place, the voices of women are frequently ignored. In one village, for example, women complained that the scarcity of fuelwood meant that they had to spend up to three hours a day collecting a headload of leaves and twigs for cooking fuel. Only six of the 97 VFC members in the village are women, however, 'so there was little objection when the VFC decided to sell off all the firewood from their 30 hectare JFPM plantation instead of using it to meet local consumption needs' (ibid.). In such circumstances, women often have no option but to violate the rules of the VFC rather than let their families starve. 'When this happens,' reports Mariette Correa in a study commissioned for the Dhaward-based India Development Service, 'they are considered offenders liable for fines and are beaten by their husbands' (Correa 1995: 5). Indeed, Correa argues, far from improving the position of women, the project may, in important respects, have undermined it further: 'Earlier, when forest management was under the control of the Forest Department, women offenders at least had the support of the men in their families. Now the policing role of the government has been taken on at village level by male-dominated VFCs and may have succeeded in further exacerbating gender inequalities within the household' (ibid.). Unsurprisingly, some NGOs have responded by creating all-women VFCs, which have, to a considerable degree, managed to overcome the silencing of women's voices.

Although the project was intended to ensure that poorer people, women, tribals and other disadvantaged groups who are dependent on the forest 'are not worse, and preferably better off', it has in many cases caused considerable hardship to local villagers. The ODA-funded plantations have been mainly on village commons, from which villagers (particularly poorer villagers) derive pasture for animals, fuel, manure, medicinal plants, and other products to fulfil their basic needs. Women have been particularly affected by the planting of common lands, since they now need to travel longer distances to obtain firewood which, increasingly, they must take from forest lands. The result is often further forest destruction.

In some villages, landless families who have encroached on common land for lack of land to grow food have been evicted to make way for the plantations, depriving them of their livelihood, without any compensation (although it should be said that some richer villagers who have encroached on land have also been evicted). However, as the independent review team notes, such evictions provide only the most visible examples of how the project has undermined the security of poorer villagers:

> A disturbing feature (of the project) is either the continuing irrelevance of

> JFPM to the livelihood related needs of marginalized but highly resource dependent communities ... or the evident danger of marginalized groups within more differentiated and heterogeneous communities being systematically further marginalized through reduction, rather than an increase, in their access to forest resources through the present JFPM implementation process. In [some] villages, it is not through dramatic interventions of poor encroachers being evicted from forest land, for which the project has been criticized by some NGOs, but through the more invisible and subtle processes of exclusion, delegitimization of their traditional resource use patterns, use of monetary and wage incentives from plantations instead of making existing forest dependent livelihoods more sustainable, that the project and the current implementation of JFPM are subtly, but systematically further disempowering the already marginalized and resource poor. (Saxena et al. 1997: 64–5)

The project has brought particular problems for poorer groups who rely on herding or raising cattle, such as the Gowlis, a local tribal group, who have also been badly hit by the decline in grazing land, as have many sharecroppers whose ability to engage successfully in a tenancy is often dependent on ownership of livestock, particularly draught animals (Feeney 1997).

NGOs also warned that, despite a commitment to allow villagers to plant trees of their choice, the project would encourage the further conversion of natural forest to monoculture plantations. Under the WGFP, gaps in the forest are to be planted with 'valuable timber species', with the aim of restoring the natural mix of the forest. Shortly after the project began, such practices led an ODA review to warn that 'the project is open to the criticism of promoting of monoculture at the cost of biodiversity' (Khare n.d.).

In 1997, after NGOs had raised these and other problems with the project authorities, the ODA and KFD commissioned an independent review of the project. Although the independent review noted that the project had brought 'substantial gains' in terms of 'greater interaction between [the] KFD and local communities' (Saxena et al. 1997: 190), it confirmed the majority of the NGOs' concerns, recommending a number of important changes to the project.

The review argued that 'VFCs can meaningfully participate as partners of the Forest Department only if they grow into robust, self-governing, autonomous people's organizations', and recommended that the obligations placed on communities through JFPM should be balanced by clearly defined rights – not least of which is the right of VFCs to govern themselves and to exercise authority over a wider range of areas. A number of conditions, the review argues, must be met if the VFCs are to succeed: a) communities must have a full understanding of the agreement with the forest department; b) the agreement must be worthwhile; c) the community must be able to devise easy and practical ways of ensuring that each member adheres to the agreement; d) the community must be able to impose graduated sanctions in case of non-compliance; and e) structures and processes for self-governing must be firmly in place (ibid.: 220).

Power, Participation and Political Space

For all their failings, there is no doubt that, in some instances, villagers have been able to use the VFCs and the Western Ghats project in general to open up a political space that might otherwise not have been available. In one village, for example, villagers were able to use the authority that the VFC nominally gave them to close a polluting mine, in another, to secure a long-promised road. More generally, by providing 'a sharp focus on questions of equity and local livelihood systems', the project has provided some villages the opportunity to challenge the power exercised by dominant and powerful village groups over the forest. It has also 'opened up the door for redefining the relationship between [the field staff of the KFD] and communities' (Khare n.d.: 41).

The key point, however, is that few of these gains have come about as a result of the project *per se*. Almost all have been won only as a result of villagers taking the project and using it to create their own futures. Moreover, the procedural changes that have been introduced in the project – for example through the independent review – have almost all come about only as a result of intense NGO lobbying.

A second key point is that NGOs and villagers are not the only actors to have found political space within the project. By rightly highlighting the inefficiency and corruption of the Forest Department, for example, the project has also proved useful to those seeking to privatize forestry in India. Whose agenda gets heard, and implemented, will depend not on rational debate but on the relative bargaining power of those now seeking to push the project in their various chosen directions. Failing to be aware of the different agendas being pursued is thus a potentially dangerous game – one that could end up marginalizing those for whom political struggle is not just another campaign but a defence of livelihood.

Indeed, a participation that fails to engage with the distribution and operations of power within local communities and the wider society in which they live is likely to offer little to marginalized groups.

Many participatory projects rest on the dubious assumption that simply identifying different 'stakeholders' and getting them around the table will result in a consensus being reached that is 'fair' to all. Such an assumption only holds, however, if all the actors involved are deemed to have equal bargaining power (which they do not) or if the inequalities between stakeholders is viewed as a purely technical matter, the only challenge being to ensure that correct procedures are formulated for bringing the parties into contact, changing the behaviour and attitudes of those who are used to dominating, and giving 'primary stakeholders' more chance of voicing their view of the world (Wright and Nelson 1995: 6). As Wright and Nelson note, however, society is not made up of 'free-floating actors, each with different interests which they pursue by bargaining with each other in interactional space'. Facilitating measures may be important in negotiations but they are not enough to grant marginal groups the bargaining power they require to overcome the structural dominance enjoyed by more powerful groups. On this view, participation requires wider processes of social transformation and structural change to the system of social relations through which inequalities are reproduced. Behavioural changes, though necessary, are not enough.

Addressing the structural causes of inequality demands not only policy changes – for example agrarian reform – but, arguably, rethinking the means by which such change is achieved. Many NGOs, for example, are drawn to participate in projects whose framework neither they nor the communities with whom they work have any substantive role in designing because their conception of power as something that a small minority (the 'powerful') 'have' and that others (the 'powerless') 'lack' dictates that participation in such projects is the only way that they will exert influence.

The ability of dissenters to effect change through the 'powerful' is hampered still further by the fact that the 'real world' of the 'powerful' bears little resemblance to the real world the dissenters know. Planners sit about discussing countries where people exist only as numbers, where government structures are assumed to act as politically impartial conduits for implementing projects, where local landscapes are mapped not in terms of forests or fields but in terms of cubic feet of lumber or yields per hectare, and where people are assumed to behave in strict accordance with sociological theory. Activists should not therefore be surprised that the planners' programmes, however carefully prepared, generally flounder the moment they leave the drawing board. By the time they are implemented, they are frequently unrecognizable even to their authors. Projects aimed at increasing public participation or 'decentralizing power' end up excluding 'target populations' and strengthening elites and local power relationships that the planners may not even have known existed.

Such a view argues for NGOs and others to take a more political-committed approach to participatory projects – and to press donors and governments to do likewise. If international and national development agencies are serious about addressing issues of equity, sustainability and poverty reduction, they should give primacy to the needs and political demands of marginalized and oppressed groups. Not only may this require them to take measures that actively disempower dominant groups (for example, through the implementation of agrarian reform or, as in the Western Ghats project, promoting women-only VFCs), it also calls for funds and other forms of support to be offered in the spirit of active solidarity – not in order to co-opt stakeholders to a preconceived agenda or with a view to empowering from outside.

Such active solidarity may take many forms. At a minimum, however, it would seem to demand that development agencies make hard choices as to whom they work with. Blaming client governments or their departments when a project stifles participation of local people in resource management, for example, should have no place in agencies that are committed to fostering genuine participation and local control. It should be the responsibility of agency staff to evaluate in advance whether or not a partner government is likely to support local participation and not to become involved if this evaluation is negative (Lohmann 1994). If a positive evaluation turns out to be incorrect, then at the very least it should have an effect on the career prospects of the relevant staff members. It would also seem to demand that staff members themselves take seriously their commitments to the marginalized groups they seek to support.

They cannot 'give' empowerment to their 'beneficiaries', 'targets of development' or 'clients': to be 'participants', people have to be able to use their 'power to' to negotiate and transform those hopefully willing partners who have institutional and structural 'power over'. Indeed, perhaps the first step that agencies that are serious about participation and pluralism might take is not to reach for the latest handbook on participatory techniques, but to put their own house in order: to consider how their own internal hierarchies, training techniques and office cultures discourage the receptivity, flexibility, patience, open-mindedness, non-defensiveness, humour, curiosity and respect for the opinions of others that active solidarity demands. Dictating and PR techniques may 'get things done' – but they inevitably end up reinforcing the problem that, in theory, the done things are intending to solve.

Notes

1. Of the failure to translate the projects documents, Lohmann comments: 'Let's put this in perspective. Imagine that a government official arrives at your house and announces that certain modifications are going to have to be made in its structure which will make it impossible for you to live there. He hastens to add that you are encouraged to participate in this renovation, and explains that you are free to ask for the documents which describe in detail what is to be done. Unfortunately, however, these documents are in Chinese. He is sorry about this, but the fact is that he has insufficient staff to translate them for you right now. He invites you to sympathize with his plight. The bright spot is that the documents, for those who can read them, describe how you will be "empowered" in a way which will enable you to seek a better life once you have been moved out of your house.'

2. Although the government order has since been amended to allow VFCs to be implemented in areas of high forest density, the order permits this only where there are forest-dependent tribals.

5

Participatory Development at the World Bank: The Primacy of Process

Paul Francis

Introduction

In his 1998 Annual Meetings speech, the president of the World Bank informed the world that: 'Participation matters – not only as a means of improving development effectiveness, as we know from our recent studies – but as the key to long-term sustainability and leverage.' The concept of participation has become central to the repertoire with which the Bank has sought to remake its public face.

World Bank operations now regularly, though not consistently, incorporate participatory methods in preparation or implementation. Three methodological approaches to participation may be broadly distinguished: Participatory Rural Appraisal (PRA), Beneficiary Assessment and Social Analysis. These approaches have several characteristics in common. All are justified in terms of the shortcomings of conventional development planning methods, which are seen as lacking in a 'human' or 'social' dimension. All, too, stress the importance of incorporating the actor's, or 'emic' view – that is, the perceptions, values and priorities of local or 'beneficiary' populations. However, despite these common features, the rationales, methods and epistemologies of the three approaches differ quite widely, as do the assumptions about social reality, explanation and the nature of development upon which they are based.

This chapter focuses primarily on PRA. It explores in particular its conception of the social and its vision of the role of the professional, in both of which the method is distinct from Beneficiary Assessment and Social Analysis. The chapter then assesses the relative influence of the PRA and the other two approaches to participation on operational practice in the World Bank. It argues that the adoption of a participatory agenda, while promoting consultation and highlighting process concerns, has for the most part neglected the need for accompanying social and structural analysis.

The following sections provide very brief summaries of Beneficiary Assessment and Social Analysis before considering some of the main features of PRA as used within the World Bank. Some of the key characteristics of the three approaches are presented in Table 5.1.

TABLE 5.1 Three 'social development' approaches compared

	Beneficiary Assessment	Participatory Rural Appraisal	Social Assessment
Precursors/ affinities	Market research	Rapid Rural Appraisal Farming Systems Research Action Research Freire Indigenous Technical Knowledge	Academic sociology and anthropology
Perspective of data	Emic and etic	Mainly emic	Emic and etic
Methodological orientation	Priorities, attitudes	Attitudes, values, perception, etc.	Social and historical processes; caste, class, etc.
Product orientation	Data extraction	Local empowerment	Research/advocacy
Professional role/orientation	Low specialization	Charismatic specialist	Specialized mediator (social scientist)
Ritual analogy	Evangelist	Shaman	Priest/mediator
Action orientation	Analysis and feedback	Local empowerment	Analysis and design
Hierarchy compatibility	+ + +	Ambiguous	+ +
Market compatibility	+ + +	+ +	Potentially good

Beneficiary Assessment Beneficiary Assessment (BA) is a method most associated with Salmen (1987; 1995), who has defined it as: 'an approach to information gathering which assesses the value of an activity as it is perceived by its principal users … a systematic enquiry into people's values and behaviour in relation to a planned or ongoing intervention for social and economic change' (Salmen 1995: 1).

BA has become the most widely used participative methodology in World Bank operations. Its rationale lies in the spatial and social distance perceived to exist between project management and beneficiaries, a 'gap', as Salmen describes it, between 'two worlds' (Salmen 1987: 2).

BA seeks to close this gap by obtaining 'the view from the ground … the grass roots' (ibid.: 2), accessing the 'voice' of the beneficiary in a way which sample or formal discussions are unable to do: 'development planners and managers need to develop their antennae, to extend their eyes and ears into the communities where they are planning and carrying out projects' (ibid.: 51). The method owes as much to market research as to social research, and Salmen frequently draws the parallel between the method and the methods of managers in private business, who are obliged to pay attention to the needs of both customers and workers. While Salmen asserts that 'the sociopolitical dynamics of a community are as important to understand as the technical aspects and design of [a] project' (ibid.: 40), for the most part the clean, modernist lines of BA are uncluttered by any notion of social structure. Methodologically, BA generally combines participant observation with some degree of quantitative data collection.

Social analysis The work of Michael Cernea, the doyen of social science at the World Bank, illustrates some of the achievements and dilemmas of applied social science in development. Cernea's introduction to *Putting People First* (1991), a collection of writings that documents the contribution of social science to the work of the World Bank, is a programmatic statement on the application of social science to development problems. The rationale for anthropological and sociological involvement in development projects and policy, Cernea argues, lies in the neglect of a missing domain, the 'social dimension', 'a structure of social relations' in which 'people's economic activities are embedded' (ibid.: 9).

The role of the social analyst is to 'identify, conceptualize, and deal with the social and cultural variables' that make up this missing dimension (ibid.: 10). Even if the financial aspects of a project are apparently proceeding smoothly, these sociocultural factors 'continue to work *under the surface*. If the social variables remain unaddressed or mishandled, then the project will be unsustainable and fail, no matter which government or international agency promotes it' (ibid.; emphasis added).

For Cernea, the social scientist is, above all, a social engineer. By this account, replete with construction analogies, his role is to formulate 'efficient social construction strategies', 'social adjustments' (ibid.); 'methodologies for social action', and 'social infrastructure' (ibid.: 24). These are the 'institutional and social scaffolding' without which 'the new edifice is not durably constructed' (ibid.: 9).

Cernea argues that the 'beneficiaries' of development should have a say in implementation, and sees social scientists as playing the central role in granting this voice. Hence Cernea recognizes the tension between human agency and scientific determinism. The fact that people are social actors as well as the objects of social engineering gives rise to the 'unpredictability of development interventions, and requires built-in learning mechanisms and flexible adjustment procedures' (ibid.: 31). More radically, putting people first is held to be 'a reversal because it proposes another starting point in the planning and design of projects than that taken by current technology-centred approaches' (ibid.: 8). Social science now appears to play a role quite different from that of engineering, as:

> a means to democratize the planning process itself by facilitating broader participation in it of the development actors themselves ... The social scientist is the only kind of expert who is professionally trained to 'listen to the people'. Social knowledge thus developed becomes a 'hearing system' able to amplify the listening for managers and policy-makers, too. (ibid.: 29, 31)

Nevertheless, Cernea's project is conceived in the image of a science, in which understanding of social, organizational and cultural variables results in the development of new operational tools, even if it is acknowledged that 'the accumulated experiences of applied social scientists have not yet been systematized, conceptualized, and codified [and] an overall theory of induced social development has not yet been articulated' (ibid.: 3).

Participatory Rural Appraisal

Although the language of participatory development is now widely current in mainstream development, its roots lie in part in the radical philosophy of *conscientization* associated with Paulo Freire and the alternative vision of development articulated, largely by NGOs, in the 1960s. In the English-speaking world, perhaps the most influential writer on participatory methods has been Robert Chambers, and the method with which he is associated, Participatory Rural Appraisal (PRA), has now begun to feature quite commonly in World Bank projects.

Chambers defines PRA as: 'a family of approaches and methods to enable rural people to share, enhance, and analyze their knowledge of life and conditions, to plan and to act' (Chambers 1994a: 953). The original impetus for the development of PRA lay in dissatisfaction with both the biases of field visits (towards easily accessible areas, community leaders, men, etc.) and the slow, expensive and inflexible nature of formal surveys. Increasingly, however, PRA has been seen as a means of validating local knowledge and empowering local populations. PRA methods have now been applied in many sectors, and have generated a substantial literature (Stewart et al. 1995).

Methodology of PRA PRA practitioners have built up an extensive repertoire of research tools and methods, including ranking, mapping and diagramming, and these are described in a growing number of manuals (see Theis and Grady 1991; Pretty et al. 1995). Distinctive though some of these methods are, the defining character of PRA lies less in its techniques than in the attitudes brought to the task. PRA seeks to avoid the biases that result from the assumptions of the investigator and from differences in power, status and culture between investigator and informant. Two of the core values of PRA are self-critical awareness (whereby 'facilitators continuously and critically examine their own behaviour') and personal responsibility (relying on one's own judgement rather than the authority of manuals or rules). 'Use your own best judgement at all times,' is one of the movement's maxims. Other precepts include: 'improvise in the spirit of play'; 'embrace error' and 'being relaxed and not rushing' (Chambers 1994b: 1254–5).

The training of participatory research practitioners is thus concerned as much with the development of interpersonal and communication skills and the transformation of attitudes as the acquisition of technical skills: building good rapport by paying attention to both the verbal and non-verbal messages given by interviewers; adopting a learning, rather than lecturing, mode; and showing respect for informants, their skills and knowledge.

PRA also stresses the *sharing* of data. In traditional research information is collected from local populations and taken away for analysis and interpretation. PRA, in contrast, offers ownership and control to 'respondents', who thereby become participants:

> Outsiders are facilitators, learners and consultants. Their activities are to establish rapport, to convene and catalyze, to enquire, to help in the use of methods, and to encourage local people to choose and improvise methods for themselves. Outsiders watch, listen and learn. Metaphorically, and some-

> times actually, they 'hand over the stick' of authority. (Chambers 1994b: 1225)

Epistemology of PRA PRA has not elaborated a formal theory of knowledge, but it nevertheless embodies distinctive notions of knowledge and evidence. Of particular significance are: its attitude to local knowledge; its means of assuring the reliability of findings; its focus on exception; and the preference for visual over verbal data.

First, in its 'reversal of learning', PRA privileges the *emic*, or actor's, over the *etic* (observer's) view. Local constructs and indigenous knowledge are thus valued over scientific taxonomies.

Second, PRA, while eschewing formal sampling and survey techniques, has developed concepts of representativeness and verification that define an alternative vision of rigour. Drawing on the work of Lincoln and Guba (1985), Pretty argues that the participatory inquirer uses four criteria to establish the trustworthiness of their findings. These are credibility, transferability, dependability and confirmability. Credible information is built upon trust and rapport with informants, knowledge of the local context, and the convergence of information obtained from different sources, by different methods, or by different investigators (known as 'triangulation' by PRA practitioners) (Pretty 1994).

The third feature of PRA's epistemology is its emphasis on differences rather than absolute measures. Comparison takes precedence over measurement, and learning comes from exceptions, oddities, discrepancies, dissenters, rather than averages (Chambers 1994a: 960; 1994b: 1254, 1259).

Finally, PRA privileges visual over verbal data. While interviews are an essential part of PRA, the techniques that distinguish it from other approaches (participatory mapping, matrices and diagrams of all kinds), are almost exclusively visual in nature. Visual media, being independent of alphabetical literacy and near-universal, are argued to empower the weak and disadvantaged.

> Participatory mapping exercises can enable marginalized women to express their preferences and properties in a physical form which does not entail personal confrontation with otherwise dominating men ... Visual diagramming is thus an equalizer, especially when it is done using the accessible and familiar medium of the ground. (Chambers 1994b: 1263)

As this suggests, the distinctiveness of PRA lies not only in the contrast between visual and verbal: the medium is itself clearly part of the message:

> The media and materials are often those of insiders – the ground, stones, sand, seeds as counters, sticks as measures, and so on. (ibid.)

The new paradigm represented by PRA is sometimes presented as a series of reversals: from the etic to the emic; from individual to group; from verbal to visual; from measuring to comparing; from reserve to rapport; from frustration to fun; from extracting to empowering; from top-down to bottom up; from centralized-standardized to local diversity; from blueprint to learning (Chambers 1994b). All in all, for Chambers, PRA entails a 'radical personal and institutional change', and the values of PRA amount to a foundation for 'a New Professionalism' (Chambers 1994a: 958; 1993).

The World Bank *Participation Sourcebook* PRA was one of the influences behind the development of the *Participation Sourcebook* (World Bank 1996), the most important document to come out of the 'learning process' through which the vocabulary and practice of participatory development began to enter the mainstream of World Bank operations. The opening chapter of the sourcebook sets its tone, contrasting the 'participatory stance' with the 'external expert stance' (ibid.: 3). In the former, 'sponsors and designers take a stance that places them inside the local social system being addressed; that is, they demonstrate a willingness to work *collaboratively* with the other key stakeholders' (ibid.). Rather than the application of technical principles to externally defined 'problems', interventions are formulated and adapted on the basis of a joint learning experience, engendering inventiveness and commitment on all sides. The *Sourcebook*, building from 17 project case studies written by World Bank Task Managers, presents practice pointers in participatory planning and the involvement of the poor, and offers guidance on participatory methods and tools.

Community and Professional in the Production of Participation

This section examines PRA's conception of social reality, and of the role it implies for the development professional.

Individual and collectivity In Participatory Rural Appraisal, the 'social' is manifested in a heightened sense of 'community', a level privileged both methodologically and morally. Most PRA exercises are collective. As in other participatory discourse, however, the community orientation of PRA means that often insufficient attention is paid to social differentiation. Further, community may be inappropriately imbued with agency.

Murphy's (1990) analysis on Mende public discourse shows that the appearance of community consensus may be just that – an appearance. Through local and private exegesis of what is said at public meetings, Murphy concludes that the orchestration of a public consensual order is an achievement that frequently conceals, rather than resolves, alternative orders of opposition. While some PRA techniques, such as wealth ranking, do explore differentiation and inequality within the community, the practice, if not the theory, of much PRA consists in the elucidation of 'community priorities' or 'community plans'. PRA emphasizes the creation of conditions for good communication *between* investigator and community in spite of differences in status between them (which are seen as the major causes of 'bias'). However, differences *within* communities may be as critical. It seems naive to assume that, simply by wishing themselves into a 'participatory stance', investigators will be able to lead the community in transcending historically and culturally rooted differences and conflicts between genders, factions, castes and occupational groups within a few hours or days. As Mosse (1994) has argued, the degree to which forums for participatory investigation, regarded as 'informal' by investigators, are likely to elicit the spontaneous opinions of subordinate groups is open to question.

A second consequence of community orientation is the portrayal of 'community' as an agent capable of planning and implementing collective initiatives (a level that appears to acquire moral authority simply by virtue of its 'community-based' nature). Experience teaches that this is frequently not the case: collectivities above and below the community level (such as individual, household, lineage, work-group, occupational association) are frequently the critical units for decision-making and action. It would be unfair to assert that other levels are ignored or dismissed by PRA practitioners. However, as the method becomes more widely used in operations – for project planning, needs assessments and participatory monitoring, etc. – the notional community is frequently emphasized to the neglect of other social groups and institutions.

Professionalism and mediation: shamanism and personal transformation PRA's distinctive combination of personal transformation, political empowerment and methodological practice is above all embodied in and transmitted through specialized training. If Beneficiary Assessment makes a professional of the listener and a listener of the professional, and

Social Analysis promotes the view of the applied social scientists as a professional and scientist alongside economists and technicians, then PRA questions the notion of professionalism itself. Although usually relatively brief, PRA training, and the attitudes and values that it imparts, are considered more important than the educational background of the investigator. Indeed, it sometimes seems that the goal of PRA training is to *unlearn* the 'expertise' of traditional professionalism and the condescending attitudes to local knowledge that it is considered to carry. Experienced PRA trainers are scarce and surrounded by something of a mystique.

The importance of charismatic specialists with esoteric training, combined with the centrality of the moral dimension, the inner-directedness expressed in the precept to 'follow your own judgement', and the symbolism of 'reversal' (cross-culturally a marker of ritual events), taken together, recall the role of the shaman. To the anthropologist, the association with the social marginality that characterizes both the investigated and the investigator (although the latter is increasingly threatened by professional respectability) are further parallels with the phenomena of ecstatic religion and spirit possession (Lewis 1971). Investigating outsiders have a dual and ambiguous status: cast as 'facilitators, learners and consultants', equipped with the paraphernalia of authority and status of more conventional professionals, four-wheel-drive vehicles, clip-boards and baseball caps, they clearly also represent to their hosts the power and resources of the state and its international patrons.

If PRA represents a rite of communion between reborn professional and community towards the redemption of both, its performance also enacts an exorcism, of sorts, of the phantoms of 'conventional' development practice. We have already noted PRA's rejection of two of the masks of technocracy – spurious quantification and the tyranny of the mean – introducing a subversive view of reality as fragmented and differentiated, rather than, as the organograms in the capital would have it, unitary, hierarchically structured and normally distributed. Suspicion of the formal, the linear, the ordained is reflected, too, in the celebration of the visual, as against the verbal, and especially against the written. 'The word' (synonymous with the truth, in the Judaeo-Christian tradition), is subordinated to direct experience (the 'vision' of Indo-European cosmology). Hence the report and the manual, those secular versions of dead scripture, embodying as they do the values of bureaucracy, and of the *clerical* class, which lives 'by the book', are not to be trusted:

> One view was that manuals of methods should be avoided; that the PRA

> principle of 'use your own best judgement at all times, permitted' and encouraged creativity; that manuals led to teaching and learning by rote, the ritual performance of methods for their own sake, and a loss of flexibility. (Chambers 1994a: 959)

PRA, indeed, advocates not simply a privileging of the visual over the verbal, but a revaluation of all senses against the dominance of the 'word'. Thus PRA practitioners are encouraged to 'do-it-themselves':

> asking to be taught, being taught, and performing village tasks – transplanting, weeding, ploughing, field levelling, mudding huts, drawing water, collecting wood, washing clothes, stitching, thatching. (ibid.: 960)

Echoes of Gandhi at his spinning-wheel. Here is a recognition that knowledge of place is not captured by the word alone, but that rural life is polymorphous: tactile, smelt, lived-in, worked-in experience (to continue our analogy, a polytheistic world), which can never be captured in numbers marshalled in a column.

And yet if the eye is the organ of truth, the gaze may also be a means of subordination, threatening the transient equality that the rites of PRA seek to sanction. During PRA, 'eye contact, and the insider's awareness of the outsider, are low' (Chambers 1994b: 1263). 'The Look', the imperial gaze, reinforces and objectifies status differences, between man and woman, between master and slave:

> We can not perceive the world and at the same time apprehend a look fastened upon us; it must be either one or the other. This is because to perceive is to *look at*, and to apprehend a look is not to apprehend a look-as-object in the world. It is to be conscious of *being looked at* … I fix the people whom I *see* into objects; I am in relation to them as the Other is in relation to me. In looking at them I measure my power … To be looked at is to apprehend oneself as the unknown object of unknowable appraisals – in particular, of value judgements. (Sartre 1972: 347, 356, 358)

Is it, then, fanciful to see in PRA, in its *vision*-ary rejection of formal methodology, of the dreary questionnaire, of the tyranny of *logos* and its linear, hierarchical, 'logic', an underlying rejection of the 'top-down' patriarchy of monotheism; an Oedipal act in which God the Father is slain, and 'the stick' 'handed over' for good? And does the Professional, with the in-*sights* of PRA, throw off at last the oppressive *voice* of the super-ego, to renew himself in reunion with the earth mother, with the plain, wholesome, fertile soil on which the ritual diagrams of PRA are inscribed, and her fruits – the seeds, stones and beans with which those charts are made? Who can say? And if so, why does it refuse to acknowledge the power of its own gaze?

The risk of PRA's neo-animism is that facing all confrontations between formal knowledge systems and indigenous knowledge. In short: which system is absorbing which? And is indigenous knowledge a 'system' at all (Richards 1993)? Certainly, PRA encourages the opening of channels not available in conventional data collection. But does it not also insist on preferences being transitive? Make time (as 'time-lines') linear? Reduce subtle multi-dimensional and multi-sensory knowledge to flat, two-dimensional, portable and photographable matrices, free of language? How much is gained and how much lost in reflecting this impoverished vision back to its authors as their 'indigenous knowledge'? The spoken word may be limited and power-laden (and incomprehensible to the international specialist), but it is also the medium of debate and accommodation, of allusion and allegory, of poetry and myth.

This transformational aspect of the method is an essential, rather than an incidental, feature of PRA: the ultimate proof of its validity is experiential (and, of course, visionary):

> The evidence of personal experience convinces ... Local people ... say they *see* things differently. (Chambers 1994b: 1266; emphasis added)

> The most striking *insight* of the experience of PRA is the primacy of the personal ... Responsibility rests not in written rules, regulations and procedures but in individual judgement. (Chambers 1994c: 1450; emphasis added)

A philosophy that is founded on personal values and commitment and seeks its confirmation in personal experience would appear to have abandoned the modernist fold of positive science. However, the transformational aspect of PRA, and its call to the well-springs of the moral imagination, are essential to its wide appeal, as an analysis of the World Bank's own *Participation Sourcebook* reveals.

The *Participation Sourcebook* is an unusual Bank document in that it does not present findings as the distillation of truth and experience of general application. Instead, it attempts to convey an alternative way of looking at the world, adopting a tone that at once recalls a self-improvement manual and a mythical text. The set of case studies that make up the body of the book repeat a mythic cycle of alienation and redemption, an Odyssey in which the World Bank task manager, after being tested and proved by a series of trials, is granted entry to the promised land of participation.

The cycle exhibits the classic stages, common to saints and addicts in recovery, of departure, initiation and return (Campbell 1968). Each legend in the cycle starts with a *crisis*: 'What had gone wrong?' (p. 104); 'The project was going to be cancelled' (p. 29); 'The electricity sector is bankrupt ... can you help us solve the problem?' (p. 39). In response to the crisis there is an *inspiration*: 'A light went on' (p. 62); 'One forester had a different idea of how to save the forest ... he felt that people living in the forest were not thieves' (p. 53); 'We realized we would need to remedy the situation by getting local people involved' (p. 104). The adventure continues with our hero facing the scorn of the world in the form of *denial*: 'They did not see the need to hold a workshop or to identify other priority areas of change' (p. 118). And even *rejection*: '"Final clearance has been denied"; this was the message I received upon arrival at R.' (p. 79); 'The new team member flatly vetoed the participatory approach' (p. 40); 'Distrust for the consultant kept bubbling up' (p. 97); 'We were faced with a prevailing reluctance to participate' (p. 76). At the same time, our hero is assailed from within by *doubt*: 'I returned to Washington in a state of depression' (p. 63); 'Doubts start creeping in' (p. 78). He (or she) faces, even succumbs to, occasional *regress*: 'I kept falling back into old habits and had to struggle to bridge the gap' (p. 65); 'The Forest Department Head disavowed the previous work and presented us with a new proposal' (p. 58).

But our hero is not daunted in his faith: 'I persisted ... because I believed' (p. 76). He perseveres until the *realization* of the truth occurs: 'with that, the attitude of the Director changed dramatically' (p. 80); 'everyone wanted to attend' (p. 79); 'the participants liked it from the start ... they were actually doing the work themselves to their surprise and delight' (p. 119). The final stage is *reintegration* as the benefits of the approach become clear across the land: '[The initiative] has opened up a realm of possibilities for involving local people in their own development' (p. 81); 'Government ministries, who only last year showed marginal interest in this initiative, are now keen to be the main conductors and sponsors' (p. 81); and the Wanderer returns to Washington from the wilderness to claim his birthright: 'it went through the peer and management review process quickly and easily' (p. 14).

Again, the parallel drawn here may seem facetious. But the point is fundamental: the key to behavioural change is seen to be as much a shift in the imagination of what is possible as the generation of a new set of methods, rules and guidelines.

Uptake in the World Bank

As the social development agenda has acquired growing prominence within the World Bank, tools for participation and social analysis have increasingly come to be used in the design and implementation of projects. An important step in incorporating social concerns into Bank operations was the promotion of 'Social Assessment' (SA). SA, according to the brief guidelines produced in 1994, is 'a framework for incorporating participation and social analysis into the design and delivery of Bank-assisted projects'; and 'a process which provides an integrated and participatory framework for prioritizing, gathering, analyzing and using operationally relevant social information' (World Bank 1995a). SA can thus address both the participatory and the structural dimensions of the social, encompassing a range of issues including stakeholder participation, the appropriateness and social acceptability of programme objectives, the prediction or mitigation of social impact, and the development of local institutional capacities. SA is in some ways similar to Environmental Assessment (EA), and like EA has been associated with an attempt to classify projects by types according to their potential impact. However, while EA is obligatory for projects considered likely to have significant environmental impacts, the social assessment guidelines have no mandatory force in the Bank (Francis and Jacobs 1999).

As the terms are not always used with consistency and precision (indeed, debate continues over the definition of Social Assessment), and data on the use of participatory or social analysis methods are not collected systematically, it is not possible to assess the relative uptakes of participatory methods with much reliability. However, a 1998 review noted that about 110 projects since 1983 had used BA, these being widely distributed across countries and sectors (Salmen 1998). The concentration of these BAs in the last five years of the period reviewed (during which perhaps one project in ten incorporated BA or equivalent methods) confirms the method's increasing popularity, especially in social funds, which are a rapidly increasing category of operation.

Figures for Social Assessment also show a rising trend. A 1995 review identified 42 SAs as having been initiated in the Bank since June 1994 (World Bank 1995b). By 1998, there were apparently 125 SAs completed or under way (although this count seems to include at least some BAs).

PRA lacks a high-profile internal champion within the World Bank, and it could be argued that its values are antithetical to the culture and procedures of a large bureaucracy.[1] The emphasis on personal values and individual judgement, and the premise that power distorts communication, make the spirit of PRA quite out of tune with bureaucracy and its hierarchical, rule-bound culture (shamanism is nowhere a state religion). Nevertheless, PRA methods have become quite widely drawn upon in the organization, especially in rural sector projects and social funds, and have also been influential in the emerging methodology for country participatory poverty assessments (Norton and Stevens 1995). In this most modernist of organizations, the philosophy also answers what appears both an individual craving for redemption and a collective search for a renewed relevance and more appropriate public image for the institution. Strong echoes of PRA are to be found in the 'village immersion program', through which senior Bank managers spend up to a week living with the poor, unfailingly returning with a reinvigorated sense of mission. Chambers was also consultant to the 'Voices of the Poor' initiative, which used PRA methods. World Bank President James D. Wolfensohn drew on this study in his speech to the 1999 Annual Meetings:

> My colleagues and I decided that in order to map our own course for the future, we needed to know more about our clients as individuals. We launched a study and spoke to them about their hopes, their aspirations, their realities. Teams from the Bank and from non-governmental organizations have gathered the voices of 60,000 men and women in 60 countries.

'Clients as individuals'. Even those without material means can still be consumers of development, at the price of being reduced to atoms of poverty with no more social identity and history than being 'poor'. The irony of the Bank's adoption of the social development agenda is that the 'social' is primarily interpreted in terms of process, consultation and partnership. Little attention is given to the underlying structural determinants of well-being: such as the distribution of assets, income and power across ethnicity, class, gender and caste. Despite its radical forebears, the 'new professionalism' of Chambers is one of individual, rather than collective, transformation.

Although calling on the tradition and vocabulary of empowerment, PRA has paid little attention to the articulation of the alternative vision of development that this abstraction implies, and has largely been contained by methodological concerns. The justification finally offered is that PRA does the job faster and more cheaply than the alternative product (Chambers 1994a). The failure of participatory approaches such as PRA to map alternative strategies has left their rhetoric vulnerable to the opportunism and co-option to which they inevitably succumbed. The vocabulary of dissent, pilfered by the keepers of Washington's wardrobe, is subverted and regurgitated in a discourse of obfuscation, portraying a processual promised land of:

> more holistic approaches: creating and building partnerships, capacity building of local institutions, and creating synergies across sectors ... to achieve effective targeting by fostering local ownership, developing local partners, and facilitating the creation of enabling environments that provide transparent and accountable mechanisms for the delivery of goods, services and resources at the community level. (Aycrigg 1998: 8)

More concrete evidence for the upstaging of content by process is found in the results of a review of a hundred projects by the Banks' Quality Assurance Group (QAG), perhaps the most systematic assessment available of recent progress in the operationalization of social issues (World Bank 1999). The report speaks of 'positive change', 'significant achievement' and 'overall improvement in integrating participation into lending programs'. However, as regards structural issues, it notes that 'basic questions of social attributes were quite marginal in a large number of projects'. Even on gender, an issue to which the Bank has for years given attention and resources and regarding which it has an operational policy, progress in implementation was found to be disappointing, the report finding that 'gender issues were widely neglected'. The same predilection for participatory form over structural content is indicated in the review's finding a 'high degree of neglect of social impact monitoring'. Most seriously, social factors were 'routinely neglected' in the design of structural adjustment programmes, notwithstanding the fact that they account for the majority of Bank lending and that explicit poverty reduction requirements are articulated in the Bank's own directives on adjustment. (According to the report, these directives 'did not seem to be widely known'.) Overall, it was concluded that 'the team cannot offer definitive conclusions about the impact of social assessments on overall loan quality'.

It is therefore far from clear how the increased attention and resources being devoted to the social agenda in the Bank is reflected in the form taken by actual operations. The rise of social development has been accompanied by a subtle, but in its consequences fatal, slide from the structural to the consultative and from substance towards process. Even within the processual sphere, it seems, there is a danger of semantic devaluation of the terms under which 'partners' are incorporated. A recent review of the Bank's participatory achievements notes:

> a tendency to call any activity along the continuum of participation (information sharing to consultation to participation) 'participation'. Information sharing and consultation occur more frequently than participation in decision making or implementation. Many project examples could be cited in which primary stakeholders were consulted as to project components or implementation strategy, but did not participate in the identification/selection of project components. Yet these projects are still referred to as 'participatory'. (Aycrigg 1998: 19)

In a hall of mirrors, anything may seem true, even the slur that the price of admission for a new profession has been its collusion in the manufacture of a collective dream of participation and community, behind the screen of which the levers of business remain quite intact. Better the warm allure of partnership than the discomforting blade of social analysis. For who would hold a glass too closely to the elephantine Narcissus of H Street, rehearsing its new dance in such ill-fitting and ill-gotten clothes?

Note

1. In his discussion of the dangers facing PRA, Chambers lists: 'faddism' (doing it because it is fashionable); rushing; formalism (following the letter but not the spirit); one-offs (doing it once); PRA by command (doing it because the boss ordered it); and routinization and ruts (Chambers 1994c: 1441). These are, for many, precisely the defining characteristics of bureaucracy, national or international.

6

Beyond the Formulaic: Process and Practice in South Asian NGOs

John Hailey

Introduction

This chapter raises questions about the role and purpose of the formulaic approaches to participative decision-making that have been promoted and even imposed by donors and other development partners. It offers different explanations for the ambiguous attitude of NGO staff to the use of such participatory technologies, and concludes by suggesting that informal, non-formulaic, personal interactions are a key element of participative decision-making. The current emphasis on formulaic participative technologies has meant that we have possibly overlooked the significance of such highly personal criteria as respect, trust, and even friendship in determining the success of many development projects.

Evidence from recent research into the development and growth of South Asian NGOs suggests that much of their success depends on their understanding of, and responsiveness to, the needs of the local communities, and the way they balance social and institutional development (Edwards 1999; Fowler 1997). Obviously, there is nothing exceptional in this conclusion. However, what is surprising in the research and the case studies on which this chapter was based was the lack of reference to participatory technologies such as Rapid Rural Assessment (RRA), Participatory Rural Assessment (PRA), or Participatory Learning Analysis (PLA), and their associated tools and techniques. Instead there are plenty of examples of how decisions, operational issues and programme design were shaped through a process of personal engagement. This implies that such participative technologies may be of less consequence than the mainstream development literature suggests.

In reviewing the evidence from successful South Asian NGOs it has been striking how important informal, personal interaction has been. Over the last 25 years staff appear to have engaged with, and listened to, the communities with whom they work in an unstructured, informal manner. Participation came easily and naturally. This highly personalized interaction has clearly shaped their programmes, and created a bond of trust between key staff and the communities with whom they work. This chapter highlights the importance of such informal, non-formulaic and often highly personal modes of interaction between NGO staff and local communities. It argues that research into NGO–beneficiary relations should not overlook the importance of such personal interaction in shaping the development agenda at a community level. In turn this raises concerns at the increasing role, and even 'tyrannical' nature, of some of the formulaic participative technologies that have been introduced at the cost of more personal, process-based approaches. The chapter concludes by suggesting that formal participative tools and techniques may play less of a role than has otherwise been expected, and that we need to encourage researchers to do more to explore some of the political, cultural and even psychological reasons why this may be so.

This conclusion comes from an analysis of case studies of the organizational and management issues facing such NGOs. This research had been commissioned by the Aga Khan Foundation of Canada, and detailed case studies have been prepared on such NGOs as: BRAC and Proshika in Bangladesh, BAIF and Sadguru in India, and AKRSP and IUCN in Pakistan. The purpose of this research was to analyse the key characteristics of the growth process within development NGOs, and identify some of the strategies and management practices they adopted that have led to their success. It was hoped that this research would identify key lessons that these organizations learned as they adapted over time to new challenges. These include the challenge of working with local communities and building internal capacity to implement an increasingly complex set of programmes, as well as the challenges of mobilizing financial and technical resources, and of motivating a range of staff and volunteers. The research was undertaken in 1998 by a team of researchers with extensive experience of the NGO sector in South Asia. Each case study was prepared by local researchers, and supplemented with detailed follow-up interviews conducted by the author and other members of the Project's Steering Committee.

Participation or Personal Interaction: Case Studies of South Asian NGOs

Studies into how successful South Asian NGOs handle growth and change highlight the way in which leaders of these organizations invest time in building personal relationships with groups and individuals in the community. They place great store by listening and learning from villagers or junior staff, and demonstrate an ability to build networks of trusting relations among a variety of staff and local people. It was also noteworthy that all the leaders of these NGOs had a strong commitment to social justice and helping the rural poor. They had a clear vision of the how they contribute to local development, which underpinned all their work and interaction with local communities.

A total of nine organizations took part in this study: two in Bangladesh, three in India, and four in Pakistan. The oldest was established in 1967, and the youngest in 1989. They range in annual income from half a million dollars to over a quarter of a billion dollars. Their work ranges from political activism and policy development to health, education, micro-finance, environmental and agricultural development. All have confronted political, financial and managerial challenges, but all have determinedly maintained close ties with the local communities with whom they work. They were chosen for this study in part because of their openness and willingness to be studied, but also because they are exemplars of a new type of organization that is beginning to change the face of South Asian development.

The NGOs in the research sample all invested considerable resources in building credibility and trust in the local communities with whom they worked. Respondents and researchers were at pains to point out that this process was not based on a set of formal tools or participative techniques designed to elicit local needs. Trust and respect were based on regular contact, personal ties and shared values. During the start-up phase NGO staff invested considerable time, emotion and energy building up relationships of trust and shared understanding between themselves and local people.

Four examples from the different case studies exemplify this point. First is the process by which Shri Manibhai Desai initially established the Pune-based Bhartiya Agro-Industries Foundation (BAIF) in 1967 to create opportunities of gainful self-employment for disadvantaged rural families. In 1946, as a disciple of Gandhi, he committed himself to the service of the rural poor, and for the next 20 years he worked alongside local farmers on horticultural and cattle-breeding programmes. Only having established his expertise and credibility in the local community did he feel it appropriate to establish BAIF. This 20-year process of 'learning by doing', which can be seen as the basis of Manibhai's relationship with the local community, was a highly successful, if somewhat lengthy, means of engaging with the needs and priorities of the local community.

Once he had established BAIF he then ran it in a highly personalized manner. Within the organization and the communities with which BAIF worked he was seen as a patriarch. As reflected in staff comments that: 'He was like a father to us'; or: 'Manibhai knew us and our families, he visited our homes, inquired after our wives and children.' His style was inimitable. As one senior staff member commented after his death in 1993, 'He did not manage people – but people followed him.' Throughout his life Manibhai Desai continued to emphasize the importance of grounding all development work on dialogue with the local people. It is therefore no accident that the quotation from Manibhai used to introduce a booklet produced by BAIF in his honour begins: 'To conceive some beautiful ideas for a programme for the people is one thing, but sitting with the people working with them and developing the programme ... is quite different and most important.'

Second is the process by which Harnath and Sharmistha Jagawati established the credibility and focus of Sadguru, an NGO established in 1974 to promote rural development through natural resource management in the tribal districts of Northeast Gujerat. Initial funds for this venture came from the Mafatlal Foundation with the understanding that no projects would be imposed on the local people. The Jagawatis were insistent that they would become involved only if they were free to take their time and build a personal understanding of the needs of local communities, and only then decide what intervention was most appropriate. As a result they spent the first two years of their work walking up to 30 kms a day, and talking with villagers in over two hundred villages. By doing this they gained an understanding of the needs of local people, but more importantly they built friendships, developed trust, gained credibility on which their future work could be based. This two-year process of 'walking and talking' was of immense operational benefit, but it was also highly symbolic, and was the foundation on which Sadguru's relationship with the local community is based.

Third is the role of Shoab Khan in establishing the Aga Khan Rural Support Programme (AKRSP) in Northern Pakistan in 1982. He was the organization's founding leader, and was genuinely committed to the values inherent in community-based development. At one level he was an inspirational leader, and there is still talk about the way people hung on to his every word. He was able to develop strong personal loyalties among both local villagers and AKRSP staff, and there seems to be a sense of awe and reverence in the way they refer to him. At another level his leadership style was highly personalized. It was based around a set of personal relations. He had the ability to empathize with all sorts of people, and to listen to their needs in an appropriate manner. Respect and empathy characterized much of AKRSP's early work. In the early days planning meetings and staff training were based on village discussions and simply conversations with all sorts of local people. Their success, as compared with similar government initiatives, was because they had, in the words of one senior staff member, 'no preconceived packages, and were willing to respond to what the people were saying'.

A similar picture emerges when reviewing the growth of the Bangladesh Rural Advancement Committee (BRAC). The organization has always placed great emphasis on the importance of learning from, and dialogue with, local communities. BRAC's executive director, Fazle Hasan Abed, emphasizes that planning and learning is a two-way process. After nearly thirty years in a leadership position he still makes a point of going to the field and talking with villagers and field staff. From the very beginning BRAC adopted a 'target group' approach, and focused their attention on working with and for the poor. At the time in 1972 this was seen as a radical departure, and staff faced considerable opposition from community leaders and politicians suspicious of their motives. However, BRAC persisted and has placed community dialogue at the heart of its work.

This approach demands a considerable investment of staff and time, and often is at odds with BRAC's strategy of growth and expansion throughout the country. However, experience suggests that dialogue and personal contact are crucial to their work. For example, in an attempt to expand the scope and impact of its health programme, staff were 'mobilized on motorbikes'. Unfortunately, they became so focused on meeting growth targets and completing tasks quickly that they 'dashed' around the countryside on their new motorbikes and failed to spend time to sit and talk with families and village leaders. It was soon apparent that, as one of BRAC's field staff noted, 'when we walked and went by bicycle, we did much better', and so BRAC reinstituted its traditional approach to community development. Although this was a more demanding, time-consuming process, it was rooted in dialogue, listening and learning. They knew from experience these were essential to their work, and were more reflective of the community-based values so central to BRAC's work.

The lack of reference in the case studies to the more formulaic participative approaches was quite striking. It either reflected a remarkable blind-spot and bias in the twelve different researchers involved, or it implies that such participative tools and techniques are of less consequence than the mainstream development literature suggests. This is not to say that such tools and techniques are of no value or are not used by such NGOs, but that they are of less significance in explaining the growth of such organizations than we in the West might have expected. If this is so it is obviously useful to try to explain why formal participative tools and techniques are of limited significance in the eyes of the local NGO managers interviewed. In trying to answer this quandary, detailed analysis of the case studies and interviews suggested three different explanations. One is that such approaches are operationally inappropriate and suffer from practical limitations. A second explanation is that the cultural context and local circumstances in which many South Asian NGOs operate is more conducive to informal, personalized methods than functional, formulaic approaches. A third explanation is that they are seen as alien techniques imposed by outsiders keen to promote certain values or political agendas.

Explanation one: operational limitations One possible explanation is based on the increasing awareness of the operational limitations of formalistic participative approaches. This is supported by the growing body of literature that in analysing the pros and cons of such techniques as RRA, PRA and PLA has identified a number of problems in the way they are implemented (Mosse 1994; Gueye 1995; Leurs 1996; Biggs and Smith 1998). Underlying many of these critiques is a concern that there is a tendency for too much confidence to be vested in the techniques themselves. They are merely tools, not recipes guaranteeing the success of a project. Moreover, each approach has its own dynamic, which is contingent on the circumstances, culture and political climate in which it operates.

There is also the suspicion that such participative techniques are merely another development fashion unsupported by suitable training, or any real in-depth understanding of the behaviour and attitudes needed to facilitate effective field practice. Even Robert Chambers, one of the main protagonists in this area, has identified and elaborated some of the pitfalls and bad practice that have beset the successful application of such participatory technologies. For example, he is concerned at the rapid spread of bad practice because of the superficial understanding of the techniques, limited training, and the inappropriate style adopted by some facilitators. His worry is that 'PRA has become an instant fad ... that has been made to go to scale too fast' (Chambers 1997: 211).

Another concern is that these processes are not as inclusive as might be expected, and that they commonly rely on a small sample of self-selecting participants. The nature of group dynamics also suggests that power often lies in the hands of the most articulate or politically adept. Not only may this jeopardize personal confidences and threaten relationships built up over time, but it also serves to reinforce the status and power of existing cliques within the community. This is hardly the outcome expected of such participative processes. Furthermore, there is a worry that because these activities have their own unique dynamism, they yield unique results that are difficult to replicate or quantify. Consequently it is fairly easy for outsiders, such as government officials or donor representatives, to dismiss results that are contrary to their own expectations as being unrepresentative or merely the product of artificial circumstances.

Criticism has also been voiced at the role and status of 'participatory facilitators'. These are seen as 'outsiders' who can use their position and authority to override existing decision-making processes within the community (Cooke 1997). Also, agency theory and analysis of 'insider–outsider' interaction have uncovered the inherently political nature of such transactions. Power and status can determine the outcome of many participative processes, and coalitions have a key role in influencing decisions (Biggs and Smith 1998; Guijt and Shah 1998). The mere presence of external facilitators can influence outcomes and the shape of discussion. This phenomenon should come as no surprise. The impact of outsiders on group decision-making processes has been well documented in management research since Mayo and Roethlisberger's analysis of the Hawthorn experiments in the 1930s (Mayo 1933; Roethlisberger and Dickson 1939). Facilitators may encourage intensive discussion, and raise expectations that cannot be met. Their role may cut across institutional boundaries and jeopardize other long-term development strategies. There is also the fear that such a public process may jeopardize confidentiality, provoke unnecessary conflict, and even raise questions as to the cultural appropriateness and ethical efficacy of such approaches (Schein 1987; Blunt 1995).

Clearly there are a number of political, ethical and operational problems in applying such participative tools and techniques that may explain their limited significance. But the evidence from the case studies suggests that operational difficulties are not sufficient to explain this diffidence. Many NGO staff clearly value the role and importance of such technologies in structured self-assessment, project formulation and community-based planning processes. They understand their qualities and their operational limitations. They see these technologies as being one of the many tools in their developmental toolkit. However, the lack of reference to them in the interviews as the key tool in handling community–NGO relations or programme design and management suggests that there are other forces at play. Therefore, alternative explanations are needed.

Explanation two: local culture and internal power relations A second hypothesis or explanation worth testing is that the highly personalized interaction between key NGO managers and staff or local people is a product of the society and context in which these NGOs operate. This is a context partly shaped by the local culture and associated political systems, partly by their financial dependence on aid donors and government departments, and partly by their own ambitions, aspirations and management style.

The evidence of the case studies is that key decision-makers interact and operate on a very personal level. They invest considerable time in building personal contacts and developing relationships of trust. They work alongside local farmers, care for families, walk and talk with villagers, listen and learn. They place great emphasis on informal contacts, unstructured dialogue and mutual learning. Their relationships, although highly personalized and even paternalistic, are rooted in a genuine commitment to helping the poor and disadvantaged. But above all their success depends on their understanding of, and responsiveness to, the needs of the local communities with which they work.

It is clear from detailed analysis of the case studies and evidence from similar research (e.g. Uphoff et al. 1998) that the staff of many successful NGOs involved in rural development work do share certain characteristics. These include a fundamental belief in participative development, an ethos of close collaboration with local communities, and a clear vision based on a strongly held, well-articulated set of values. Their work is based on the conviction that the poor and uneducated can take control of their lives with some outside encouragement, assistance and support. As a result, NGOs bring to local communities new technologies, new organizational capacities, and management competencies compatible with local experiences and preferences. Their staff demonstrate a willingness to experiment and learn, to listen and discuss, and also to initiate and inspire.

The picture that emerges is that the staff and leadership of effective development NGOs in South Asia work closely with local communities in a highly collaborative, but personal, way. Their interaction is based not on formulaic, structured processes, but more on common sense, shared beliefs, and mutual dialogue. This process is open to criticism in that it smacks of paternalism and is easily manipulated by educated, articulate individuals whose power is derived from their access to funds, political contacts and new technologies.

Quite clearly there are many NGOs that operate in such a cynically manipulative, paternalistic manner, but few of them grow successfully or gain a reputation for effective, sustainable work. Moreover, there is some concern that such criticism is rooted in a very alien set of values that fails to account for the dynamics of the culture and context common to much of South Asia. Too often critics base their analysis of the way organizations should operate or make decisions on Western perceptions of good practice.

Cultural researchers have noted that South Asian cultures are marked by their collective nature and a general acceptance of innate social differentials. Hofstede (1991) suggests that South Asian societies have 'high power distance' levels, with the implication that less powerful members of an organization expect and accept that power is distributed unequally. His findings also suggest that these societies are highly 'collectivist', with the implication that people are integrated into strong, cohesive social groups form birth. Trompenaars (1993) also identified the highly collectivist nature of South Asian society, and the importance of 'ascription' in South Asian cultures. He sees this as the extent to which position and power is ascribed by virtue of birth, kinship, education, networks and connections.

Thus we have a cultural context in which cohesive group relations are paramount, and where it is accepted that the power and status of key decision-makers is dependent on kinship ties, personal relationships and connections. This is seen as alien to the highly individualistic, 'low power distance', achievement-orientated meritocracies of Western Europe and North America. In organizational terms this would imply that strong personal relationships between the leadership and the staff or communities with whom they work is essential to their success and survival. These are not cultures where relationships are mediated by mechanistic planning tools or structured participative technologies. These are cultures that depend on a network of highly personal relationship. Consequently, it is no surprise to find in many South Asian NGOs that informal, highly personal relationships are at the heart of the decision-making and planning process.

It appears that key individuals mediate an informal consultation process, and facilitate a shared decision-making process with local communities. This not only enables them to maintain their networks and contacts, but also enhances their profile in the community and reinforces their power and authority. This raises crucial questions, and clearly further research is needed to assess the motives behind this. For example, does such informal mediation reflect a genuine belief in the value of collaboration and participation, or is it merely a way to reinforce their power-base? Does the highly personalized nature of the relationship mean that key NGO staff manipulate and hi-jack decision-making processes? Do local people have any real power in shaping decisions or prioritizing activities?

We also need to develop a greater understanding of the impact of culture on participative processes. Can the Western concepts of participation and democracy inherent in many participative technologies really be translated into a different cultural environment (Blunt 1995)? Certainly the work of Hofstede or Trompenaars would suggest that the collectivist, high power distance cultures commonly associated with the developing world have a very different perspective of participation than the individualistic, low power distance cultures of the West. This would imply that the process of participation is not universal and is contingent on different cultural norms or assumptions.

Explanation three: external power and control As has already been noted, it is feared that participative technologies have become a 'development fad' – a 'mantra' articulated by NGO staff, donors and development agencies alike. However, there are some mutterings of criticism as to the assumptions and the underlying motives of those who actively promote the use of such technologies. As one Bangladeshi NGO manager commented: 'The way donors make us use PRA implies they have little trust in the way we have successfully worked with local communities over the last twenty-five years.' Alan Fowler noted that donors now expect participatory self-assessment tools to be an essential component of any attempt to formulate an aid proposal. However, in so doing, donors have reduced participation to a state of tokenism that is not embedded in any long-term process (Fowler 1997: 99).

There is a suspicion that those 'experts' who advocate participatory approaches to development appear to sit on some high moral ground and as such are immune to criticism. It is also noteworthy that there has been surprisingly little research that offers a critical perspective on the motives, actions and agendas of those who promote these participative tools and techniques. The early work of French philosopher, historian and sociologist Michel Foucault would suggest that unless we understand why the development community in general, and development 'experts' in particular, promote such participative approaches we will never gain a critical insight into their real role and influence.

The writings of Foucault in the 1970s highlighted the importance of critically analysing the formation and content of discourse. In simple terms he saw discourse as the complex processes by which we communicate with each other about a particular topic. He proposed that such analysis is necessary if we are to understand the underlying assumptions that have shaped a particular discourse – its internal rules, how it operates, as well as how it changes over time. These are all commonly reflected in texts, conversations and practical application. Foucault's own work looked at writings in specific areas of technical knowledge. For example, he analysed discourses on 'madness' as produced by 'experts' (such as doctors, psychiatrists), which showed not only how our concept of 'madness' has transformed over time, but more importantly how 'experts' are key to shaping our understanding of the term (Foucault 1973). Thus, as many critical theorists argue, the knowledge embodied in a discourse should not be seen as being representative of a universal truth, but rather should be seen as an exercise of power (Calás and Smircich 1997). Consequently, a study of any kind of discourse, for example about participatory development, must include an investigation of the motives and ideology of the 'experts' who advocate such an approach.

Quite clearly there is need for research to help our understanding of why Northern-trained 'experts' and donor agencies are keen to promote formulaic participative approaches. Such analysis may provide an insight into what power or control it gives them. This in turn may offer some explanation as to why certain successful NGOs in the South do not appear to give much credit to such participative tools and techniques. Such studies are clearly problematic because researchers are frequently immersed in the very same discourses they are trying to uncover, as well as being involved in detailed surveillance of all texts, conversations and actions, while still attempting to interpret meaning and apply judgement. But such research may offer possible explanations as to the momentum behind the spread of participatory technologies, and open discussion as to the motives behind the current fascination with participative development.

A number of hypotheses or explanations exist as to why 'development experts', and the donor community in general, promote such participatory technologies. The experts themselves most commonly claim that existing project planning techniques or community development methodologies were inappropriate, destructive, and 'a waste of money and a bloody mess' (Chambers 1997: 15). In hindsight, the conventional, technocratic, top-down approaches to development common to many development projects of the 1960s and 1970s were seen as not working. They were inherently dirigiste, and consequently failed to address the reality of local circumstances, and the priorities and needs of the community. As a result too many aid programmes failed to achieve the desired result or had any sustainable impact. We now recognize that such technology-driven, externally planned, expert-led development was inappropriate to the exigencies of community development. In their efforts to ensure that such projects were more effective, both multilateral and bilateral donor agencies experimented with different approaches, and promoted the application of different types of participative tools and technologies. They were motivated by a desire to encourage qualitative improvements in the design and product of development projects, but also to ensure that aid funds were better utilized and had lasting impact. Thus one can argue that they became another 'management tool' promoted by donors to ensure value for money and sustainable impact (Bond and Hulme 1999).

From a donor perspective these technologies had the added advantage in that they were wrapped in a patina of radical politics. They are arguably the operational consequences of the work of Ivan Illich (1990) and Paulo Freire (1973). Thirty years ago their writing on social justice and grassroots development was seen as revolutionary and threatening. However, by the 1990s their analysis had entered the mainstream and had apparently been accepted by the development establishment. One of the challenges for those working in this field, though, has been to marry the 'political' school of participation, with its radical, anti-establishment agenda, with the operational priorities of donors and their concern for effectiveness and value for money.

But there is possibly a more sinister historical genesis to the use of such participative technologies that may also be worth considering and may in part explain the willingness of the 'development establishment' in the North to accept and encourage such participative technologies. Further research is needed to undertake historical studies or longitudinal analysis that track how much participative development owes its genesis to attempts by Western governments, and by virtue of their funding position, Northern aid donors, to limit the power and influence of political dissidents, freedom-fighters or radical Marxists. Certainly, some have argued that the tools of development administration more generally have served Western Cold War aims (e.g. Dwivedi and Nef 1982). Researchers may find themselves examining how 'participative' or 'democratic' processes were used in the villagification strategies adopted by the British in Malaya in the early 1950s, and the 'pacification' campaigns used by the USA in Vietnam in the late 1960s. In both these campaigns communities were relocated, and new 'democratic' decision-making processes and institutions were introduced (e.g. Thompson 1966; Sheehan 1989). There is also some suspicion that US development agencies working in India in the 1970s encouraged the use of formal participative technologies in their efforts to break the stranglehold of Marxists over the community development process.

In other words, the researcher would have to test to what extent the momentum to participation beneath the ostensibly radical rhetoric is merely symptomatic of efforts by the political right (and financially prudent donor agencies) to shift the development agenda to the middle ground of resource provision and technology transfer, away from any radical engagement in social or political restructuring. If this analysis has any validity then it may explain in part why many older-generation NGO leaders are resistant to the push to participative technologies. They could be suspicious of the cynical abuse of the language of participation to fit the agenda of the political establishment or different donors. They may also be concerned that the structured, formulaic nature of the various technologies ensures that power still lies in the hands of the facilitators who are seen to represent donor interests. Thus one must question whether they are an extension of donor power or even some form of control mechanism. Also, to what extent do they vitiate against the application of insight and personal judgement, or even exist to constrain the work of local activists?

Conclusion

Quite clearly there are still crucial questions that researchers need to ask about the way in which NGOs interact with local communities. There is concern about the operational limitations of participative tools and technologies, and there are fears that they are inherently culturally inappropriate. There are worries about the real agenda of those promulgating such techniques, and concerns whether the move to impose such approaches is merely another level of donor conditionality. If this is so, one must question whether this is reflective of the 'tyrannical' nature of the way participative technologies are being imposed regardless of the circumstances or cultural context. These concerns may help explain why some successful NGOs appear not to rely on formulaic participative technologies, but place greater reliance on personal contact and a process of personal engagement. Further research is needed to explore these limitations and also to analyse the extent of planning decisions and efforts to prioritize activities based on informal processes of personal interaction and dialogue. In other words, how critical are personal interaction, respect, and the ability to build a relationship of trust to the success of the way NGOs plan and prioritize activities with local communities?

In trying to answer the question why formulaic participative technologies may be of less consequence than the development literature suggests, three explanations were offered in this chapter. They are not complete, nor are they exclusive. But together they point to some of the limitations of such technologies. These explanations pull together some diverse strands of thinking from different literatures, research and experience. They are obviously interrelated and reflect different facets of the same problem. We clearly need to explore these in more depth and to develop a greater understanding of how these dimensions interact. Although there is some research that has examined the operational limitations of such participative tools and techniques, little has been written exploring the underlying motives of the 'experts' or the institutions promoting such technologies, or to what extent are they culturally appropriate or relevant.

In conclusion, this chapter should partly be seen as a call for more research into the genesis of such formulaic approaches, their applicability in different cultural contexts, and the role of informal personal relations in local decision-making processes. However, the chapter should also be seen as a reminder that personal dialogue, conversation and discussion are crucial to the success of shared decision-making. Effective personal interaction is dependent on a degree of affection, friendship and trust. Participative decision-making should not therefore be reduced to some formulaic process, but should be rooted in a dynamic relationship of mutual trust and respect.

7

The Social Psychological Limits of Participation?

Bill Cooke

Introduction: Social Psychology and Participatory Development

Social psychological analyses of what happens when people work together in groups suggest that the very processes of participation can restrict the ability of participatory development to deliver what is claimed for it. Specifically, participation can cause decisions to be made that are more risky, with which no one really agrees, or that rationalize harm to others, and it can be used consciously or otherwise to manipulate group members' ideological beliefs. According to Allport (1968: 3) social psychology is concerned with 'how the thoughts, feelings and behaviours of individuals are influenced by the actual, imagined and implied presence of others'. Social psychology is therefore about the relationship between individuals' cognitive processes (thoughts), affective processes (feelings, e.g. anger, fear) and what they do on the one hand, and the interaction between these and other people on the other.

In that it calls for attention to 'irrational' affective processes, this chapter gives no succour to those who critique participation from the perspective of disciplines based on assumptions of rationality (e.g. economics). But it does argue that unless well-documented (outside development) limitations of participation are acknowledged, it will continue to contain within it the seeds of its own destruction, and, worse, harm those it would claim to help. It also raises a question about development's willingness to visit participatory processes on the Third World without mention of the reservations and critiques applied to participation in the First.

The focus of the chapter is what social psychology tells us about interactions within groups of people, drawing on the subset of social psychology theory typically described as being concerned with 'group processes' or 'group dynamics'. In particular, it will consider how group interactions manifest themselves in four different ways that are problematic for the proponents of participatory development. These are, first, *risky shift*, second, the *Abilene paradox*, third, *groupthink*, and, fourth, *coercive persuasion*.

Group process theory is of relevance given the almost definitional use of what Mosse, speaking of Participatory Rural Appraisal (PRA), calls 'public social events' (1994: 497), that is, face-to-face interactions between a group of people in participatory development. Such events are not limited to PRA, however; they are equally prevalent in development projects in a range of sectors (e.g. public sector reform), where they might be called 'workshops' (see for example, Joy and Bennett n.d.), and ostensibly more radical Participatory Action Research (PAR) processes, as in PRA with rural communities (e.g. Fals-Borda and Rahman 1991). Thus the group in question may consist of a group of ministers and/or civil servants, a project team, or 'a community' of the rural poor and dispossessed. What they have in common, and what gives them their status as a group, is their shared and face-to-face involvement in a participatory process. There is also typically an outsider present, often labelled a researcher, facilitator, consultant, animator or change agent.

An event with this outsider presence is, from a social psychological perspective, known as a participatory 'intervention', the point being that it would not have happened without the outsider (or those she or he represents), and that the very presence of the interventionist changes things. For Argyris, 'to intervene is to enter into an ongoing system of relationship, to come between or among persons, groups or objects for the purpose of helping them' (1970: 15). Argyris' work is part of a literature on intervention practice *per se*, which this chapter does not address directly, and which is by and large ignored by the participatory development literature (but see Cooke 1997; Brinkerhoff and Coston 1999). However, this chapter does have implications for how the interventionist works.

Claims made for participation Social psychology challenges the claims made for participation both as a means and as an end (Nelson and Wright 1995: 1). Claims for participation as a means focus on its ability to deliver more effective development. Here it is seen to lead to better planning, implementation, monitoring, evaluation, investigation and training and action (e.g. Chambers 1994: 961), and indeed evaluation (e.g. Acharya et al. 1998). Participatory analysis is seen to be better informed, because the data on which it is based have been generated collectively between interventionist and participants. The methods that are used also enable the generation of data that are particularly rich in comparison to data collected by other means. Participatory action builds a sense of commitment, and again allows local knowledge to contribute to how the plan is implemented. Participatory evaluation gives 'beneficiaries' themselves the chance to comment on the effectiveness of a given development intervention.

Advocates of participation as an end in itself see it as delivering empowerment. At one end of the scale this means giving people control over development processes from which they had traditionally been excluded, through their very participation in analysis, planning and action (e.g. Chambers 1997). At the other, participation is seen as leading to empowerment by transforming consciousness. Thus engaging in PAR will, it is claimed, enable the poor and oppressed to become aware both of the structural sources of their own oppression and of how their own views of the world and thought processes (for example, with respect to gender relations) – that is, their consciousness – sustain this oppression. Once this awareness is achieved the group in question will be in a position collectively to challenge the causes of their oppression (again, see Fals-Borda and Rahman 1991).

Of course it is recognized that proponents of participatory development do identify potential problems with it. However, descriptions of such problems are almost invariably grounded in the worldview of development and/or in the light of problems that have manifested themselves in participatory practice, and do not lead to any questioning of the legitimacy of participatory development *per se*. Examples include the acknowledgement of the problems in assuming the homogeneity of community, the contradictions of top-down donor-led participation and inappropriate behaviour, attitudes and training among practitioners (e.g. Guijt amd Cornwall 1995). Co-optation of participation, by and for those who do not have the interests of the poor and oppressed at heart, is also identified as a potential problem by both Chambers (1997) and Rahman (1991).

There have also been more critical analyses of participation, which both extend some of these points and add new criticisms. For example, Craig and Porter (1997) argue that participation in the hands of development professionals can become an instrument for control. White (1996) suggests that there has been a failure to address the political dynamics of participation, not least the complex conflicts of interests between those driving it 'top-down' and those involved from 'bottom-up'. Mosse (1994) suggests that existing social relationships influence the way knowledge is constructed in participatory public social events. Stirrat (1997: 70) identifies 'the new orthodoxy' of participation as neocolonialist, noting for example its usage of terms like 'community', 'village', 'local people', which arose from colonial anthropology, and all of which are elements in colonial and postcolonial discourses that depict the world in terms of a distinction between 'them' and 'us'. He also argues that the seductive yet ultimately vague rhetoric of 'empowerment' associated with participation serves to justify the activity (or interventions, in Argyris' terms) of outside agencies, ignoring autonomous organization, resistance and self-empowerment.

We will return to these problems and critiques in the conclusion, having considered risky shift, the Abilene paradox, groupthink and coercive persuasion. What we will find, first, is that these social psychological analyses suggest that the problems faced by the proponents of participation are greater than they surmise. Second, while all of the four analyses are individually within the social psychological (and managerialist) orthodoxy, contrasting this orthodoxy with that of participatory development reveals a gap between the two. This gap reinforces the arguments of those who are more critical of participation.

Conceptual underpinnings There is an extensive range of different approaches to the study of groups to be found in social psychology. The field is often depicted as arising from a seminal workshop in 1945 run by Kurt Lewin and his associates. In passing, that workshop is also often cited as the birthplace of action research (Lewin 1946), and, ironically, its purpose was community development (Cooke 1998), the resulting account entitled *Training in Community Relations* (Lippitt 1949). The study of group processes continues to thrive, and be documented, for example in journals like *Group and Organization Management* and *Journal of Applied Behavioural Science*. Within this field there is, it should be recognized, research that recognizes value in group processes. Shaw (1971) summarizes a range of research that suggests that, among other things, there is evidence that group membership motivates individuals, that groups usually produce more and better solutions than those working alone, and that they learn faster than individuals.

But against this has to be set a concern about what can go wrong in groups – so-called *group dysfunction*. The four analyses considered here have been selected because they offer particular insights into the limitations of participatory development. They are, however, also some of the most widely cited and reproduced, particularly in managerial texts and readings aimed at practitioners working participatively on behalf of senior managers in organizations in the North (see, for example, Dyer 1987; Kolb et al. 1991; Robbins 1998). Taking each in turn:

1. *Risky shift* is an example of an empirical approach to the study of group processes. Here a hypothesis about individual and group behaviour has been identified and tested, with further replication studies to check whether initial findings are generalizable.
2. The *Abilene paradox* is at the opposite end of the methodological and conceptual spectrum. Its basis is in theory rather than experimentation. It derives from a psychodynamic view of human behaviour, which suggests that unconscious psychological process shape how we think, feel and act.
3. *Groupthink* is developed from a grounded approach to understanding group processes. That is, the theory of groupthink arose from an attempt to construct a theoretical framework that explained how a particular type of group process came about. In this case the concern is with processes leading to decisions that to an outsider are obviously wrong.
4. *Coercive persuasion* also tried to provide a conceptual explanation of a particular type of group process – that which led to 'brainwashing' – as its starting point. However, its approach was to use and adapt existing psychological and social psychological theory to construct this explanation.

It is not claimed that these analyses are representative of group dynamics/processes as a field, conceptually or methodologically. The Abilene paradox, with its psychodynamic foundation, is on the fringes of group dynamics theory. There are also other group process approaches that provide insights into the conduct of participatory development. There are, for example, studies that have considered the impact of a range of different variables – e.g. group size, physical location and circumstances, member diversity – on group functioning (summarized in Handy 1985). Another is that associated with group interaction analysis (starting in the 1950s; see, for example, Bales 1950), which provides us with straightforward, established and tested methodologies for addressing questions like 'who participates' in participatory development. Interaction analysis suggests we address this question by using the group process and its interactions as a source of data. Thus we record who participates (and who does not), how often, who addresses whom, in what sequence, and what (in broad categories) they say.

Risky Shift

Risky shift defined Studies of group decision-making have found that group discussion leads group members to take more risky decisions than they would have taken as individuals – hence risky shift. The phenomenon was originally suggested by Ziller in 1957, and subsequently confirmed by Stoner in 1961 (see Stoner 1968). Stoner's experiment, and the work of those who followed him, was based on asking subjects to decide between two courses of action that varied in riskiness and reward for a range of hypothetical situations, with the greater reward for successfully taking a greater risk. They were first asked to make and record the decisions on their own, and then to make the same decisions again following group discussion. In a significant number of cases the latter decisions were more risky.

Researchers following on from Stoner attempted to find out how far his results were shaped by his research design. For example, Stoner's original work had used only male graduate students studying management, so attempts were made to see whether risk-taking was associated with gender and management roles. However, risky shift was found in groups of women and of liberal arts students, and has been widely replicated. Among the explanations for risky shift the following three recur:

1. Risk-taking is a cultural value, the argument being that in US society risk is valued, 'and that in the group situation most individuals want to appear to be willing to take greater risks than the average person in order to enhance their status in the group' (Shaw 1971: 73). Reviewing this research, Shaw suggests that there is some research evidence that suggests that cultural attitudes towards risk 'probably' have some determining effect, but cannot explain every incidence of risky shift.
2. The risky individual is the most influential. Shaw argues that this has been a difficult hypothesis to test, with studies producing less than definitive findings. Moreover, while there may be a link between the presence of individuals with a propensity to take risks and overall group riskiness, cause and effect is hard to prove. Shaw suggests that this means that at best the risky individual is not the only cause of risky shift, and perhaps not even an important one. He also suggests that high risk-takers have the opportunity to use more colourful, and thus more persuasive, rhetoric than that open to the risk averse, which is inherently conservative.
3. Diffusion of responsibility. The actual sharing of responsibility means that individual accountability for a given decision is blurred. Again, Shaw's review of the research literature suggests that this is one of the most likely explanations of risky shift, but that again, this does not explain every occurrence of risky shift.

Risky shift and participatory development It is not that difficult to identify circumstances within participatory development where any of the three potential causal factors can be present, in, for example, a project management process or a community-based participatory development programme. The language of participatory development is in itself often colourful and persuasive, as can be the individual behaviours of its proponents, who often find their way into the influential role of facilitator. At a community level, getting participation in the first place requires facilitator persuasiveness. In a project-planning process participation may be formalized, for example, in the development of a logframe. But even though logframes require participants to identify assumptions, and by implication consider risk factors, this still inevitably involves group judgement and thus the danger of risky shift.

We should also note that risky shift is not completely explained by the presence of the three factors listed above, and by implication that it can occur in their absence. More generally, in both project management and community development scenarios we might also anticipate individual and collective decision-making processes to be shaped by individual assumptions about other group members that are never articulated or tested. These could be about what powers (e.g. in terms of resources and capabilities) and responsibilities members have – and where responsibilities lie. Again, the interventionist, by acting in that role, sends out a message about his or her own level of power and responsibility.

Risky shift is an empirically supported example of how the very processes of participation can influence outcomes, in this case leading to group decisions that are more risky than those that would have been taken by members of the group as individuals. The probability of risky shift occurring therefore has to be set against claims made for participation as a means, particularly for its effectiveness and rigour in analysis, planning and action. It also has to be set against claims for participation as empowerment, in the sense of giving participants control over their own development. Is participants' control increased when they are put into a situation leading them to commit to more risky decisions than otherwise would have been the case?

The Abilene Paradox

The Abilene paradox described 'The Abilene paradox' is the title of what can only be described as a parable, written by Harvey (1979) about unconscious collusion to produce false agreement. The story, quite simply, is of a family spending an agreeable afternoon at home in Coleman, Texas, when it is suggested that a trip is made to Abilene. Everyone agrees to go. On returning after a gruelling, uncomfortable four-hour trip, one family member ventures that they hadn't really wanted to go, and had only agreed because everyone else was so enthusiastic about going. At this the family bursts into argument, each member claiming they hadn't wanted to go either, and had only agreed to keep everyone else happy.

The Abilene paradox in organizational terms is 'that organizations frequently take actions in contradiction to what they really want to do and therefore defeat the very purposes they are trying to achieve' (Harvey 1979: 127). In a development context we can easily substitute 'communities' or 'project teams' for organizations. The six symptoms of the paradox (summarized from Harvey 1979: 130–1) are:

1. The agreement, at a private level, on the nature of the situation being faced.
2. Agreement on what is to be done to deal with it (in the Abilene parable, this was 'nothing').
3. Group members fail to communicate accurately their actual desires, and indeed they do exactly the opposite, leading 'one another into misperceiving the collective reality'.
4. On the basis of this misperception actions are taken by the group that are actually contrary to what everyone wants to do.
5. This leads to anxiety, frustration, anger, and the search for someone to blame.
6. If 'the generic issue – the inability to manage agreement' is not dealt with the cycle is likely to repeat itself.

The Abilene paradox and participatory development Harvey illustrates the paradox with cases from corporate and political decision-making, and analyses the causal dynamics at increasing levels of depth using an individual psychoanalytical framework. However, it is fairly straightforward to transpose these cases to a participatory development context. We can use a hypothetical public sector reform planning workshop to illustrate. Actors in this hypothetical workshop would include an interventionist paid by the bilateral donor concerned; local representatives of the donor; ministerial and civil service representatives of the government department concerned; and a locally based project manager and other stakeholders, for example those with professional expertise.

Each actor could well assume that, contrary to their own personal belief, everyone else wants the project to go ahead, that its outputs should be of a certain kind, and that its processes should take a certain form. In such a scenario, it can be envisaged that a least some of the causal dynamics Harvey proposes are likely to be present, beginning with 'action anxiety', which occurs as each one present struggles to find a compromise between what one thinks should be done and what one assumes others want to be done. To illustrate, Harvey relocates Hamlet to a corporate context; but the president and V.P. he mentions might equally be heads of state or any other perceived superior (1979: 135):

> To maintain my sense of integrity and self worth, or compromise it, that is the question. Whether 'tis nobler in the mind to suffer the ignominy that comes from managing a nonsensical ... project, or the fear and anxiety that comes from making a report that the president and V.P. might not like to hear.

According to Harvey, action anxiety arises from a combination of there being genuine, 'real' risk to the individual who confronts consensus, and risk that is imagined. Harvey calls imagined risk 'negative fantasies' about what will happen if one acts according to one's true beliefs. These include, for example, 'loss of face, prestige, position, and even health' and 'being made scapegoats, branded as disloyal, or ostracized as non team players' (ibid.: 135). But these fantasies have an important purpose for those who have them. They provide absolution, specifically 'the excuse that releases him (*sic*), both in his (*sic*) own eyes and frequently in the eyes of others from the responsibility of having to act to solve ... problems' (ibid.: 135).

Harvey describes living with the consequences of risk in psychodynamic terms. He claims that risk aversion arises specifically from the fear of separation, of being excluded from others, and from an unwillingness to accept risk-taking as a condition of being human ('existential risk'). This leads to what Harvey calls a paradox within a paradox, that negative fantasies about imagined risk can lead people into paths where we take wrong decisions (perhaps meaning greater real risk) and consequently suffer greater real adverse consequences than those imagined.

Harvey's prescriptions for avoiding the trip to Abilene include avoiding blaming and fault-finding behaviour, and at the same time challenging collusion in risk avoidance. Each individual, in their 'own collusive manner, shares responsibility for the trip, so searching for a locus of blame outside oneself serves no useful purpose. What is required is that assumptions about the nature of reality and knowledge are confronted' (ibid.: 138). Later he continues: 'change and effectiveness may be facilitated as much by confronting the organization with what it knows and agrees upon as by confronting it with what it does not know or disagrees about' (ibid.: 140). For Harvey, anyone in the group is able to play this confronting, risk-taking role, and should be prepared to take the risk involved. We may get plaudits if this works out, we may find ourselves disliked, we may get fired if it doesn't. But whatever happens, our self-esteem remains intact, and this is what matters.

There is a range of explanations for people not wanting to take risks. In the case of our participatory workshop it might be because of real concerns about jobs and careers. In community-based participation it may be because participants do not want to lose the resources they assume the interventionist has under his or her control, or because they do not want to antagonize elders, family members or neighbours who have the power to visit real (or imagined) consequences on them. Given this, it is tempting to argue that we can accept that false consensus in the form of the Abilene paradox can arise in participatory processes, and even that risk aversion is its cause, without necessarily having to accept Harvey's psychodynamic explanations for it. There are those for whom psychodynamic explanations of behavioural processes are inherently unsound, given that they derive from a paradigm that does not see the need nor offer the opportunity for empirical testing (see, for example, Blunt 1995).

Accepting the paradox without its psychodynamics would still undermine participation's claims as a means. Clearly, we do not have more effective planning, analysis and evaluation, nor do we have commitment if people subconsciously collude to make decisions they know are wrong. Chambers does of course acknowledge the potential for practitioner and beneficiary to engage in 'mutual deception' (1997: 89). However, the Abilene paradox suggests that participation is not necessarily a remedy; indeed, it suggests that face-to-face interaction can make things worse. Likewise, people are not empowered in the sense of being given control over their own development if they come to decisions with which they disagree, but which they feel unable to publicly contest. The implication of the Abilene paradox for those who see empowerment as consciousness-raising is that participatory processes may lead a group to say what it is they think you and everyone else want to hear, rather than what they truly believe.

Furthermore, we should be wary of writing off psychodynamic understandings of what happens in group processes, and their insights for the practitioner. Psychodynamics is, as we have said, about the relationship between the unconscious mind and how we think and feel. As such, they pose important questions for participatory interventionists. For example, what psychodynamic processes make people want to be interventionists in the first place? How do psychodynamic processes affect how the interventionist thinks of and interacts with participants? And what does psychodynamics tell believers in participation as consciousness-raising empowerment about how consciousness is shaped?

Groupthink

Groupthink described Harvey does acknowledge that there are other valuable accounts of dysfunctional group consensus – what he calls group tyranny. In particular he cites Janis' concept of groupthink. Groupthink is the term for a set of group dynamics that leads to evidently bad or wrong decisions being taken. Groupthink is perhaps the best known of the three concepts discussed here, and is used in political science as well as in management and organization studies as an explanation of how bad decisions are taken in the face of strong contrary evidence. The concept centres on there being an *ingroup* and an *outgroup*, and its main principle is:

> The more amiability and esprit de corps there is among a policy making ingroup, the greater the danger that independent critical thinking will be replaced by groupthink, which is likely to result in irrational and dehumanizing actions against outgroups. (Janis 1991: 262)

Janis' arrival at the concept was based on his analysis of the Bay of Pigs fiasco, but he went on to analyse the USA's entry into the Korean War, Johnson's escalation of the Vietnam War and Watergate on the same terms (ibid.). The eight symptoms of groupthink are described in Box 7.1. Of these, symptoms 6 and 7 parallel the Abilene paradox.

Groupthink and participatory development The development of the concept came about from Janis' research into high-level policy-making, and it is tempting to point to evidence of groupthink at the policy level of the development process. It is also possible to identify symptoms of groupthink in the very discourse surrounding participatory development (and, anticipating, in the reactions of the participatory development community to the book in which this chapter appears). The point here, though, is that groupthink can occur in participatory processes at the micro level, in the participatory project management process described above, or even in community-based participatory processes in which donors are supposedly not directly involved. In either circumstance there are likely to be

Box 7.1 Janis' eight symptoms of groupthink

1. *The illusion of invulnerability* An over-optimism about the power of the group and the lack of any real threat to the prevailing status quo ('laughing together at a danger signal, which labels it as purely a laughing matter, is a characteristic manifestation of groupthink') (1991: 262).

2. *Rationalization* Along with the collective ignoring of warning signals there is a collective construction of rationalizations that allow any negative feedback to be discounted, so that assumptions never need to be reconsidered each time decisions are recommitted to.

3. *Morality* Ingroup members 'believe unquestioningly in the inherent morality of their ingroup', inclining 'members to ignore the ethical or moral consequences of their decisions' (ibid.: 263).

4. *Stereotypes* Group members hold stereotypical views about 'enemy groups', which lead to the assumption that they must be eliminated rather than compromised with. Such stereotypes often focus on the inherent badness or evil nature of 'the enemy' (ibid.: 264).

5. *Pressure* This is directly applied to anyone who momentarily expresses doubts about the group's shared illusions. Such pressure often is masked as amiability, in an attempt to 'domesticate' the dissenter, so long as doubts are not expressed outside the ingroup, and fundamental assumptions are not challenged.

6. *Self-censorship* 'Individuals keep silent about their misgivings, and even minimize to themselves the importance of their doubts' (ibid.: 265).

7. *Unanimity* An illusion of unanimity exists with the group, with silence assumed as concurrence with the majority view.

8. *Mindguards* 'Individuals sometimes appoint themselves as mindguards to protect the leader and fellow members from adverse information' (ibid.: 266) that might confront complacency about the effectiveness and morality of decisions, to the extent of taking it upon themselves to exclude dissenters from the group.

ingroups and outgroups, and the eight symptoms of groupthink may well occur.

Thus, taking our project planning workshop example, let us go on to depict it as being about 'employment reform' in the civil service (i.e. about downsizing, rightsizing or retrenchment). The ingroup – the same actors as before – diverse as it is, might positively stereotype itself as *the modernizers*, and equally, share all sorts of negative stereotypes of the outgroup (e.g. the civil service in general) it is seeking to reform (words like bureaucratic, corrupt, inefficient, or self-seeking, flowing freely and uncritically). The illusion of invulnerability is sustained by the actual power that results from being within the ingroup, and the surrounding trappings of hotels, chauffeurs and high salaries/fees. That rationalization occurs is evident in the (implicit or explicit) belief that there is no alternative, and in the virtual ignoring of the substantial data that suggest that retrenchment might not work, that money is often not saved, and that organizational effectiveness is often impaired (summarized by McCourt 1998). The morality of development is often seen as unquestionable, particularly when associated with intentions that few could criticize – poverty alleviation, sustainable development or, indeed, empowerment.

So deep are the professional and disciplinary socialization processes that precede entry into the group that dissenting views are rarely expressed. The assumptions that dissent is never insurmountable, and that consensus can always be achieved, are implicit in the very use of participatory processes. These processes themselves also often provide the mechanism for the domestication of dissenters in which group members are permitted to express concerns in a way which does not challenge fundamental aims.

Chambers suggests that in PRA games or exercises can be used with names like 'saboteur or dominator which then lodge as words, often used jokingly by participants' (1997: 215). This apparently amiable labelling of dissenters is, from Janis' (1982: 115) position, an indicator of domestication processes at work:

> The non-conformist can feel that he (*sic*) is still accepted as a member in good standing. If on occasion he goes too far, he is warned about his deviation, in an affectionate or joking way and is reminded only indirectly of his potentially precarious status by the labels others give him … The others in the group … can even pat themselves on the back for being so democratic about tolerating open dissent. Nevertheless, the domesticated dissenter repeatedly gets the message that there is only a very small piece of critical territory he can tread safely and still remain a member in good standing.

Thus while the group as a whole may feel invulnerable, individual feelings of vulnerability – not least to exclusion from the group – are high.

This in turn points to the need to consider whether groupthink can occur in so-called community-based approaches to participation. Chambers himself is not beyond stereotyping (e.g. his 'uppers' and 'lowers'). Moreover, once we acknowledge Mosse's point that communities are not one homogeneous group, we must also recognize that ingroups and outgroups may exist of which the interventionist is not even aware. These in/outgroups might be differentiated on the bases of gender, age, ethnicity, tribe, caste, class, sexuality, occupation, location, nationality, and so on. Once again, 'developmental' purposes and the rhetoric of empowerment sustain a belief in the inherent morality of what is being done. Power actually derives from being a member of the participatory community group – one's voice is heard. All sorts of actual and potential benefits may be ascribed to being a member of the group; fear of their loss may lead to self-censorship, and a desire to present unanimity. Likewise, there may be a fear of presenting what the interventionist may perceive as adverse information (Chambers' mutual deception again). The extent to which the illusion of group invulnerability might occur is open to question, and perhaps the least likely of the symptoms of groupthink to occur. However, an ingroup that is seen as invulnerable in a community – for example, elders or men – is likely to have that sense of invulnerability reinforced if it is the focus or gatekeeper of a participatory intervention.

The potential presence of groupthink undermines claims for participation as a means and as an end. End-wise, groupthink is defined by processes and decisions that lack rigour and are worse than ineffective, in that they can cause harm. As a concept it also reveals some of the subtle and unwitting processes that can occur within supposedly empowering group activities that have a disempowering effect. Real control is removed from individual 'ingroup' members, who are loath to lose that status, and of course outgroup members can be left with real cause for concern. Groupthink is not inevitable, and unlike risky shift we cannot point to empirical studies that tell us the statistical likelihood of it occurring. However, as the Bay of Pigs and the decision to escalate the US war on Vietnam show, one-off occurrences can cause harm enough.

Janis' antidotes to groupthink are less reliant than Harvey's on individual heroism, and depend more on structural arrangements. They include the setting up of more than one decision-making group to counterbalance each other, the assignment of someone to the devil's advocate role, individual group members checking with non-group members for their opinions, having subgroups meet separately, and the removal of time pressures on decisions to allow for reflection. Janis also suggests that outside interventionists be called in. These are not mere facilitators, but trained behavioural science experts who have both the legitimacy and the expertise to confront groupthink. In sum, groupthink poses three questions for proponents of participatory development. First, is its potential recognized anywhere in the vast literature on participatory development? Second, to what extent are the antidotes built in to participatory development? Third, to what extent are the antidotes – for example, the need for highly trained interventionists – actually counter to the anti-professionalism espoused by participatory development (e.g. Chambers 1993)?

Coercive Persuasion

Coercive persuasion described Both the Abilene paradox and groupthink are presentations of how underlying psychological or group dynamics lead members unintentionally to shape group processes, which in turn ultimately lead to 'bad' or 'wrong' decisions. Schein's analysis of coercive persuasion works the other way round. It shows how group processes can intentionally be shaped to set up specific psycho- and group dynamics to achieve a particular outcome. This particular aspect of Schein's work has been dealt with in depth elsewhere (Cooke 1998), so is summarized in brief here. Schein is a respected mainstream managerial/organization psychologist, who has written standard texts on organizational culture (1990), and can claim to be the inventor of process consultation, widely used as a term in development, albeit with little reference to Schein's principles (Schein 1988; Joy and Bennett n.d.). I have also argued elsewhere that development practitioners should learn from Schein's concept of 'the clinical perspective' (Cooke 1997). The particular concern here, though, is his early work funded by the US military on the 'ideological conversion', or so-called brainwashing of US prisoners by the Chinese. Schein's purpose was to explain how US forces personnel came to make public statements, while prisoners, in which they apologized for atrocities they had perpetrated, and denounced US imperialism in pursuing the Korean War.

Schein's method was to take a range of psychological and social psychological theories, and analyse the extent to which they were able to account for the so-called brainwashing process. What he came up with was a synthesis of Goffman's ideas on face work and presentation of self, and Festinger's work on the importance of self-image and the need for an attractive, coherent picture of oneself as a prerequisite for social existence, constructed around Lewin's three-stage model of the change process. Box 7.2 is Schein's presentation of the model in *Process Consultation Volume 2* (1987). He describes the model thus in *Coercive Persuasion* (1961: 118):

> it is a basic assumption of the model that beliefs, attitudes, values and behaviour patterns of an individual tend to be integrated with each other and tend to be organized around the individual's self image or self concept. This integration, even if imperfect, gives continuity and stability to the person, and hence operates as a force against being influenced, unless the change which the influence implies is seen to be a change in the direction of greater integration

Thus I have described Schein's method of attitudinal and behavioural change as 'one of social disintegration (unfreezing), social reconstruction (change) and social reintegration (refreezing) of individuals' cognitive frameworks' (Cooke 1998: 48). 'Participatory' group processes are used by

Box 7.2 Schein's three-stage model of the change process

Stage 1

Unfreezing: Creating motivation and readiness to change through:

a) Disconfirmation or lack of confirmation
b) Creation of guilt or anxiety
c) Provision of psychological safety

Stage 2

Changing: Through cognitive restructuring: helping the client to see things, judge things, feel things, and react to things based on a new point of view obtained through:

a) Identifying with a new role model, mentor, etc.
b) Scanning the environment for new relevant information

Stage 3

Refreezing: Helping the client to integrate the new point of view into:

a) The total personality and the self concept
b) Significant relationships

(*Source*: Schein 1987: 93, Table 6.1)

'change agents in the day to day business of producing ideological change' (Schein 1961: 12) in order, first, to unfreeze. Guilt or anxiety are produced – in the case of prisoners of war, by, for example, producing and collectively discussing the evidence of the consequences of US bombing raids; this in turn disconfirms individuals' feeling of self-worth; at the same time some psychological safety is produced by group members being all in the same boat; and the so-called 'lenient policy' of Chinese captors in which understanding and re-education rather than punishment appear to be the primary motives (although, at the same time, the alternative to participating in these group discussions clearly was severe punishment). The 'change' process was facilitated by encouraging prisoners to identify with their captors, by the introduction of fellow prisoners who had had already recanted, and the ongoing provision of information, for example, through news media. Refreezing was encouraged by rewarding captors with privileges, reinforcing the perception that what they had done was the right thing to do.

Coercive persuasion and participatory development It was Schein who labelled and described the change process in this way. The captors, although, Schein suggests, relying heavily on Maoist traditions of thought reform, did not see or describe themselves as going through a process of unfreezing, changing and refreezing; nor indeed is there any evidence that they saw what they were doing as brainwashing. From the evidence that Schein provided so-called brainwashers can equally be represented as doing what they believed was right to bring prisoners round to what they perceived was an objectively correct analysis of the situation, and to get them to act accordingly. Of course, in participatory development we have participants rather than prisoners. However, it is not necessarily safe to assume that participants participate completely out of free will. Schein himself went on to argue soon after his initial work that his three-stage process could and should be used managerially, the safeguard being the benign intent of a highly trained practitioner. His model of change was to become a generic model in his own work, and one that was explicitly and implicitly to underpin other models of, and approaches to, the management of change.

Let us take our participatory project workshop once more. In this one workshop the unfreezing is brought about by all sorts of 'evidence' that things cannot go on as they are – the state must be reformed or bad things will occur (disconfirmation); donors will withdraw funding, development will be impeded (creation of anxiety); however, there is a way out if we follow certain prescriptions and processes of good government (provision of psychological safety). The logframe becomes a talisman that will ensure our survival. Changing is brought about by providing examples of how other people have done it – we look at the case examples of New Zealand, the UK, Chile. We identify real and fictional organizational and individual models of what we want to look like (identifying with new role models), and set up research programmes into the functioning of our and other civil services (gathering new information).

Refreezing perhaps only begins within the first workshop, which is why there is a strong managerialist emphasis on change as an iterative process. However, within that initial workshop, there may start to be a realignment of how people see themselves – for example, from bureaucrat to reformer, from academic to consultant – all which begin to change the self-concept. Those whom one identifies as important begin to change as other workshop participants come to be seen as more significant, and some of our absent colleagues less so. This is reinforced by the actual and potential rewards of being associated with the change process that become apparent at an early stage.

The work of the community facilitator can be described in the same way. Indeed, the very presence of a facilitator can begin the unfreezing process, and be seen as suggesting that things will not carry on as before. Unfreezing is also achieved through the use of data collection processes that reveal things – to interventionist and participants collectively – that have hitherto been concealed or unspoken. This in itself can create anxiety or insecurity. A counterbalancing sense of security is provided by the very presence of the interventionist, and indeed by the language of helping and of development that is likely to be used. The role models upon which change is to be based are often provided by the interventionists' descriptions of how things will be different, and examples of communities that have already changed through participatory processes. Refreezing is fostered by rewards for acting/behaving in a different way – at a collective level, by funding further development, individually, by providing further career opportunities (e.g. the chance to become a 'local' facilitator).

Schein's work undermines claims made for participation as a value-free or benign means, suggesting that participatory processes never take place in an ideological vacuum. What is seen as a positive outcome from a participatory process, indeed what effectiveness means, will depend on an ideological position. But the more profound challenge is offered to claims for participation as a consciousness-raising end. This is, paradoxically, because Schein shows participation to be no more than a technique or technology, or a means, for consciousness-changing. There is nothing in participatory processes themselves that brings about a particular state of consciousness; rather, that state is shaped by the interventionist.

PAR facilitators seeking to empower through changing consciousness can equally and legitimately be described in the same terms as Maoist cadres, as 'in the day to day business of producing ideological change' (1961: 12). As Schein puts it:

> on the level of social process, I saw many parallels between what the Chinese Communists were doing and what we do every day ... the goals are different but the methods are remarkably similar. When we disapprove we call it a cult and deplore it; when we approve, we call it an effective indoctrination programme. (ibid.: 234)

or, we might add, an effective consciousness-raising activity.

Finally, there was a development agenda that underpinned the Chinese use of thought reform processes on the broader Chinese population that has resonances with that of contemporary participatory development. Hence there was a strong emphasis on the creation of social and economic change to benefit the poor and oppressed, the creation of a non-Western, indigenous, anti-capital 'Asian way' (see ibid.: 82–4) and a grassroots, participatory, peasant-orientated rhetoric. Schein argues that what was created as a consequence was an ideological unanimity that facilitated Maoist oppression and, it can be argued with hindsight, development programmes that led to devastating famine and authoritarian oppression (see, for example, MacFarquhar and Fairbank 1987; Chang 1991; Yang 1998).

Conclusion

Whether considered on their own or collectively, the four analyses suggest that there are social psychological limits to what can be achieved through participatory development. Moreover, each can reinforce and be reinforced by the other problems with participatory development acknowledged by its proponents. To illustrate, an assumption of community homogeneity on the part of the interventionist is likely to mask even further the false nature of an 'Abilene' consensus; and any tendency to false consensus is in itself likely to conceal difference and heterogeneity from the interventionist. Coercive persuasion suggests that participation can indeed be co-opted for a range of agendas other than those with the needs of the poor and oppressed at heart – hence the co-optation of

Maoist brainwashing processes for managerial ends in Western work organizations. However, it also suggests that participatory development with an espoused and genuine commitment to meeting the needs of the poor and oppressed and to raising their consciousness on the part of the change agent are not in themselves, if we take the Maoist illustrations, a safeguard against disastrous outcomes from participatory development.

The four analyses discussed here also lend strength to the more critical analyses of participation. Craig and Porter's (1997) view of participation as an instrument for control is almost provided with a practical 'how to do it' guide by Schein. The political dynamics and complex conflicts of interests identified by White (1996) can now be seen as source of, for example, groupthink, and as potentially manifesting themselves in any of risky shift, Abilene paradox, groupthink and coercive persuasion. Likewise, construction of knowledge in participatory public social events, which Mosse (1994) argues is shaped by existing social relationships, can now also be seen to be shaped by the social psychological processes of participation itself.

But it is by building on Stirrat's (1997) identification of 'the new orthodoxy' of participation as neocolonialist that we arrive at our most important concluding point. This chapter suggests that the poor of the world, particularly but not exclusively those in 'developing countries', are the victims of a disciplinary bias: put simply, the rich get social psychology, the poor get participatory development. Chambers' claim that, while 'group dynamics can present problems', 'how best to convene and facilitate groups remains an area for learning and invention' (1994: 148) ignores the substantial amount about groups that has already been learned and invented since 1945. As we have noted, the four analyses here represent but a small sample of this work, but they are standard fare in texts aimed at practitioners working for First World work organizations.

The absence of social psychology from participatory development therefore identifies it as yet another technology used with the Third World without the care and concern that would be expected elsewhere. Those of us who are participation's technocrats should reflect on why this is the case, what it tells us about the limitations of our own practice, and how that practice should change. A starting point might be to counter the proselytizing euphoria that surrounds participatory development with a more mundane but clearly essential understanding of when participatory processes must not be used.

8

Insights into Participation from Critical Management and Labour Process Perspectives

Harry Taylor

Introduction

Participatory discourse and practices, and the social relations of which they are constitutive, are not confined to the development arena. They are also of significant interest in the fields of management generally and human resources management in particular. This chapter shows how participatory discourses in mainstream management generally, and the set of values and practices that have come to be known as Human Resource Management in particular, mirror closely the participatory discourses in development in terms of its comforting ethos, its practices and the deception it attempts. In mainstream management this is articulated in the rhetoric of employee participation and involvement.

But why is a critique of participatory approaches in management of relevance to the development practitioner? I would suggest three reasons. First, such a comparison provides confirmation that participatory discourse and practices are part of a wider attempt to obscure the relations of power and influence between elite interests and less powerful groups such as the 'beneficiaries' of development projects in local communities in developing countries and employees of organizations in the developed world. Second, mainstream and critical debates on employee participation add new arguments and dimensions that may deepen our understanding of the use of participatory approaches in development. Third, there is evidence to suggest that organizations operating in the development arena are becoming increasingly influenced by Western managerialist thinking, including approaches to Human Resource Management and employee participation. They may thus come to espouse and be seduced by the rhetoric of participation for both their 'beneficiaries' and their employees.

The next section argues that the beneficiaries of development projects and employees within organizations are comparable in terms of their dependency and powerlessness in relation to the organization and their similar social relations within global capitalism. This is followed by a consideration of the arguments for participation stemming from mainstream management that shows how, even from within the mainstream, there are doubts about the feasibility and desirability of employee participation. The subsequent section critically examines approaches to Employee Involvement and Participation (EIP) through a discursive analysis of the concept informed by Foucault, and from the labour process perspective of Marxist approaches. The concluding discussion explicitly draws attention to the similarities between participation debates within management and those within development, and offers some suggestions as to why disillusionment with participation is apparent in both these arenas before proceeding to speculate on the prospects for 'genuine' participation.

Participation for 'Project Beneficiaries' and Employees: Comparable Dependencies?

At first sight, the project beneficiary in development projects and the employee have a different relation to the organizations they interact with. First, the beneficiary of a project is a client of a development organization but outside it, whereas the employee has a close contractual relationship in which the organization imposes an authority relationship. Second, improvements in the beneficiary's livelihood are intended to be the end of the development organization's activity, whereas the employee is primarily a means to the ends of the work organization's activity. Third, the beneficiary's involvement is only a temporary one whereas the employee enjoys (?) a long-term relationship with the organization and develops through the career structure a degree of commitment and loyalty (even though such commitment may be more instrumental than affective).

These differences can, however, be overstated. While the beneficiary may be seen as a 'client', it is often the case that they are highly dependent clients who are not competent to or not allowed to explicate their demands. Thus often the 'clients' of development organizations have little power or influence and are required simply to confirm the preconceived notion of orderly, rational and measurable development as defined by donors. This may be the case even when the donor formally espouses a participative approach (see Chapter 6). Thus the 'client' may become the means to the end in a way analogous to the employee. Also it can be argued that the timescales of involvement of the two groups may not be so different. Few employees, especially in development organizations, enjoy a 'job for life' status and many may view the organization in the same instrumental and opportunistic way as project beneficiaries might. Moreover, and perhaps more fundamentally, both the employee and the beneficiary are both weak and dependent partners in the relationship, depending on the organization for their livelihood and subject to the ultimate sanction of withdrawal of capital. In most cases neither the employee nor beneficiary can exercise a commensurate countervailing power.

This dependence of both beneficiaries and employees on development and work organizations respectively is, of course, not just a 'local' dependency but part of the wider social relations of capitalist production. Global capitalism requires the extension of market relations and the extraction of surplus value to all areas of 'production' in both the developed 'metropolitan' centres and the less developed 'peripheral' countries. In the developed, industrialized nations formal employment is the primary means of achieving these two goals. However, even in the less developed (or peripheral) countries, where formal employment applies to only a minority, surplus value and market relations are created by other means. An illustration of this is the notion of 'peasants as proletarians' which, although of long standing (see Cohen, Gutkind and Brazier 1979) nevertheless shows similarities between 'peasant production' and 'proletarian wage labour'. Cohen (1991) outlines three elements of this thesis. First, through the 'commoditization of production' (i.e. production for the market rather than subsistence) in the countryside the local farmer is drawn into market relations and productivity improvements that mirror those in the employed sectors. Second, 'capital has subordinated the countryside informally through a "concealed" wage relationship in which surplus value is none the less realised' (ibid.: 82). Third, through the increasing direction of the conditions of production by agencies acting on behalf of capital, there arises a control of labour time. In sum, 'peasants are (as it were) outdoor proletarians. The physical structure of the factory is absent, as is the gang boss or foreman, but the impelling necessity to work for capital is constructed by other institutional means' (ibid.).

Cohen does not indicate what the 'other institutional means' are, but Henkel and Stirrat (Chapter 11, this volume) see the 'development industry' as functioning to integrate the beneficiaries into 'national and international political, economic and ideological structures' by creating rational farmers increasing GDP, participants in the labour market, consumers for the products of capitalist production, and citizens of the institutions of the modern state. I argue that many development projects, including those purporting to be participatory, whatever their ostensible purposes, have these overarching but often unstated objectives. This incorporation of farmers and rural populations into quasi or actual capitalist modes of production, while it does not and is not intended to establish an argument that beneficiaries and employees have *identical* social relations in the capitalist system, nevertheless sets out some similarities that are not obvious from a cursory analysis.

Dependent relationships, such as those of employee and project beneficiary outlined above, require a legitimatory justification that obscures the nature and full extent of the subordination of these groups. As someone whose background is in management and human resources I am immediately struck by the similarities between the participatory discourse in development and its critiques, on the one hand, and debates about EIP in mainstream and critical management thinking on the other. These similarities will become apparent in later sections, but my contention is that this similarity is neither accidental nor surprising. Indeed, Chambers approvingly makes explicit the link between thinking in development (in particular PRA and RRA) and new thinking in business management (among others):

> RRA and PRA have been validated and reinforced, as modest partners, by parallel developments in the natural sciences, in chaos and edge of chaos theory, in the social sciences, and in business management, sharing with them a new high ground. (Chambers 1997: 192)

In both business management and PRA, according to Chambers, the important values emerging are creating a move away from top-down approaches towards decentralization, open communications, sharing knowledge and expertise coupled with 'empowerment' and diversity.

I would argue, however, that participatory discourses are utilized in both the development and managerial contexts because they serve essentially the same purpose of giving the 'sense' and warm emotional pull of participation without its substance, and are thus an attempt to placate those without power and obscure the real levers of power inherent in the social relations of global capitalism. This is my first rationale for arguing that the discourses and practices of participation in development and management have relevance and connection to each other.

My second rationale for this position is that 'managerialism' is spreading from the private sector in industrialized countries to all kinds of organizations globally, including state bureaucracies, NGOs and bilateral and multilateral donors (Morgan 1990). This attempt at transplantation is based on the technocratic view that 'management' is a universal, rational process capable of being successfully applied to all kinds of organization by impartial managers finding technical solutions to organizational problems more or less irrespective of the organizational context (Alvesson and Willmott 1996). Thus managerial practices developed in the West, including employee involvement and participation, are making inroads into development organizations. The extent to which this is happening is not clear. While some hold the view that 'notions of distributed leadership and empowerment, participation and co-operation and the facilitation of learning' (Valentin 1999: 1) have been explored in public and voluntary sector organizations, others draw attention to the irony of organizations that profess to empower communities but have no equivalent mechanisms for empowering their own staff (Nelson and Wright 1995). Irrespective of the extent to which managerialism has spread to the development industry to date, and regardless of whether the uncritical adoption of managerial ideas developed in one context can be successful in other quite different contexts, it is clear that 'progressive' and 'enlightened' managerial thinking, including the participation and involvement of employees, is being embraced by development organizations and has confirmatory resonances with the participatory discourse in development.

The meeting of these two discourses may thus provide mutual reinforcement and legitimation. Chambers provides a good example of this mutual reinforcement of participatory ideas in development organizations in claiming that PRA has been most effectively adopted in organizations (mainly NGOs) that have structures and cultures that are flexible and adaptive, have lateral communication and are democratic and participatory (Chambers 1994: 1447). By the same token, however, by bringing these two discourses together it may be possible to expose the partiality and deception that they both involve and bring to the surface the common interests that they serve. The next section begins to examine the discourse of employee involvement and participation, its social science and management underpinnings, and questions its efficacy from within the orthodox managerial paradigm.

Employee Involvement and Participation in Orthodox Managerial Thinking

As indicated above, debates about EIP from a mainstream perspective have an extremely long history, possibly as long as the history of industrialization itself. Many managers would agree with the Marxian analysis that the problem of management is about turning 'labour potential' into 'labour power' but may disagree about the best way to achieve it. During the early/middle stages of the industrial period, with a few notable philanthropic exceptions, direct and close supervision and the application of top-down hierarchical authority structures were adopted as the solution. However, this approach was later seen to be lacking in that it often resulted in the alienation of employees, and individual and collective resistance, which threatened productivity and managerial control. The 'human relations' movement, having its origins in the 1930s (Mayo 1933; Roethlisberger and Dixon 1939) was seen as the corrective to the overtly exploitative nature of coercive control. The literature on human relations is immense but the work of Likert (1961), who distinguished between authoritarian and participative systems, Burns and Stalker (1961), who emphasized participation through democratic 'organic' systems, and Blake and Mouton (1964), whose 'managerial grid' emphasized 'concern for people', are exemplars of the view that participation was 'good for business'. Anthony (1977: 241) reports a 1950s account from a US company that stated that 'participation in management decisions actually converted radical workers into "sound" management-oriented employees'. Thus, although the call for EIP has been given greater emphasis in the last 10–15 years through developments in the nature of jobs requiring greater involvement and commitment, and the rise of new employment policies under the broad banner of Human Resource Management (HRM) attempting to deliver it (see following section), the case for participation by employees in management has been part of mainstream thinking for a long time. However, this is not to say that human relations has completely or even significantly displaced earlier direct control or 'scientific management' approaches. Rather these earlier approaches have been assimilated into the repertoire of management and are used in combination with more 'enlightened' methods in an opportunistic and contingent way to achieve the optimum managerial result.

The actual implementation of these human relations ideas of participation into employing organizations has taken a number of forms. In common with the participatory development discourse there is little agreement on basic definitions of involvement and participation, but there is a recognition of different levels or a continuum in practice ranging from top-down management communication to workers at one end to full workers' control at the other. Intermediate levels of participation identified are:

- job level, where employees are given the opportunity to influence decisions regarding their own jobs and immediate environment;

- management level, where employee influence extends to the planning and allocation of work and other resources;
- policy-making level, where employee influence extends to strategic aspects of the organization; and
- ownership level, where employees either own equity in the company along with external investors, or where employees exclusively own the business (a worker cooperative) (summarized from Armstrong 1999: 744).

It is probably not too much of a generalization to add that the actual incidence of participation decreases as we move up through the various levels, but also that as the level increases the more likely it will be that the influence is restricted to *post facto* communication or consultation rather than prior joint decision-making.

These mechanisms of participation enjoy considerable support and legitimacy, at least in theory. Various statutory provisions in the UK provide a legal base but additionally management associations such as the British Institute of Management, the Institute of Directors and the Institute for Personnel and Development (the professional body for HR/personnel specialists in the UK) provide varying levels of enthusiasm. A joint Code of Practice by the Industrial Participation Association and the IPM (forerunner of the IPD) was produced in 1990 offering principles and practical guidance to employers in setting up EIP mechanisms (IPA/IPM 1990).

However, notwithstanding the long lineage of management thinking promoting respectability with regard to notions of employee involvement, and its recent encouragement by the state and other influential managerial bodies, evidence of a track record of success, even on management's own terms, is extremely hard to find.

Recent empirical work has failed to demonstrate clear links between, first, EIP and organizational commitment and second, EIP and individual and organizational performance and productivity. A recent substantial survey of employee relations in British workplaces (WERS 1998) found that while most British employers utilized at least one method of EIP and most workers would prefer to have some influence rather than none, a substantial minority of employees were sceptical about its motives and outcomes. This is echoed by Marchington's earlier study: 'whilst employees see benefits from EI, these had not generally been so powerful as to change their overall attitudes or perceptions ... nor as yet leading to widespread increases in commitment' (Marchington et al. 1992: 57). Moreover, the literature suggests that there is often a sizeable gap between espoused policy and practice, and that participation is more about an attitude of mind, or part of organizational culture rather than a set of mechanisms that can be closely prescribed and measured. Hyman and Mason (1995) summarize the main reasons for the failure of EIP in the UK:

- many EIP techniques have been introduced in an uncoordinated way unrelated to organizational systems, culture, context and practice;
- many initiatives have foundered on the rock of line manager hostility who have perceived a threat to their authority;
- senior management support has either not been available or has not been sustained in the face of more 'urgent' business pressures; and
- many initiatives are a result of hype and 'fad-surfing' by HR and Organization Development specialists, consultants and management gurus.

A recent and related trend may also suggest that the current wave of interest in EIP may be in jeopardy (see Ramsey 1983). Participation is often associated with the decentralization policies of the 1990s; however, there is evidence to suggest that some organizations are quietly recentralizing their activities in order to reduce costs and rationalize activities (Arkin 1999). Recentralization, to the extent that it is occurring, puts in jeopardy the lower levels of participation: if managers lower down the organization have little influence themselves, they can hardly share it with employees.

So, even from within the mainstream managerial paradigm there are significant doubts about the ability of EIP to deliver either improved performance, or employee satisfaction and commitment. The implications of this analysis for participation in the development arena will be considered in the concluding discussion. Attention will now focus on more radical analyses of EIP.

Radical Critiques of Employee Participation and Involvement

Disillusionment with employee participation is not new. Almost fifty years ago, Clegg and Chester (1954: 344) wondered why 'a device which is given almost universal public approval has met with such limited success'. More colourfully, Anthony (1977: 256) speculated on why 'the stink of rotting fish' was associated with participation. Mainstream critiques, as outlined above, go only so far in explaining its continuing failure and the willingness of some managers to go 'once more into the breach'. My contention is that the underlying motives for the introduction of EIP, and the reasons for its continuing failure and reappearance in different guises, can only be satisfactorily explained by utilizing more radical and critical analyses. These comprise the following four elements. First, there is a rejection (whether in management, development or any other area of social life) of 'common sense' and 'obvious' notions of the 'natural order' of social arrangements. Second, there is a sustained attempt to understand and make explicit the underlying social processes and sites of power within capitalist society. Third, unlike mainstream managerial analyses the ends of productive activity are open to rigorous questioning as well as the means. Fourth, an attempt is made to seek out opportunities for transforming social and productive relations.

Within these broad parameters of a radical agenda there are different approaches. The two approaches I examine here are the discursive analysis advocated by Foucault (1980) and the labour process theory, exemplified by the material analysis of Marx (1959) and Braverman (1974) among others. While these approaches utilize different conceptions of 'reality' and 'ways of seeing' there is a degree of complementarity between them. Following Mitchell (1997), I argue that purely cultural and linguistic constructions of participation ignore structural and material constraints, and thus the two approaches must be analysed in tandem.

The managerial discourse of employee involvement The discursive and socio-linguistic critique of management and EIP is based on the idea that 'implicit assumptions can be revealed by focusing on social relations, power structures and meanings, *contained within the language used*' (Valentin 1999: 3, emphasis added). Thus the bases of power and domination are essentially linguistic: discourse is used as a set of statements, concepts and expressions which constitute a way of understanding particular issues and 'framing' the subject in such a way that what can be talked about and what the subject comprises is formulated so that they reinforce existing power relations. For example, Mosse (Chapter 2, this volume) describes development projects not only as systems for the delivery of development but also as a 'system of representations – a set of validating ideas … which need to be maintained'. Thus power does not exist as an objective reality. Rather, power and knowledge are inextricably linked and mutually causal. The task of managers of employees, and development project managers, then has to do with the creation and adaptation of shared meanings and 'representations'. This analysis of managerial activity has developed because of a perception that the direct control strategies of the early/middle industrial period are being displaced by 'social technologies of control' that operate through affective and attitudinal means.

Turning now to the elements of the particular discourse of participative management it can be argued that the discourse 'frames' the subject in such a way as to close off more fundamental notions of participation by presenting as radical and fundamental a version of participation that is essentially quite 'conservative' and non-threatening to powerful interests. Among academics and consultants, for example, post-Fordist and post-industrial 'paradigms' are represented as radical transformations of the organization of work leading to the inevitable democratization of work practices (see, for example, Matthews 1989). However, such 'paradigm shifts' leave existing power relations undisturbed and thus, whatever kind of post-something they are, they are not post-capitalist.

Moving closer to the level of the practitioner the broad HRM discourse (of which EIP has come to be a constituent part) displays great subtlety by generally appealing to warm emotions through mantric statements such as 'our people are our greatest asset' – an assertion that is hard to disagree with. At the same time HRM discourse displays different faces for differing audiences. The 'hard' model of HRM focuses on employees' contribution to the 'bottom line' and 'required behaviours'. This version emphasizes rationality and is intended for consumption mainly by chief executives and senior managers. By contrast, in the 'soft' model of HRM, although it uses the same starting point as the 'hard model', i.e. employees' contribution, the emphasis switches to showing how eliciting that contribution allows employees to 'self-actualize', to develop their creativity and become 'empowered'. The intended audience here is employees and possibly those elements of management who incline to more humanistic values and for whom this approach provides a warm but non-threatening outlet (for a fuller account of the 'hard' and 'soft' models of HRM see Storey 1987).

The EIP elements of the HRM discourse display this ambiguity by combining the warm emotions of the 'soft' HRM approach with talk of inclusivity, equity and equality, the valuing of contribution and the positive-sum aspects of 'partnership', with the 'hard' aspects of participation holding out the promise of improved commitment, and more fundamentally, greater productivity.

The practitioner management literature is replete with examples of how the enthusiasm and hype for the initiatives of EIP draw attention away from its restrictive 'framing'. Leaving aside the fantastic terminology of, for example, *Liberation Management: Necessary Disorganization for the Nano-Second Nineties* (Peters 1992), the possibilities of liberation from rigid Fordist-style work practices and authority structures are presented and re-presented as organizational and individual salvation in the face of accelerating change. Nevertheless, space is usually found to insert some warnings about the limits to participation. For example, in a British Institute of Management report managers are counselled to be clear about its objectives for participation 'so that they can select the appropriate form of participation and *avoid the creation of unwarranted expectations*' (British Institute of Management 1979: 1, emphasis added). Even the quote marks around words can form part of the discourse. For example, the word ownership is used extensively within the HRM and EIP discourses to indicate that participation creates a sense of at least psychological ownership of the ideas and decisions jointly produced. However, the quote marks around 'ownership' that frequently appear in both the practitioner and academic literature reveal that any ownership is nominal rather than 'real' or 'realizable'.

The labour process approach and EIP The labour process approach, unlike the approach discussed in the previous section, sees power and social relations in the context of a material and structural reality. The starting point is, of course, Marx (1959), who argued that the logic of capital accumulation necessitated the continual and increasingly intensified 'extraction of surplus value' from employees. Therefore managerial practices and the design and control of work cannot be understood without considering the capitalists' imperative to intensify production pressures while at the same time reducing labour costs to the minimum. Braverman (1974) explicated this analysis of the labour process and predicted that through continual work simplification and increased division of labour work would become deskilled and workers would become increasingly marginalized and alienated. Braverman's analysis has been criticized for its simplistic view of deskilling as the only employer strategy, for its lack of recognition of employee resistance to the extraction of surplus value (Jermier, Knights and Nord 1994) and its failure to take account of changes in the structure of capitalism and corresponding changes in the structure and nature of employment (Crompton et al. 1996). Later and more subtle analyses, while acknowledging the need for capital to continually revolutionize the production process to extract surplus value, delineate a range of employer strategies. Friedman (1977) has developed a model of employer strategy linked to a contingency approach. The 'direct control' strategy, which basically corresponds to Braverman's concept, is appropriate for mass production, low skill, and competition based on cost and price minimization rather than quality. Here supervision is detailed and coercive, tasks are highly specified and there is little discretion for the worker.

However, in other situations a control strategy of 'responsible autonomy' is seen as more appropriate (ibid.: 58). In situations where the 'production' process requires not physical effort or prescribed manual skill but personal service, flexibility, application of knowledge in varied situations, and the 'affective' and attitudinal engagement of the worker, direct prescription and supervision is much less effective. However, control is maintained through processes of socialization, attitudinal structuring, careful selection, and training that produces employees who can be trusted to do the right thing without the need for close supervision. Thus the 'responsibly autonomous' employee is subject to controls demanded by the labour process, but these controls are more subtle and less visible than those under direct control strategies.

Changes to the structure of global capitalism and a new 'international division of labour' (Hirst and Thompson 1992) that result in the movement of low-discretion manufacturing jobs to low-labour cost areas (i.e. developing countries) and their replacement (to some extent) in the developed countries by professional services, 'knowledge' industries and specialized, high-technology manufacturing require more workers who have a 'hearts and minds' commitment to their jobs and their employers, where the emphasis 'becomes the total behaviour of the individual rather than specifically productive behaviour' (Townley 1989: 106). Hence the introduction of EIP initiatives by management can be seen as one part of the attempt to create a committed and 'responsible' workforce aligned to the goals of the organization without the need to cede control in any substantive way. Another element of the strategy is that EIP initiatives are introduced by management in order to offer an alternative to trade union power and collective bargaining, which because they often arise as a result of a spontaneous collective challenge from workers are more threatening to employer interests. However, even these processes can be subject to 'accommodation' and 'incorporation' within the broad structure of capitalism (see Allen 1971).

The idea that EIP initiatives are part of an employer strategy to retain control of the labour process rather than relinquish or share it is supported by research. Boreham in his study of 'post-Fordist' (i.e. participative) management practices in six developed countries (Britain, Canada, Germany, Japan, Sweden and the USA) found that 'there is little evidence in the data presented here to suggest that participative organizational practices have made any significant incursion into traditional managerial prerogatives in the workplace in any of the countries studied' (Boreham 1992: 23).

Moreover, even where a particular organization is held up as an icon of best participative management practice and where these practices are seen as part of the 'Japanization' of manufacturing management in the UK (Oliver and Wilkinson 1988), the reality falls short, as in the case of Nissan's much-hyped involvement practices at their new Sunderland plant: 'Real autonomy for the workforce is largely cosmetic, as production decisions and all quality targets are dictated either by management decreed goals or "customer needs"' (Blyton and Turnbull 1994: 222).

Managers thus still expect and enjoy the right to make unilateral decisions regarding job design and work allocation, product design, production and marketing of goods and services and the allocation of resources, despite the rhetoric or discourse of participation and its partial implementation in the service of the employer's interest.

The implementation of EIP practices is, however, not the sole element of this employer strategy that appears to offer discretion in work practices and redefined authority relationships to employees but effectively denies them. In contemporary organizations EIP is part of a constellation of practices that can be broadly described under the banner of Human Resource Management.

The previous section outlined the discursive dimension of HRM (see Townley 1994 for a fuller exposition), whereas the analysis here is more in terms of its actual practices. HRM is essentially an attempt to redefine and reshape the problem of managing employees for the 'enterprise culture' of 'advanced' and possibly post-industrial capitalism. Although it contains within it some of the practices of its predecessor, personnel management, such as selection, appraisal, reward, and employee development, these HR practices have as their clear goal 'strategic integration', i.e. the subjugation of these previously non-strategic administrative routines to the requirements of the profit and efficiency concerns of the employer. HRM's values emphasize commonality of interest of employer and employees, a focus on the individual as the unit of analysis in prescriptions of managing performance and rewards, flexibility in the use of 'human resources' (though not necessarily employees), and an orientation to quality and continuous improvement (Storey 1995). EIP is intended to contribute to this agenda by delivering committed workers who share management's 'vision'. In a sense EIP can be seen as the 'soft' and acceptable face of HRM that attempts to make acceptable the 'hard' elements of HRM, i.e. insecurity and work intensification.

EIP's managerial agenda is muted in much of the literature and is presented with at least some acknowledgement of employee needs. For example, the IPA/IPM (1990) Code of Practice sets out the aims of participative management in terms of commitment to organization goals, satisfying customers, and improving organizational performance and productivity, but also goes on to list employee satisfaction – although this is included almost as an afterthought, and later it refers to management's continuing responsibility to 'making business and organizational decisions falling within the area of their own accountability' (IPA/IPM 1990: para. 2.8). Others, however, are less circumspect: 'don't do participative management for your employees' sake; do it for the business' sake. We believe the purpose is business stability and growth, not employee fulfilment' (Plunkett and Fournier 1991: 4).

Employees themselves also have few illusions about the efficiency-driven purpose of EIP. Hyman and Mason (1995: 190) in their survey found that a 'majority of employees believe that management objectives for EI are to increase efficiency and encourage people to work harder'. In a review of an 'Empowerment Programme' at a large UK chain of restaurants, Harvester Restaurants, the Programme was seen to be inextricably linked to 'delayering' and one manager, presumably without any sense of irony, declared that 'the staff are empowered to do virtually anything ... except decide whether they will be empowered' (Pickard 1993: 22).

The foregoing arguments may give the impression of an all-knowing, competent, completely united and focused managerial group deliberately conspiring cynically to extract maximum 'surplus value' from the workforce, and of a weak, manipulated workforce with no resources available to resist. Without wishing to deny the general weakness of employees in the employment relationship, managers are not often so well organized or united and often have difficulty 'papering over the cracks' in this edifice of mystification. Despite the rhetoric of HRM, often in the support of the sectional professional interest of HR specialists, initiatives such as EIP may not be well implemented or may clash with other aspects of organization structure and culture. In some cases, then, EIP may not be deliberately part of a grand design of deceit but rather may be misguided 'muddling through' (Watson 1994) by managers who, under pressure to get results, will grasp at new managerial ideas (or reformulations of old ones) in an attempt to resolve their people management problems. Therefore, although an understanding of how EIP initiatives may serve employers' interests in the labour process, this is not to say that the situation is predetermined, or that workers have no opportunity to gain some control, whether overt or covert.

Participatory development and employee involvement and participation There are implications of EIP for participatory development and this concluding section identifies some of the similarities between the discourses, and makes some final comments about the prospects and requirements for 'genuine' participation.

First, it appears that participatory approaches are not working in both arenas, or at least have not had the impact that was expected of them. Employees continue to be cynical about participation and have not developed the commitment to organizational goals that was expected as a consequence of 'empowerment'. Moreover, the link between employee commitment and productivity has not been established (see Hyman and Mason 1995; Marchington 1992). Similarly, many project beneficiaries, as evidenced elsewhere in this volume, exhibit an instrumental approach to participatory development projects rather than seeing them as liberating experiences (see Nelson and Wright 1995).

Second, it has been argued that participation has become deradicalized. My contention is that in both arenas participation has *never* been radical. To be genuinely radical, I argue, it is necessary for there to be a 'challenge from below' and a spontaneous coming together of different individuals and groups who see their common subordination to the social and economic power relations of capitalism. In both participatory development and EIP, however, participation has been sponsored by the powerful and, indeed, EIP is itself part of the much broader managerial project of HRM. While in the realm of employment, it is possible to identify the 'challenge from below' as coming from trade unions and the institutions of collective bargaining. This represents only a modicum of genuine countervailing power, and is quite distinct from the mechanisms of EIP discussed in this chapter. Furthermore, even this countervailing power has been subject to accommodation and incorporation.

Third, participation in both arenas is largely cosmetic (see Mosse, Chapter 2, this volume) and fulfils the role of a deflecting device in order to give a 'sense' of participation without its substance. Where there is some participation it is usually restricted to the determination of means to achieve a predetermined outcome (such as profit, efficiency, project outcome, disbursement of funds) rather than participation in determining the ends sought. As Mosse indicates, in the development arena participation can be used as a commodity or 'formula' by agencies which can be marketed as part of a corporate image to assist with reputation-building. This has some clear parallels with EIP, where the existence of participative management is used as a selling point by employing organizations to build a concept of 'employer brand' (Weston 1999).

Fourth, the explanation of the reasons why participation is not working, why it has been sponsored by the powerful, and why it is largely cosmetic is that for both arenas it is used as a 'hegemonic' device to secure compliance to, and control by, existing power structures. The control is more subtle than direct domination, taking the form of seeking the 'commitment' of those to be controlled and then allowing a degree of 'responsible autonomy' within limits. Whether we describe the deception as involving a 'discursive practice' or as a 'legitimatory ideology' is less important than its recognition and the proposal of possible alternatives.

Much of the literature of EIP and participatory development is presented as a universally 'good thing'. Its ideals may well be so, but in searching for opportunities to extend genuine participation perhaps it is necessary to be more focused, analytical and realistic about the specific contingencies that need to be put in place to bring it about. Such explanatory frameworks are becoming more prevalent in the EIP literature, where there are attempts to locate the levels and extent of participation by reference to two sets of contingencies. First, there are the characteristics of those who are to participate and include such factors as age, gender, job tenure, job role, education and social status. Second, there are the external environmental variables such as technological factors, market 'imperatives', cultural norms, government policies, and centralization/decentralization in the organization (Drago and Wooden 1991). Poole (1986) attempts to construct an explanatory framework for workers' participation and control which, I suggest, could be relevant for participatory development. This is reproduced in Figure 8.1.

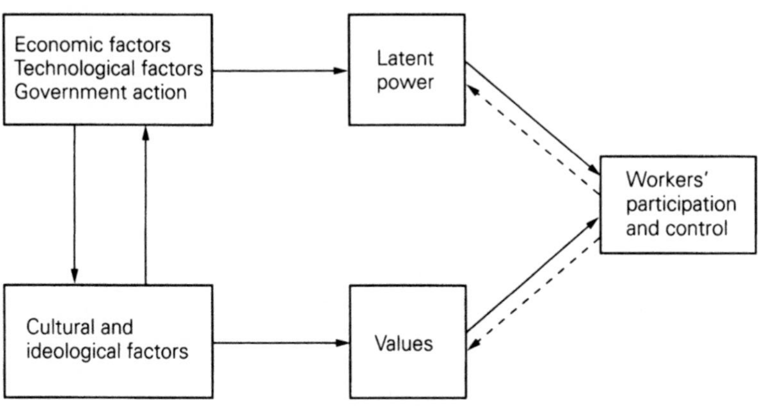

FIGURE 8.1 Framework for workers' participation and control
Source: Poole (1986: 29)

The advantage of the model presented in Figure 8.1 is that it combines elements of the material/structural dimension and the cultural-linguistic approach. Again, the model may or may not be applicable to the development arena, but the point is that we do need some models as a starting point. Cotton (1993) also reviews a wide range of models of EIP that may be of value. These frameworks may not be exhaustive and may not be directly relevant to the participatory development area, but the point is that similar analyses need to be carried out from a participatory development perspective to tease out some of the contingent forces that influence the extent and nature of participation. Having done this, attention needs to be directed to increasing elements of both the 'power to' and 'power over' of subordinate groups. Elements of the former include encouraging subordinate groups to 'represent themselves' (see Kothari, Chapter 9, this volume) and, to use an older concept, raise the consciousness of the deception of participatory development. These would comprise the main elements of a deconstruction/reframing approach. However, it is now necessary to address the material and structural realities of power relations. To say that this is not going to be easy is a gross understatement, but labour process theory, in its more recent offerings (see, for example, Jermier et al. 1994), attempts to describe in numerous situations of the seeming hegemony of employers, locations of resistance and sources of power in organizations for employees, which may offer some lessons for the powerless and marginalized in participatory development.

The urgency of the task of introducing genuine participation is underlined by the fact that alternative critiques of participation do not simply arise from critical/radical approaches. There is also a 'conservative' analysis, which claims that participation is overvalued, that generally experts and the state do know better, that managers of organizations and projects need freedom to act quickly to achieve results, and that people are more interested in short-term substantive livelihood improvement than participation (see for example Henkel and Stirrat, Chapter 11, this volume, for participatory development and Clarke 1999 for an analysis of 'unavoidable economic rationality' in management). If we are to counter such authoritarian, oppressive and interest-protecting approaches we need to identify realistically what opportunities exist for employees and project beneficiaries to gain an increased measure of countervailing power, and to gain participation not as a placatory gift from the powerful but as a genuine shift in the social and power structure of capitalist society.

9

Power, Knowledge and Social Control in Participatory Development

Uma Kothari

> Power is tolerable only if it masks a substantial part of itself. (Foucault 1979: 86)

Participation: A New Grand Narrative of Development

In recent years there has been widespread adoption in the development aid industry of participatory approaches to development in an espoused attempt to enable those individuals and groups previously excluded by more top-down planning processes, and who are often marginalized by their separation and isolation from the production of knowledge and the formulation of policies and practices, to be included in decisions that affect their lives. The arguments supporting participatory research are many, and include the notion that development policies and practices based on research with intended beneficiaries of development are more likely to meet the interests and needs of primary stakeholders, and that those development interventions based on local knowledge and experience are more likely to be relevant, 'home-grown' and therefore sustainable. Furthermore, and fundamentally, a central concern for many proponents of participatory development is that the methods of enquiry used should encourage a process of empowerment.

There have recently been numerous reviews and critiques of populist participatory approaches (Bastian and Bastian 1996; Mosse 1994; Nelson and Wright 1995; IIED 1995). These take two main forms: those that focus on the technical limitations of the approach, which stress the need for a re-examination of the methodological tools used such as in PRA, and those that pay closer attention to the theoretical and conceptual limitations of participation. In this chapter, I want to move between these critiques by examining the techniques of knowledge accumulation and processes of information exchange that take place during participatory research and planning in order to identify and highlight the forms of control and power articulated by participative approaches through the particular social interactions that take place. It is not my intention to homogenize all participatory development practitioners or their practices, but there are some identifiable tropes within the participatory discourse that suggest a regularity or consistency of approaches at least at some levels.

Since participatory research is a technique for knowing particular kinds of subjects, underlying the discussion in this chapter is an analysis of the techniques of power and the particular types of knowledge that the methodology creates and reproduces. This analysis, I argue, will challenge some of the truth claims made by participatory practitioners about the validity of the data collected and raise questions about the extent to which it represents 'true' local knowledge. What is significant here is that the participative technologies used are effective in producing what is considered as 'truth' or at least closer to the 'truth' than other less participative, top-down methods of enquiry and knowledge accumulation. These claims to acquiring 'truer' knowledge and, for some practitioners, to also empowering participants through their involvement in the process, have led to the overwhelming adoption of participatory techniques within development policy and practice. Within participatory discourse a number of binaries, or oppositions, are presented (see Chambers 1997), such as 'uppers' and 'lowers', North and South, professional knowledge and local knowledge, which are continuously evoked and rehearsed as popular slogans of participation and empowerment. These dichotomies set up oppositions invested with notions of the morally 'good' and the morally 'bad' (see Henkel and Stirrat, Chapter 11, this volume), and it then becomes the main aim of participatory approaches to development to set about reversing them, as reflected in the title of one of Chambers' books, *Rural Development: Putting the Last First* (1983). Participatory methodologies, then, require the formulation and adoption of a framework in which the micro is set against the macro, the margins against the centre, the local against the elite, and the powerless against the powerful. However, the almost exclusive focus on the micro-level, on people who are considered powerless and marginal, has reproduced the simplistic notion that the sites of social power and control are to be found solely at the macro- and central levels. These dichotomies further strengthen the assumption that people who wield power are located at institutional centres, while those who are subjugated and subjected to power are to be found at the local or regional level – hence the valorization of 'local knowledge' and the continued belief in the empowerment of 'local' people through participation. Foucault, however, argues that,

> Power must be analyzed as something which circulates, or rather as something which only functions in the form of a chain. It is never localized here or there ... Power is employed and exercised through a net-like organization. (Foucault 1980: 98)

Thus Foucault's analysis of power requires us to shift our concentration from the centre and national institutions such as the state not because this enables the powerless to speak and be heard, but because those macro-spheres of authority are not necessarily the only focal conductors of power. He stresses, instead, the need to explore further the local and micro-points of power because,

> Hegemonic or global forms of power rely in the first instance on those 'infinitesimal' practices, composed of their own particular techniques and tactics, which exist in those institutions on the fringes or at the micro-level of society. (ibid.: 99)

So power is everywhere, and can be particularly analysed through the creation of social norms or customs that are practised throughout society. This disrupts the dichotomies of macro/micro, central/local, powerful/powerless, where the former are sites and holders of power and the latter the subjects of power. Instead, all individuals are vehicles of power. An analysis of the ways in which power extends and transforms in different micro- or 'everyday' contexts can further our understanding of the more readily identifiable types of social control and domination traditionally seen to be located at the 'centre', be they at the level of the state or other global institutions or in the hands of local elites. Power is thus found in the creation of norms and social and cultural practices at all levels. Within much participatory development discourse, 'people's knowledge' or 'local knowledge' is seen as a fixed commodity that people intrinsically have and own. Instead, as is argued here, knowledge is culturally, socially and politically produced and is continuously reformulated as a powerful normative construct. Knowledge is thus an accumulation of social norms, rituals and practices that, far from being constructed in isolation from power relations, is embedded in them (or against them). However, the creation of dichotomies of power within participatory discourse (the haves and the have-nots) allows the revealing of power not as a social and political discourse or as embodied practice, but only as manifest in material realities. Thus participatory approaches can unearth who gets what, when and where, but not necessarily the processes by which this happens or the ways in which the knowledge produced through participatory techniques is a normalized one that reflects and articulates wider power relations in society.

This chapter focuses on participatory techniques as methods of knowledge accumulation and attempts to unravel the sorts of power that are reproduced at the micro-level through the use of these approaches, and how participants and participatory development practitioners are themselves conduits of power. The arguments presented here are that participatory development can encourage a reassertion of control and power by dominant individuals and groups, that it can lead to the reification of social norms through self-surveillance and consensus-building, and that it 'purifies' knowledge and the spaces of participation through the codification, classification and control of information, and its analysis and (re)presentation. The chapter also explores the limitations of participation in terms of how it demands certain kinds of performances to be enacted. It is suggested here that individuals and groups can and do subvert the methodology and, in doing so, gain control by shaping the form of their participation through their 'performances' on the PRA stage and in their selection of the information they conceal or choose to disclose. Thus they become social agents and actors by subverting the power of development and disrupting participatory discourses. This subversion does not always require their inclusion in processes of participation as advocated through such methodologies as PRA; indeed, they are often found through acts of self-exclusion and non-participation.

Reassertion of Power and Social Control

Participatory approaches to development research and planning attempt to challenge the apparent power relations in society by recognizing the control that certain individuals and groups have over others. This is based on the recognition that those who wield little power have limited opportunities to express their interests and needs and are generally excluded from key decision-making processes, and that their knowledge is considered insignificant. However, despite the aims of participatory approaches and the claims made by participatory practitioners, particularly with respect to empowering the disempowered, it is argued here that participative methods of enquiry simplify the nature of power and are thus in danger of encouraging a reassertion of power and social control not only by certain individuals and groups, but also of particular bodies of knowledge.

The very act of inclusion, of being drawn in as a participant, can symbolize an exercise of power and control over an individual. As Geof Wood suggests (1999), there are forms of 'adverse incorporation' where the act or process of inclusion is not always to the benefit of those groups who have previously been excluded. Cohen (1985) similarly refers to insidious modes of inclusionary control. He suggests that programmes designed to bring the excluded in often result in forms of control that are more difficult to challenge, as they reduce spaces of conflict and are relatively benign and liberal. That is, those people who have the greatest reason to challenge and confront power relations and structures are brought, or even bought, through the promise of development assistance, into the development process in ways that disempower them to challenge the prevailing hierarchies and inequalities in society, hence inclusionary control and the inducement of conformity.

Participatory approaches to development are about the identification, collection, interpretation, analysis and (re)presentation of particular forms of (local) knowledge. However, it is now widely acknowledged that the production and representation of knowledge is inseparable from the exercise of power. Thus, as Mosse writes, '[P]ublic participatory research methods are unlikely to prove good instruments for the analysis of local power relations since they are shaped by the very relations which are being investigated' (1995: 29).

Power is not only manifest in the workings of the development practitioner but also more widely played out by other cultural intermediaries, such as translators. Thus there are many articulations of power through participatory processes and in the wider context within which knowledge is (re)produced. Development practitioners as interpreters of the social world further exercise economic control through the disbursement of aid and resources, which are allocated on the basis of external donor agendas and their policies, and not necessarily founded on the information gathered through PRA exercises (see Mosse, Chapter 2, this volume).

Foucault's analysis of power is useful in understanding the everyday nature of social control. He was concerned with examining how power relations of inequality are created and maintained in more subtle and diffuse ways through ostensibly humane and freely adopted social practices (Foucault 1977). So although participatory approaches to development attempt to reveal subjugated knowledges, those that have been hitherto disqualified as insufficient or insignificant, there remain in the practice of participation forms of control and dominance that are not simply articulated in the direct and immediate relationship between participant and observer but also historically constructed through all sorts of social practices and rituals. So,

> To understand power, therefore, it is necessary to analyze it in its most diverse and specific manifestations rather than focusing on its most central-

> ized forms such as its concentration in the hands of a coercive elite or a ruling class. This focus on the underside of everyday aspect of power relations Foucault calls a *microphysics* rather than a *macrophysics* of power. (McNay 1994: 3)

Foucault's thesis in *Discipline and Punish* (1977) is that the discipline of a highly controlled institution like a prison or a nineteenth-century asylum 'represents a continuation and intensification of what goes on in more ordinary places' (Sibley 1995: 82), and that the controls that are embedded in ordinary life legitimate the kind of regime practised in, for example, a prison. Foucault uses Bentham's panopticon, which was a model for a totally controlled institution, designed on the principles of discipline, surveillance and hierarchical classification, as a metaphor for control, arguing that social life becomes colonized as control, discipline and carceral forms of punishment are diffused through society (Foucault 1977).

Foucault characterizes ways in which power is wielded and, more significantly, how it masks itself; in so doing, he demonstrates how social control is not restricted to particular sites and locations, policies and practices but also colonizes the individual's body. That is, an individual's behaviour, actions and perceptions are all shaped by the power embedded and embodied within society.

This understanding of power elucidates more about its everyday nature as expressed in people's daily lives than a focus on institutions and structures of power alone can reveal. In PRA exercises individuals and groups are often selected for participation because of their disadvantaged position *vis-à-vis*, for example, their access to resources and services, or their control over decision-making. This is undeniably significant in revealing local power structures, but this identification of groups based on their structural or material inequalities may detract from considering the everyday power in people's lives, which may not be structured (solely) in these ways. While all individuals are most certainly affected by macro-structures of inequality (such as gender, ethnicity, class), if participatory approaches to development are to be bottom-up and uncover the daily oppression in people's lives, and reveal their interests and needs, they need to go beyond these conventional stratifications of power. This confirms Foucault's argument that even when individuals think that they are most free, they are in fact in the grip of more insidious forms of power, which operate not solely through direct forms of repression but often through less visible strategies of normalization (Foucault 1977, 1980).

Power is thus difficult to locate as it runs through notions and practices, can be enacted by individuals who may even be opposed to it, and is localized through its expression in everyday practices – through, for example, self-surveillance. Thus, 'the government of the self allies itself with practices for the government of others' (Foucault, cited in Rabinow 1984: 19). However, in PRA, the traffic of surveillance travels one way: towards the subject upon whom the technique is exercised. Moreover, the subject of the surveillance does not have the reciprocal power to 'observe' and comment upon the role and actions of the observer.

Building Consensus and the Reification of Social Norms

This section focuses on the more insidious modes of social control, which are not revealed through the use of participatory approaches in the collection of 'local knowledge', and challenges claims of empowering 'local' people. These forms of control demonstrate a link between power relations and the production of the 'truths' by which we live. Individuals adopt discursive and embodied articulations of power that become readily accepted as cultural norms. In this way, power and inequalities become normative and thus often remain unchallenged. By not recognizing that knowledge is produced out of power relations in society and through practitioners' acceptance of 'local knowledge' as some kind of objective truth, participatory methodologies are in danger of reifying these inequalities and of affirming the agenda of elites and other more powerful actors. If, as Foucault argues, individuals subject themselves to self-surveillance as they absorb wider notions of social control, then the purpose of participatory research should be to uncover these more normalized articulations of power. In this way, power inequalities in society and the needs and interests of the poor and marginalized can be revealed.

During PRA, what participants say and do is often accepted as individual experience, preference or choice, and less frequently seen as an articulation of wider cultural and social norms. These norms have, however, been constructed out of processes of domination and sometimes contestation, and thus are also reflections of social control in society. Participatory practitioners may interpret the actions and expressions of participants as 'local culture' when they are also the product of these processes of normalization, but are not seen to embody power relations since they appear to be articulated and believed in by all. People absorb these cultural tropes, which are then recursively practised almost ritualistically, and it is the widespread acceptance of, and conformity to, these practices that make it difficult to interpret them as expressions of power or demonstrations of inequalities. Thus, since people are constituted and represent themselves through discourses of power, the process of normalization of this or that cultural practice is an expression of power. There is a distinction, then, between social controls that are external in origin and transmitted hierarchically, and those that are internalized, in that members of a group make a commitment to norms and values producing, perhaps, a conformist community (see Davis and Anderson 1983).

Through participatory practices conventions develop and acquire the status of 'common sense' and become normative simply by being performed repeatedly. Mosse (1995) identifies a problem with participatory approaches which relates to consensus-building. A fundamental concern for Mosse in the interpretation of PRA is that:

> as public and collective events, PRAs tend to emphasize the general over the particular (individual, event, situation, etc.), tend towards the normative ('what ought to be' rather than 'what is'), and towards a unitary view of interests which underpays difference. In other words, it is the community's 'official view' of itself which is projected … [O]ften the very structure of the PRA sessions – group activities leading to plenary presentations – assumes and encourages the expression of consensus. (Mosse 1994: 510)

Hence the paradox that the more 'participatory' the enquiry the more its outcome will mask the power structure of the community (Woodhouse 1998: 144). Some of these issues have been raised by critics of participatory development; however, there is a need for a deeper understanding of the processes by which knowledge is jointly created and negotiated through the production of social norms and various types of social encounter, and for greater recognitions of the power dynamics involved.

The Purification of Knowledge and Space

Sibley, referring to the degree to which ideas become part of the wider currency of knowledge, argues that the success or failure of ideas is affected by the contexts in which they are produced (Sibley 1995: 118). Sibley's comments have resonance for development practitioners and the ways in which we acquire, interpret and represent knowledge. If the exercise of power has a role in promoting or suppressing knowledge, how is this power expressed? Sibley suggests that it takes place through a process of ranking knowledge. The question here is: What kinds of knowledge are deemed important? As Sibley (ibid.: 127) puts it, '[t]he desire to maintain monopolies over areas of knowledge encourages ritual practices designed to protect the sacred status of established approaches to understanding'.

Thus, although one of the aims of participatory research is to uncover the voices of the marginalized and excluded, this can present problems when the knowledge produced challenges knowledge conventions (see Mohan, Chapter 10, this volume; Mohanty et al. 1991; Smith 1999; Spivak 1990). Sibley argues this point when he writes: 'when dissenting, radical ideas are produced by members of social groups who are themselves marginalised and excluded from centres of power, the threat to the establishment may be more tangible than when it comes from within' (Sibley 1995: 133).

Furthermore, there is a purification of space by the exclusion or rejection of certain people and certain forms of knowledge (see de Certeau 1985). The methodological tools and techniques of participatory development, such as seasonal calendars and wealth ranking, similarly require a purification or cleaning up of knowledge and experience: a tidying up of people's lives through the exclusion of anything that is messy or does not fit the structured representations implied by participatory tools. The use of participatory techniques often requires the taking out of anything complicated, making people's lives and their social interactions linear and sterile as they fit into charts, diagrams and tables and conform to the boundaries and limitations of the methodological tools. There is also a process of controlling to produce the norm, the usual and the expected.

Participatory techniques do not easily accommodate chance happenings, or unplanned and irregular occurrences. In fact the methodology requires a normative view of people's lives to be presented. Decisions taken on the basis of a rapid participatory analysis reinforce a normative discourse that reflects a group consensus on what is usual and ordinary, while the complexities and 'messiness' of most people's everyday lives is filtered out. For example, an event such as a wedding may be rare for an individual household (although a common enough occurrence in society generally) and may not be presented in any significant way in a PRA exercise where the normal and the routine is noted. However, much of the previous lives of those involved in the wedding may in a variety of ways have been shaped and informed by this future event, such as working in order to save for the ceremony, or the choice of education for boys and girls, which may be largely influenced by their future (marital) role in society. So the event itself is occasional and infrequent, but much of the longer-term and daily activities of individuals may be shaped by it in a way that goes beyond the event itself. The PRA snapshot is unable to capture these processes.

This requires us to explore further how practitioners interpret and shape an account of what is presented during a participatory exercise. What information or knowledge is considered irrelevant and thus omitted from analysis or ignored, and how is it classified and codified through participatory analysis? For example, are ambiguities and unexpected occurrences too messy to include, and are narratives framed according to discursive conventions?

At the same time there is an implicit notion of deviancy for those who choose not to participate. This chimes with Nelson and Wright's (1995) observation that there is no positive opposite or counter to participation – it is implicitly good, constructive and productive. Processes of participatory research can purify social interactions and social space by framing and ordering people's messy and varied experiences, needs and interests, but a further characteristic of this purification process is that difference will register as deviance (Sibley 1995: 78). Classification and boundary maintenance are characteristic of participatory development and thus the potential for difference to be deviant and the subsequent exclusion of deviant individuals and groups. A paradox in participatory research is that while the flexibility of the tools and techniques is stressed, there is simultaneously a desire to fix people's lives through processes of identification and framing of social interaction and activities, revealing the rigidity of the methodology.

Participation as Performance and the Possibilities of Subversion

The focus in the above sections has been on discursive power, and the ways in which this shapes the narratives of participants. The following section explores how the metaphor of performance can be used to understand the limits of participatory research, and also the ways in which power can be seen as enabling within the participatory process as participants can and do subvert participatory methodology.

The metaphor of performance is used here to understand the ways in which participants act out their roles on the PRA stage where the practitioners or facilitators act as stage managers or directors who guide, and attempt to delimit, their performance, and the implications this has for the types of knowledge accumulated.

In this context, Goffman's ideas about the presentation of the self in everyday life can be usefully employed to understand people's behaviour and social interactions in public places. Goffman (1997) writes about the ways in which we present ourselves in everyday life, conjuring up metaphors of performance, and distinguishing between what he calls the 'front-stage' and the 'back-stage'. The 'front-stage' is where performances are enacted in order for people to create impressions in public life. The 'back-stage', on the other hand, is where unrehearsed performances take place, those that are not intended for public consumption. Back-stage performances constitute the dramas of everyday life and represent the work that goes into the making of a front-stage performance. The back-stage is ostensibly the arena of private performance, a rehearsal for the production on the front-stage, but as Goffman suggests there are also audiences who will not allow performers to be sincere by avoiding seeing or experiencing 'back-stage' realities, even when presented with such an occasion. Here we find support for Mosse's argument that PRA and the like are often carried out to give the appearance of participatory development but that the 'local knowledge' shared in the process invariably justifies or legitimizes the pre-determined project agenda rather than reshaping or influencing the project objectives or priorities.

The development practitioner initiating a PRA is asking participants to adopt and play a role using certain techniques and tools, thus shaping and, in some instances, confining the way in which performers may have chosen to represent themselves. The stage and the props for the performance may be alien to the performer. The tools provided can limit the performance so that the performers are unable to convey what they want to; the stage has been set by others and the form of the performance similarly guided by them. The resulting communication or dialogue are then fraught with confusion and ambiguity.

PRA requires a particular type of performance to be played out on a specified stage using methodological props, thus producing a contrived performance. A quote from a group of participatory practitioners writing about the need for props for research demonstrates the ways in which this manipulated or contrived performance is produced:

> The rural population ... often have difficulty in understanding questionnaire surveys. We have found that props can make it easier for them to understand the meaning of questions. We define props as tools that enable local people to visualize the theme of questions and debates. They should be made out of materials which are commonly used and locally meaningful. (Bourai et al. 1997: 91)

The above quote demonstrates well that while the props are seen as enabling knowledge-sharing and are locally relevant, they are clearly of much more benefit to the practitioner or knowledge-gatherer than to the participants. This reminds us that PRA is always a performance sponsored by the observer/practitioner.

In order to make visible to the audience what would otherwise have been invisible and would have required observation over a much longer period of time the participatory practitioner asks the participants to dramatize their lives (see IIED 1995: 28). The dramatization of a seasonal agricultural cycle, for example, can be played out 'front-stage' with the use of signs and symbols representing fields, crops, seasons and seasonal activities in a matter of hours. However, this can often demand that more time and energy be expended by the participant as it requires a clear, visual presentation of what in reality is often a more variable and less easily compartmentalized process. Participants must therefore have the ability to learn roles and be convincing in order to be 'good' participants, and the question here is: What happens to the narratives of those who do not possess the right skills, or more appropriately, the talent, to perform as required?

The more worrying aspect is that the performance comes to be accepted as reality. The performance by an individual, in front of others from the same social group, often requires incorporating and exemplifying the officially accredited values of the society, and presenting socially accepted norms. Thus, to stay away from the place where the performance is taking place, i.e. to choose not to participate, Goffman argues, is to stay away from where reality is being performed (see Lemert and Branaman 1997). He goes on to say that a bureaucratization of the spirit is expected so that people can be relied upon to give a perfectly homogeneous performance at every appointed time, although, of course, this is rarely achievable. In this way the socialization process not only transfigures but it fixes reality (see Giddens 1984). Furthermore, a form of social discipline is instituted and the performer re-presents the social norms of the group that they are representing before them. There is minimal scope for other realities to be shaped. The performer can also be misrepresented and misunderstood and must take care that the observer does not impute unintended meanings. The intentions of the performer and the reading of the performance may be different with unintended effects, particularly in the way the audience then analyses what is presented. We need also ask whether the performer is authorized to give such as a performance, how this is decided and by whom.

In the rituals of participatory research, participants are not always or necessarily recipients/victims of methodology but can also have enough power to carve out spaces of control with respect to the (re)presentation of their day-to-day lives (Foucault 1980; Giddens 1982). Giddens' work on the reciprocity of social interactions and spatial structures is concerned with both fluid and concrete social relationships. He suggests that human activities are recursive, in that they are continually being re-created by social actors 'by the very means whereby they express themselves as actors' (Giddens 1984). However, social actors are also reflexive in the ways in which they reproduce social life.

So although ritual practices can be interpreted as expressions of power relations, since they are often concerned with domination, and while control by dominating agents may seem complete, there is always the possibility of subversion (Sibley 1995: 76). Thus, although power can constrain people, it can also constitute the condition or potential for their freedom (McNay 1994: 4), and individuals as active agents have the capacity to fashion their own existence autonomously.

There is a general failing among development practitioners to recognize or acknowledge the capacity of individuals and groups to resist inclusion, resist projections about their lives, retain information, knowledge and values, and act out a performance and in so doing present themselves in a variety of ways.

Subversive participants can also choose to opt out of the participatory process completely, although they are often characterized as uncooperative or even as social deviants. Cohen maintains that:

> when ... boundary blurring, integration and community control take place, the result is that people get involved in the 'control problem' ... In order to include rather than exclude, a set of judgements has to be made which 'normalize' intervention in a greater range of human life. (Cohen 1985: 230–1)

In this sense, then, exclusion can be empowering and even necessary in order to challenge existing structures of domination and control (see also Wood 1999).

But participants can also subvert expectations of themselves by choosing how to perform and present their lives through PRA exercises. If, as Goffman suggests, all actions are a performance and 'all the world is staged', then there is a possibility of resistance or subversion through people's performances in participatory exercises. Just as the PRA 'expert' is performing, so too are the participants or recipients of development aid. Through their performance they can invert power relations in small and big ways.

Conclusion

In this chapter I have stressed the importance of examining how power relations run through a particular social body and are not confined to particular central sites or located solely among the elite. Instead, through processes of normalization of social and cultural rules and codes, power circulates and can be expressed in a variety of ways. By constructing dichotomies of power and oppositional social groupings, participatory approaches simplify highly complicated social relations. Thus participatory techniques can conceal inequalities and in certain circumstances reify them. What counts as 'local knowledge' is very often the effect of specific kinds of techniques of power, of regulation and of normalization. As has been shown in this chapter, those drawn in under the gaze of participatory development practitioners can and do represent powerful cultural norms.

Donor-backed participatory practitioners are also not without power; they are able to regulate or at least delimit the ways in which people choose to represent their lives and in so doing shape the type of knowledge accumulated and influence the extent to which participants can become empowered in the process. Debates around the identity and positionality of the researcher (see Long 1992) are increasingly familiar within, for example, anthropology, human geography and sociology. Some researchers within the social sciences have become more self-critical in recognizing and analysing how and to what extent their privileged positions *vis-à-vis* the subjects of their research will influence their research experience and shape their research findings. These debates are important; however, there seems to be little discussion within them on the perceptions of those being asked to participate, i.e. the subjects of research, and the experiences of being researched (see Smith 1999). While this chapter does not directly address this issue, it suggests that an understanding of theories of power, social control and performance borrowed from disciplinary traditions, often marginal in debates within development studies, may offer some insights into the ways in which power, embedded in knowledge and the forms of its accumulation, affects the processes and findings of participatory research and planning.

This chapter has raised some concerns about participatory methodologies, particularly the claims made of acquiring more appropriate and relevant local knowledge, of including those previously marginalized in decision-making processes, and of their subsequent empowerment. At the same time, within the methodology there is the potential for reflexivity and subversion and, as Goffman writes, there always remains the possibility that the performer may delude the audience. It is also in this way, perhaps, that participants can become empowered.

10

Beyond Participation: Strategies for Deeper Empowerment

Giles Mohan

> community action programmes and non-governmental sponsored projects ... are surely projects that lead to greater autonomy and independence, factors vital for decolonisation. That these forms have existed separately from the enunciation of postcolonialism should not be forgotten. (Goss 1996: 248)

Introduction

This chapter has two major aims. The first is to critique existing participatory practices, especially the ways in which local knowledge is generated as a necessary first step in reversing the 'top-down' approaches of many development initiatives. This critique is realized largely through the use of concepts derived from postcolonial studies. In order to do this effectively, the following section outlines some of the major themes within postcolonial studies, as it is a relatively recent and poorly defined area of the social sciences. These critical insights are then used to examine the ways in which participatory research methods tend to reinscribe relations of authority between the outside facilitator and the grassroots. The second aim is to rework approaches to participatory development in light of the preceding criticisms. This is done through both theoretical considerations and a case study of a small NGO working in West Africa. While I do not want to portray the NGO as having overcome all barriers to participation, it is instructive in demonstrating how a reflexive, 'outside' organization can deal with problematic power relationships at the local level.

Postcolonialism and Local Knowledge

In this section I review the field of postcolonial studies and draw two major themes, which have a bearing on the practices of participatory development. Recently, scholars and practitioners have challenged 'externally' imposed knowledge and policies and sought ways to create collaborative forms of knowledge that underpin more appropriate and sustainable social development (Nelson and Wright 1995; Escobar 1995). For postcolonial scholars this involves revealing the ways in which colonialism has impacted upon knowledge and subjectivity (Ashcroft et al. 1995). As Watts notes: 'The post-colonialism literature has unleashed a ferocious debate which speaks directly to the writing of development history and the practice of development' (Watts 1995: 54; see also Kothari 1996; Power 1998). However, as Goss asserts, the postcolonial critique has become heavily textual, involving 'the study of study' or 'armchair decolonisation' (1996: 248). Despite this well-founded criticism, this section discusses areas within postcolonial studies that might 'speak directly to' the practice of participatory development.

The postcolonial critique has grown in prominence over the 1990s, but its colonization of increasing areas of social theory threatens to render it meaningless, as almost anything can be considered 'postcolonial' (Ahmad 1995, 1997; Dirlik 1994). Dirlik (1994) argues that 'postcolonial' has replaced 'Third World' in the political imagination, while other scholars (Tiffin and Lawson 1994) examine countries, such as Australia, that have historical connections with Europe and a legacy of subjugating indigenous peoples. Similarly, in terms of periodization, postcolonial studies cover broad historical epochs ranging from colonial contact onwards. These conceptual uncertainties undermine the focus of postcolonial studies as a coherent critique.

Originating in literary studies, the postcolonial critique has become a fashionable label, but one that is increasingly formless. Postcolonialism can usefully be seen as referring to a condition and/or a critique, in the sense that ontologically a given community can be considered postcolonial while postcolonial criticism attacks epistemologies that have privileged Western ways of knowing (Ahmad 1995; Dirlik 1994). Despite Ahmad's (1995: 9) warning of a self-aggrandizing circularity whereby 'we have a globalized *condition* of *postcoloniality* that can be *described* by the "postcolonial critic"' (emphasis in original), there are, I feel, two areas where postcolonialism elucidates the practices of development.

Eurocentrism and the politics of representation The first emerges from attacks on Western discourses that 'place' the non-West and thereby determine who has authority over knowledge. Clearly, Edward Said's (1979) Orientalist analysis has been the most influential (Ahmad 1994). Said argues that the West has constructed the Orient as 'other' and fashioned exclusive authority over its representation. This means that the Orient has been seen only through Western eyes, which enables other processes of domination to proceed. Similar critiques have followed that challenge Eurocentric thought (Shohat and Stam 1994) while Jonathan Crush's (1995) collection examines the power of Western discourses in shaping development interventions in the Third World (see also Escobar 1995).

While making 'us', the Western critics, sorely aware of our complicity within colonizing discourses, Said's work has been attacked for the ways in which it effectively silences the voices of the other. First, Said homogenizes and essentializes both the West and non-West and treats them as undifferentiated and unchanging (Young 1990). Analytically, he makes no 'qualitative distinctions between a variety of texts produced under a variety of historical conjunctures for a wide variety of audiences' (Porter 1994: 153). This flattening of history and geography does away with the possibility of contested discourses and, thus, any notion of political agency. Second, there is an epistemological problem in that Said claims Orientalism is mythical and creates its own truth so that nothing we know can exist outside of it. At other times he dismisses Orientalism as representations and not 'the truth', which implies that a reality exists independently of this hegemonic discourse (Porter 1994), yet he offers no clue as to how one might access it. These two tendencies, despite an apparently radical anti-imperialism, leave Said unable to suggest any alternatives to Orientalist thought. The result is that 'virtually no counter-hegemonic voices are heard' (ibid.: 152–3), which has important implications for researchers seeking to recover the subject from Eurocentric accounts of the non-West.

Recovering political agency A second strand of postcolonial criticism focuses precisely on this question. Various postcolonial scholars (Bhabha 1983, 1984; Spivak 1987, 1988) challenge the premise that colonialism was hegemonic, implying a unity of purpose and totalizing effects. Following Fanon, Lacan and Gramsci these scholars have explored questions of identity (Gates 1991) and counter-hegemony that destabilize the fixity of the colonizer–colonized dualism. Homi Bhabha (1983: 200) argues that Orientalism suggests that 'power and discourse is possessed entirely by the colonizer'. Contrary to those who see the colonial moment as one in which two, distinct cultures meet and one is subjugated by the more powerful, Bhabha examines questions of 'hybridity', which is 'the sign of the productivity of colonial power, its shifting forces and fixities; it is the name for the strategic reversal of the process of domination through disavowal'

(Bhabha 1995: 34). One such 'productive' process is that of mimicry, where the colonial subject takes on certain elements of the colonizer's culture so that s/he resembles the colonizer, but is at the same time different. Bhabha sees this as a subversive form of resistance because 'mimicry is at once resemblance and menace' (Bhabha 1983: 127; Obeyesekere 1992). Thus Bhabha challenges the depoliticizing effects of essentialist historiography and posits hybridity as a space of radical possibilities (Mitchell 1997), although Ahmad (1997) criticizes this for ignoring the overt challenges to colonial power such as anti-colonial struggles.

Other scholars have emphasized hybridity as a condition of post-colonialism (Mudimbe 1988; Gilroy 1993), but Ahmad (1995) argues that hybridization as a cultural process is common where any different people meet, so it cannot be seen as a defining feature of postcolonialism. Importantly, the focus on the subject as hybrid tends to obliterate any structural determinations (Mitchell 1997). There is a tension between an ultimately situated *localized* experience and a *global* condition. One explanation for this is that the postcolonial critics are really the only people to whom these peculiar conditions apply; scholars shaped by hybridized education systems in former colonies who now inhabit the rarefied world of the Ivy League (Dirlik 1994: 339; Ahmad 1997: 366). More important still is that in examining the cultural construction of global hybrids they tend to ignore the structural and material constraints of globalized capitalism. Politically this can be limiting since 'the term "postcolonial" in the Western academy ... serves to keep at bay more sharply political terms such as "imperialism", or "geopolitics"' (Loomba 1998: xiv). Katharyne Mitchell (1997) offers a way out, which argues for the material and cultural to be analysed in tandem rather than abstracting the cultural as a metaphorical space outside of material conditions.

A Marxian attempt to recover the voice of the marginalized has come through the work inspired by the Subaltern Studies (SS) Group. This is important for grassroots development, because it seeks to move the focus away from elite perspectives to those of the marginalized. It also opens up the question that if we can 'hear' these non-elite voices, will new social forms unfold? SS emerged from a group of Gramscian historians (Guha, Chatterjee, Chakrabarty, Prakash) who were disenchanted with the existing histories of India. Ranajit Guha describes these as elitist because the agents of history are presented as the colonial and postcolonial elites. Both colonial and postcolonial versions of history ignore 'the contribution made by the people on their own, that is, independently of the elite to the making and development of this nationalism [who are] the subaltern classes and groups constituting the mass of the labouring population and the intermediate strata in town and country' (Guha 1982: 4). The key for Guha is that this was 'autonomous' from the elite politics described in the earlier histories so that his analysis recovers the voice of the subaltern. Subaltern politics is based around resistance and horizontal community linkages rather than vertical linkages into elitist state structures.

One obvious criticism is that these analytical categories are still generalized; the 'subalterns' are the residue of the 'non-elite' and there is little differentiation within this massive category. A second criticism concerns the whole question of political organization being 'autonomous' from any elite influence, which presents a highly dichotomized view of political processes (Young 1990). SS does raise important questions about intellectuals and politics centred upon the question of *representation*. Representation can mean 'speaking of' – constructing accounts and writing texts – or it can mean 'speaking for' – advocating and mediating. The SS scholars combine the two, believing that by speaking of the subaltern experience they would change the political relations in their favour.

It is here that Spivak's (1988) famous intervention is aimed in a piece entitled 'Can the subaltern speak?' She argued that SS is blind to gender differences and that women's voices are suppressed by class, ethnicity and patriarchy. The 'Third World Woman' becomes a signifier who is unable to represent herself and is 'assigned no position of enunciation' (Young 1990: 164). Any discussion of subaltern consciousness is always intermediated by scholars who can never know the subaltern, and hence the latter cannot speak. By this logic the only true subaltern is the one who cannot speak, so attempting to recover their voice is pointless, a logic that Peet and Watts (1996: 15) describe as 'indefensible'. In deconstructive style Spivak seeks to destabilize textual representations, but does not 'confront these with another knowledge' (Parry 1987: 43). As Gates (1991: 464) adds: 'Considering the subaltern voice to be irretrievable, they devalue the actual counternarratives of anticolonialist struggles as mere reverse discourse.' He suggests that we distinguish more sharply between cultural *resistance* and the more generalized forms of cultural *alterity* or hybridity identified by Bhabha and Spivak.

Postcolonial studies alerts us to the epistemic violence of Eurocentric discourses of the non-West and the possibilities of recovering the voices of the marginalized. Yet much of this abstracts cultural processes away from material conditions and is unable to stand outside (or suggest alternatives to) the dominant epistemological frameworks against which they argue. In this sense many analyses run the risk of reinscribing authority over the non-West rather than subverting it. As mentioned earlier, similar processes of challenging Western constructions of the Third World are central to participatory development. The latter has become prevalent in development practice (Chambers 1997) and centres upon the valorization of local, non-Western knowledge. This has important implications for practitioners since it rejects the assumption that 'expert' professionals know best, and makes epistemological questions central to the process of change and not separated from concrete 'policy' actions. In the next section I demonstrate that even when a conscious effort is made to access local knowledge the reverse is often the case.

The Pitfalls of Participatory Research

In this section I use some of the insights of postcolonialism to interrogate participatory research. Participatory research is centred upon the reflexive awareness that power and knowledge are inextricably bound up (Chambers 1997), and it is PRA that has come to dominate this field (Chambers 1994a, b, c; Mohan 1999). While we should welcome approaches that seek to alter power relationships in favour of the marginalized, this section looks at participatory research as a set of practices that reinscribes power relations between expert and other. Here I disagree with Goss' (1996) argument quoted at the start of this chapter that NGO activity is likely to produce a decolonization of knowledge and action.

Western 'primitivism' and the (re)authorizing of knowledge Participatory research involves the valorization of local knowledges and seeks to empower grassroots communities. As such it raises serious questions about the relationships between expert and non-expert, how we define 'decision-makers', and the ways in which the world is represented to different groups. This sub-section examines how a subtle Eurocentrism infects and shapes the interventions of non-local development workers despite claims to the contrary.

Our current fascination with the local, community and uniqueness reflects both older traits and newer concerns of Western society in the way it confronts the non-West. Campbell (1997) argues that in participatory research one is viewing the other as 'unknowable', that their 'rationality' is different and difficult to understand. In talking of Africa, Chabal (1996: 41) makes a similar point when he writes that it embodies:

> the mysterious and the exotic. Mysterious not just in the sense that we do

> not understand its reality well but also in that its reality is not really amenable to our understanding. Exotic in that it fulfils in us the most enduring need to find in some (suitably distant) 'other' that quality of inexplicability which is both frightening in its apparent irrationality and reassuring in that it highlights our own rationality.

From the point of view of research this 'predication of mystery allows the obliteration of dialogue' (Kanneh 1999: 5) as complex societies are reduced to 'discrete entities, entirely separable from each other in space' (ibid.: 7). In this sense the ontological pitfalls of Said's dualism between Occident and Orient are repeated.

Additionally, it reflects the belief that their knowledge is more 'organic'. However, what might appear to be less energy-intensive technology may be not born out of an innate wisdom resulting from their relationship to nature, but a result of necessity. As Campbell notes (1997: 50–1) 'interpreting African dire necessity as a product of "indigenous knowledge" rather than a product of grinding poverty, the concept of indigenism can then be served up to gullible Westerners as a "sustainable" system that they should be proud to live by'. Again we see a privileging of the cultural realm over the material and its appropriation by Westerners. As Dirlik (1994: 346) observes: 'By throwing the cover of culture over material relationships, as if one had little to do with the other, such a focus diverts criticism of capitalism to the criticism of Eurocentric ideology [and] provides an alibi for inequality, expolitation, and oppression in their modern guises'.

Both Campbell and Chabal argue that this appropriation is not innocent, but stems from 'our' growing doubts about the modernist project. In Africa 'we' see the antithesis of rationality, yet one that is at the same time recognizable and, in this sense, threatens our own sense of identity and progress. Kaplan's (1994) infamous 'The Coming Anarchy' is the most bald statement of this paranoia. While Campbell perhaps stretches the point, there is an assumption, which I will return to throughout this section, that in participatory research there are distinct realms of knowledge that exist prior to the research process. One is Western, rational and familiar, the other is local, multiple and strange.

The practical effects of this 'primitivist' discourse concern the way in which PRA techniques are biased towards seeing 'communities' as consensual and harmonious, the paternalistic way in which PRA treats the 'participants', and issues of cognition and interpretation. First, the primitivist notion of the local as harmonious community is reflected in the way in which PRA tends to promote a consensual view (Goebel 1998). In Chambers' work, as Brown (1994) points out, there is a tendency to romanticize and essentialize the poor and the social systems by which they operate. The 'poor' are set against an unspecified 'elite' whose only defining feature is their 'non-poorness', with the former group operating through affective ties of, for example, kinship and ethnic group and the latter utilizing the 'modern' methods of state channels. Such binary ontologies repeat the arguments about subaltern politics being 'autonomous' while undermining the stated intentions of PRA of seeking diversity. We saw above that the early work of the Subaltern Studies Group tended to do the same by labelling 'subalterns' as all those people who were 'non-elite', which concealed the important differences within the marginalized along lines of class, gender and ethnicity. Such discourses smooth and homogenize.

As Nelson and Wright (1995: 15) observe '[c]ommunity is a concept often used by state and other organizations, rather than the people themselves, and it carries connotations of consensus and "needs" determined within parameters set by outsiders'. PRA has tended naively towards this consensual view, which conceals powerful interests at the intra-community level (Byrne 1995). The danger from a policy point of view is that the actions based on consensus may in fact further empower the powerful vested interests that manipulated the research in the first place. Pottier and Orone (1995) describe how in one case the chief purposefully failed to invite the very poor, so that, as Richards (1995: 15) notes, 'decisions made generally favour village élites'. Recently, such criticisms have been addressed with conscious efforts made to disclose difference and hetereogeneity. For example, Norton (1998) and Milimo et al. (1998) demonstrated that gendered differences exist over the importance of water availability to poverty in Zambia, while Goebel (1998) successfully analysed gender differences over resource management in Zimbabwe.

Second, as Chambers (1994b: 1255) notes: 'Local people and outsiders alike are encouraged to improvise in a spirit of play' while the experience reverses 'frustration to fun' (1997: 154). It should be noted that the emphasis on playfulness can be seen as a reaction to the stresses of contemporary capitalism whereby 'a whole generation of consumers has toddled into early middle age with the infantile desire to be surrounded by ... things that remind them of their childhood' (Bracewell 1998: 26). Hence, we should be wary of such universal claims that play is necessarily good at all times. Similarly, the PRA exercise is intended to be informal and practitioners talk of the 'relaxed' nature of the research meeting. In such cases the outside facilitators are making cultural assumptions about the best milieu in which to conduct research. Mosse (1994) notes from his experiences in India that what the outsiders consider to be informal is taken by the community as an important and highly formal event.

Third, as Mosse (1994; see also Richards 1995; Thrift 1998) warns, Western models of cognition assume that knowledge is mediated by language, but most knowledge is non-linguistic, tacit and generated in practice. The weakness of PRA is that it relies heavily on linguistic representation of knowledge (the diagrams provide a talking point or the results are written into a report), which is probably not amenable to such explicit codification. Hence much of what is important is left unknown. As Robinson-Pant (1995: 80–1) observes, various PRA techniques 'represent a way of thinking that may be peculiarly Western ... we can all see, but do not necessarily understand or interpret diagrams in the same way'. In this way research is biased away from local knowledge from the start, because only the opinions of locals who are conversant in such media are heard. In particular, Katz (1993: 104) observed, while working in Sudan that 'boys tend to exceed girls in spatial and mathematical ability', which in turn prejudices the results and decisions based upon them. Goebel (1998) argues that for PRA to move onwards it needs to allow local people to generate their own categories, concepts and criteria for understanding and changing their lives. I return to this point in the third section.

Leading on from this is the construction of texts and the authority this imposes. Such problems are also part of the 'economism' of development agencies whereby 'soft' information has to be made acceptable through its pseudo-scientism to hardened decision-makers. Dogbe (1998) on Ghana and Moser and Holland (1998) on Jamaica discuss this problem of translation, where the openness and subjectivity of the PRA findings need to be made intelligible to a sceptical audience in the major development institutions. Again, these practices represent wider ways of apprehending the non-West. In discussing ethnography in Africa, Kanneh (1999) argues that the production of 'the text' gives legitimacy to the subconscious knowledge of the informants. In doing this the ethnographer-researcher assumes that the people being researched lack the capacity for self-analysis and that only s/he can truly 'decode' and 'interpret' reality for them. Kanneh (1999: 18), echoing Spivak, adds: 'This system of unequal exchange has significant repercussions for a project of knowledge which is founded upon literacy. If written representation effectively erodes the chosen self-representation of another, how can ethnographical writing allow another to speak for herself?' In much the same way the findings of PRA are translated and interpreted by the researcher, which undermines the value of local knowledge. It also raises questions about 'chosen self-presentation', which I return to below in discussing alternative criteria and methods for PRA.

Identity, scale and politics In this part of the section I argue that the focus on the personal and local as the sites of empowerment and knowledge circumscribes consciousness and action. Participatory research assumes that local knowledge will reverse the previous interventions, which treated locals as passive recipients. However, the reversal has almost been complete, so that subjectivity and the locality are reified as the only valid political sites. For example, Chambers (1997: 14) acknowledges the 'many levels' of causality within underdevelopment, but chooses to focus on 'the primacy of the personal'. This reductionism is at odds with the increasingly globalizing tendencies of many economic and social processes. As Dirlik (1994: 336) notes, 'local interactions take priority over global structures in the shaping of these relationships, which implies they are better comprehended historically in their heterogeneity than structurally in their fixity'. This returns us to earlier discussions regarding the politics of hybridity–subjectivity versus more overt forms of action and resistance.

The participatory research agenda assumes that the insider/outsider division is the most important problem blocking meaningful development. By revealing our self-conscious appreciation of this we place ourselves back at the centre of the (under)-development process and therefore reinscribe the authorial voice, because only 'we' can really change things. As Rahnema (1990: 213) notes, they 'express this superiority by the very fact that we recognize and respect the validity of traditional knowledge, whereas nobody else does'. The familiar character of the Westerner as enlightened and omnipotent saviour reappears while the emphasis on (under)-development as cultural difference ignores the materiality of the development process.

The corollary is that by valorizing the local and being self-critical of our colonizing knowledge 'we' behave as if we do not have anything to offer. The populist line treats all knowledge from 'the West' as tainted (Young 1990; Goebel 1998) and prevents genuine dialogue and learning; even though in practice, as we have seen, facilitators intervene, which biases knowledge away from locals. This homogenizing and demonizing of Western discourses repeats earlier criticisms of Orientalism in that 'everything that originates in Europe should be consigned so unilaterally to the "heritage of imperialism", unless we subscribe to an essentialist notion of an undifferentiated "Europe" where everything and everyone is imperialist' (Ahmad 1995: 5). I return to a more hybridized conceptualization of knowledge below.

Another effect of 'going local' is that the state seems to disappear. The liberal assumption of participatory research is that better research will make bureaucrats more aware and in touch with locals so that appropriate development ensues (Rew 1985). This belief is based upon a technocratic view of the state, in which it is a 'black box' that responds to 'inputs' in a balanced and rational manner. Such an assumption ignores the ways in which the state has manipulated civil society and used 'the local' as a political discourse that disempowers. For example, colonial indirect rule and the apartheid system were at one level about celebrating and politicizing local difference in order to govern, but their corollary was that they fragmented opposition and fuelled divisions between 'ethnic' groups (Young 1988). What is needed is a more critical view of the state and central–local relations.

Alternative Possibilities of Going Local

In this third and concluding section I take on the preceding criticisms and examine the possibility of moving beyond them. So far we have seen in much participatory research and development a re-authorizing of knowledge whereby assumptions are made regarding the separate rationalities of the insider and outsider. Linked to this is an assumed homogeneity within communities, which encourages a localism and populism that leaves structural constraints relatively untouched. So are there ways of moving beyond participation as currently practised and bringing about deepened empowerment? Clearly there are problems, many acknowledged by practitioners themselves, with orthodox approaches to participatory research, but researchers and NGOs have been attempting to move beyond them. This section serves as an extended conclusion on alternative possibilities whereby I interweave general theoretical observations with my own, based on the work of Village AiD (VA) in West Africa.

Radicalizing hybridity One over-arching criticism of participatory research is that it assumes a dualistic notion of knowledge-generation. Following from postcolonialism, we can overcome this by using concepts such as liminality and hybridity, but avoid the reductionism that treats these as an 'ahistorical eternal present' (Goss 1996: 244) or collapses all hybridity into a romanticized form of resistance (Gates 1991). This can be done by simultaneously studying up, down and sideways (Schrijvers 1995; Mitchell 1997). Most participatory approaches tend to study down to the local level, but more transformative approaches would also study the global economy and transnational organizations such as the major development agencies and be prepared to criticize bad practice.

Participatory development could follow those notions of hybridity that acknowledge that inequalities of power exist, but looks at this productively rather than attempting to minimize a differential which cannot be readily removed. The first move is to acknowledge that those we view as powerless are not. Rahnema (1992) argues that '(t)heirs is a different power which is not always perceived as such, and cannot be actualized in the same manner, yet it is very real in many ways [it] is constituted by the thousands of centres and informal networks of resistance which ordinary people put up' (Rahnema 1992: 123; see also Scott 1990). Although such a recognition can be 'politically conservative' (Brass 1995), it helps to move us beyond the patronizing attitudes that 'they' need to be empowered according to our agenda. As Grossberg (1996, cited in Thrift 1997: 150) asserts, we need to give up 'notions of resistance that assume a subject standing entirely outside of and against a well-established structure of power'. Having begun from this ontological position the possibilities for a more transformative agenda are established.

In terms of research (Fine 1994; Schrijvers 1995) we need to move beyond the bounded notions of self/other and insider/outsider. Katz (1992: 504) argues that 'this is not a project of getting "others" to speak as all knowing subjects of others ... but rather to undermine this very construction and recognize that none of us are all knowing subjectivities'. This presents a very different starting point from most participatory research, which posits bounded subjectivities and, concomitantly, discrete realms of knowledge. Melhuus (1995: 106) adds that '[s]ome things can perhaps *not* be explained within the terms set by the society under study', which opens a place for our own, guilt-free analysis. As Fine (1994) puts it, we need to 'work the hyphen' between dualisms because it is within these inter-subjective worlds that meaning, knowledge and political action will emerge.

We have seen that PRA never really overcame this problem largely because while 'they' may become subjects we never lose our grip of being the originating subject. So if we are to move towards more dialogic research that involves 'a different type of relation, a different balance, between the researcher herself, the "subject" of research, and whatever is being researched, the "object"' (Arnfred 1995: 3) then the researcher him/herself must become an object of research, which may involve reversing the roles of researcher and researched. As Schrijvers (1995: 25) asserts, 'all parties create room to make explicit their points of view so that they can exchange and discuss their interpretations – among which are the images of each other and of the power relations at stake'. This strategy assumes that knowledge is generated inter-subjectively and does not *a priori* privilege one form of knowledge as more complete or essentially more appropriate.

Goebel (1998) demonstrates this in her work with resettlement communities in Zimbabwe. She shows that gender and religion are important axes of social conflict, but in neither case are these beliefs and practices lodged in enclosed and static lifeworlds: '"indigenous knowledge" or "traditional practices" should not be constructed as part of a dichotomy, with "western ideas" as the other half. It is more useful to investigate the outcome of the interaction of the "western" and the "indigenous" [since] there is very little called "indigenous" that does not have something "western" implicated in it' (1998: 294). Such a recognition opens up the possibility of constructive dialogue where 'we' do have something to offer.

One of the stumbling-blocks in the application of participatory development has been the imposition of evaluation and monitoring criteria for projects that reflect the concerns and priorities of the non-local organizations (Goebel 1998). Hence there is a real need to pursue methods that put in place criteria that are locally meaningful. VA has begun to do this in developing the REFLECT approach to literacy pioneered by Action Aid. In sharing learning with Action Aid regarding the widened application of PRA, VA argues that the application of PRA often carries flaws 'not in theory, but in practice. This is [because] PRA tools ... are developed according to values, communication capacities and processes (which are themselves politically driven), and agendas of outsiders. So, albeit indirectly, people do not have control of their literacy and political processes' (Village AiD 1998: 11). Instead they are working not to 'regenerate', but to explore the potential of 'self-generated literacy' through a programme called *Arizama*, which is a Dagbani word roughly translating as 'dialogue'. Still working within the REFLECT paradigm, this involves the identification, adoption and adaptation (where necessary) of indigenous facilitation methods, such as dance, song and story-telling. This process can be extended from communications within communities to that between them, and thereby challenge the damaging localism inherent in much participatory development.

Rescaling politics Having introduced less essentialist conceptions of knowledge and geo-political power, the space is opened for rescaling political action that moves beyond the locality. As Guijt and Shah (1998: 3) observe, 'participatory processes have been increasingly approached as technical, management solutions to what are basically political issues'. A more useful approach acknowledges the political nature of participatory development and the conflicts that this necessarily involves. In this regard it would be wrong to treat the state as separate from 'the local' and/or necessarily venal since the state can still protect and effect socially beneficial change. This suggests that 'local' action must simultaneously address the non-local. As Nyamugasira (1998: 297) observes, NGOs 'have come to the sad realization that although they have achieved many micro-level successes, the systems and structures that determine power and resource allocations – locally, nationally, and globally – remain largely intact'. Recent interventions have begun to deal with these limitations by looking at strategies for 'scaling up' local interventions (Blackburn and Holland 1998). Only by linking participatory approaches to wider, and more difficult, processes of democratization, anti-imperialism and feminism will long-term changes occur. For example, Whaites (1998: 346) argues that NGOs should 'also seek to build up the capacity of the state *as an integral part* of this localized, grassroots work' (emphasis in original) rather than creating parallel or alternative welfare systems outside of the state.

In terms of political interventions, VA's Cameroon programme works with an organization that represents the Mbororo Fulani in North West Province. The political situation is complex: the government is attempting to suppress ethnically based regional movements and local commercial interests are further marginalizing these people. In such a situation it is impossible not to deal with political conflict. The local organization, MBOSCUDA, is an NGO but is heavily involved in the anti-government and pro-democracy movements so that it receives sustained attack by the state. VA recognized that 'the deeper issues of marginalisation were central themes to address – not simply manifest "problems" of specific material needs' (Village AiD 1997: 3). In response its programme aims to link together various NGOs through traditional fora that aim to engender 'institutions of self-representation and advocacy' based upon complex psychological, emotional and cultural issues. Although in its early stages (14 months), the programme is largely about political empowerment within the state structures so that participation involves democracy and human rights rather than technical issues of material security. There is also a longer-term aim of linking communities together so that more concerted pressure can be placed upon the state, other powerful institutions of development and traditional social structures.

This leads us into the question of commitment. Although the 'rapid' in RRA has been replaced by 'participation', there remains an emphasis on short-term involvement. VA is dealing with this by moving, as it says, 'beyond participation' through a programme that seeks to end the supplicant' relationship between the NGO and villagers. It seeks to develop a situation where 'village communities set the agenda and outside agencies become responsive' (Village AiD 1996: 8). For VA participation is much more than confirming some pre-given agenda or increasing the efficiency of institutional policy-makers. It starts from the recognition that its role is not to impose external criteria for development intervention but to work with existing social realities. The process is long-term and involves 'a willingness to work with a community over many years' (ibid.: 10).

Much of this involves the notion of 'capacity-building' so that communities are able to demand action from the Northern development agency, whose role is responsiveness. The aim of VA is to move beyond traditional 'capacity-building', which strengthens the areas that ensure the success of pre-determined interventions set by the development agency. Hence more general capacity issues are being addressed where the outcomes are less circumscribed by a rigid project framework. This need has been identified by local communities who 'complained that a particular project undertaken in the past had not been a high priority for the village, but was undertaken at the suggestion of an NGO' (ibid.:7). The reversal of this begins by building upon what exists in the community, which involves acknowledging and working with traditional facilitators rather than using a rigid PRA framework for appraisal and monitoring. In the longer term it is hoped that 'this whole capacity building process is about confidence in the village in order to say "No" to organizations that do not meet the village's requirements' (ibid.: 14).

This still leaves the problem that any intervention, even one that seeks to overturn existing decision-making structures, can be criticized for 'originating' the process and thereby 'colonizing' social change. While this is clearly a potential hazard, the themes outlined in this chapter – our common subjugation to increasingly global material forces and the possibility of transformative dialogues – make the need and likelihood of collaborative alternatives more urgent and pressing.

11

Participation as Spiritual Duty; Empowerment as Secular Subjection

Heiko Henkel and Roderick Stirrat

Introduction

Since the mid-1980s, words such as 'participation', 'empowerment', 'bottom-up planning', and 'indigenous knowledge' have become increasingly common in the world of development. Such is their popularity that by the early 1990s every major bilateral development agency emphasized participatory policies. It is now difficult to find a development project that does not in one way or another claim to adopt a 'participatory' approach involving 'bottom-up' planning, acknowledging the importance of 'indigenous' knowledge and claiming to 'empower' local people. It is, we think, increasingly possible to talk of an emerging new orthodoxy in the world of development that is shared by a majority of practitioners involved in the bilateral, multilateral or non-governmental sectors of the development industry (Stirrat 1997). Even so, it has to be said straight away that there is no systematic ideology underlying this new orthodoxy. Rather it consists of a set of loosely connected ideas and approaches developed in response to what its proponents see as an older misguided orthodoxy of development. Moreover, the prominence of 'participatory approaches' is not confined to the field of development alone. It figures centrally in the post-socialist political theory of the 1980s and 1990s, notably in what has become known as 'New Social Movements' and, maybe more surprisingly, is a key term in recent management theory, which talks in terms of participation and empowerment of employees and customers (Gee et al. 1996).

Although, at least traditionally, anthropology has been very sceptical about the 'applied' usage of its discipline, anthropology (or rather, perhaps, a significant number of anthropologists) has played an interesting part in this 'participatory turn' in the development business. Because the object of anthropology has been traditionally defined as the study of 'non-European' societies, or more to the point, of the non-modern aspects of these societies, it is not surprising that anthropologists have been sceptical of the modernizing aspirations of development interventions. Much more influential than this 'sceptical' stance, however, has been the growing involvement of anthropologists in development projects as 'cultural consultants'. Starting in the late 1970s, a number of anthropological studies began to produce a body of literature that Hoben (1982) has argued clarifies 'the unique features of the social and cultural landscape or the institutional context of development issues' in the 'developing societies'. In the words of Lucy Mair (1984), anthropologists represented a new kind of specialist who, through the specific knowledge of the local culture 'can help those who are trying to make things better to avoid making them worse'. In the 1980s what is often called 'Development Anthropology' became an increasingly significant branch of anthropology both in terms of employment and in terms of academic interests. Development Anthropology, while taking the 'modern' setting of the development encounter as its arena, is nevertheless usually concerned with the 'native' side of that encounter, showing 'like a magnifying glass ... village life in greater detail and thereby reveal[ing] far more complexity of organization, thought, and behaviour than was apparent from afar' (Hoben 1982: 367).

However valuable the contributions of Development Anthropology undoubtedly are, this chapter takes a different perspective. We are here concerned with the practices, ideas and, if you like, the cosmologies of those who plan and practise 'development' projects. What we attempt is thus a contribution to an 'Anthropology of Development', and as such an anthropology if not of Europe, certainly of one of the 'frontiers' of the modern project.

In this anthropological endeavour, we take our investigations along two lines. One is an analysis of the discourse, and to some extent of the practice, of what we see as the new orthodoxy in development. This line of inquiry is based both on many years of 'participant observation' in the development world by one of the authors of the chapter and on the preliminary analysis of central texts of this new orthodoxy. The other line we follow in this chapter is an investigation into the genealogy of one of the key concepts of the new orthodoxy – participation – and the way this concept is related to empowerment.

Such a genealogical perspective is necessary, we think, for at least two reasons. First, perhaps opposed to a deep-rooted anthropological prejudice, we think the genesis of social practices and discourses is generally of crucial importance for an understanding of them. Second, and specifically related to our project of an 'Anthropology of Development', we suggest that this project is threatened by the very 'familiarity' of its object. The 'exotic' nature of the societies anthropologists normally study provides a crucial heuristic device, that is, the implicit juxtaposition of these societies with the Western way of life. In other words, one major contribution of anthropology to the social sciences has been its endeavour – sometimes implicit, at other times more explicit – by making visible and understandable exotic societies, to show that our own categories, customs and institutions are not so much 'natural' but specific and culturally contingent. An Anthropology of the West, and more specifically of Development, thus has to take this 'lack' into consideration as a disadvantage. This lack of a missing differential, we suggest, can be met by a historical perspective as an alternative device of *Verfremdung*.

The New Orthodoxy

As we have already pointed out, the most obvious mark of the 'new orthodoxy' is that its proponents set themselves up in opposition to older approaches to development work. These older concepts, they often point out, are embedded in the context of grand, and by now disavowed, narratives of 'progress', seeing development in terms of modernization theory (or theories of socialist liberation, for that matter). Within such a context development necessarily involves the 'developing' or 'underdeveloped' world (i.e. the sites of development interventions) becoming 'modern' (i.e. like the West or, more generally, the North). In contrast, the new orthodoxy stresses the cultural diversity of societies and points out that the 'Western way of life' is neither universally desirable nor inevitable.

The participatory turn in development was marked by volumes such as Cernea's *Putting People First* (1991), and Chambers' *Rural Development: Putting the Last First* (1983). Since those early volumes there has been a stream of publications with more or less similar titles, all sharing a common series of themes. These include:

- *A stress on 'bottom-up' rather than 'top-down' approaches.* In part this is an approach that claims to be based on empirical analyses of development projects. It is claimed that many projects fail because they are imposed from above rather than planned and implemented by those who used to be called 'beneficiaries'. In other words, a 'bottom-up' approach to development is more rational in that it delivers the required outputs. But at the same time, a 'bottom-up' approach is also seen as being morally superior. Projects should be planned and implemented by the 'beneficiaries' and should not be imposed on 'the people'. Furthermore, there is a sense in which beneficiaries are seen as morally bound to participate.

- *A stress on empowerment.* Usually, although not always, it is argued that people are poor because they are disempowered. Through empowerment people will escape their poverty. Precisely what empowerment involves is frequently unclear, and at the same time empowerment often becomes the objective of development rather than the means towards development.
- *A stress on the marginal.* Here, what is marginal varies enormously. It can include women, the poor, ethnic minorities, almost any group of people who can in some sense or another be seen as excluded from the mainstreams of society, usually defined in terms of formal power relations.
- *A distrust of the state.* This in effect is implied in all the features so far mentioned: that the state encourages 'top-down' development; that it inhibits 'participation'; that it 'disempowers' people. But it is most manifest in terms of the present fashion for 'non-governmental organizations' or 'private voluntary organizations' of various types. Once again, the argument is mounted that they are somehow more 'efficient' than state bodies, but again there is a set of (often) implicit assumptions that NGOs somehow embody the virtues of participation and empowerment.
- *A celebration of 'local' or 'indigenous' knowledge.* In line with the stress on the marginal, on 'bottom-up' development and 'empowerment', the new orthodoxy puts great store on the efficacy of 'local' or 'indigenous' knowledge. Scientific or external technical knowledge is frequently presented as antipathetic to development and thus to be deprecated.

With the growing influence in recent years of the new orthodoxy there has, not surprisingly, also been a growing critique of the practice of participatory approaches. On the one hand are 'conservatives' (by no means always on the 'right' of the political spectrum) who claim that participatory approaches are often naive as they overstate the value of 'local knowledge' and local potential to self-determination and assert that in general the experts and the 'state' actually do know better. On the other hand there are the 'progressives' who claim that participatory policies often do not really lead to participation and empowerment. Dominant power structures in the local communities and beyond are reproduced because participatory policies tend to be naive in regard to political issues. Also it has been pointed out that participatory approaches are frequently used instrumentally as a tool for development agencies to implement their projects more efficiently rather than seeking 'real' participation from the affected community.

Both strands of critique have, we think, relevant things to say. However, our line of inquiry in this chapter is somewhat different. In short, we want to look not at what 'participation' does not do, but at what it actually does. We will argue that the specificity of 'participation' and 'empowerment' as political concepts is often overlooked by both their promoters and detractors. Instead of asking how efficient certain policies are at securing participation we want to begin to ask what kind of phenomenon 'participation' (and thus participatory approaches such as PRA) actually is in a broader anthropological perspective. We suggest that the concept of 'participation', as it is put forward in the current debate, is indeed a specific cultural concept and part of an equally specific vision of society.

Genealogies of Participation

Much of the recent success of terms such as 'participation' and 'participatory' as a prefix for development policies is due to the ambivalent connotations of the terms. As we have already pointed out, the semantic field of these terms points in two apparently very different directions. On the one hand it refers simply to people taking part in decision-making processes. In this sense it is put forward to contrast with the heavy-handed 'top-down' approaches to development that impose policies upon people – without their participation – in the name of the authority of the state or institutions such as the World Bank. On the other hand, however, 'participation' has much more far-reaching connotations involving a specific vision of society as 'communitas' and, at times, of evangelical promises of salvation.

This ambivalence in the meaning of the term today is mirrored by its history. Besides its general meaning of 'taking or being part of something' we want to point to two distinct lines of genealogy of the term 'participation', and we suggest that a closer look at these sheds light on the current usage of the term. A genealogy, as we use the term here, is not the same as an attempt at a history of the idea of 'participation', and certainly not a social history of participatory practice. What it attempts is to draw attention to some connotations of the term that once were more pertinent, but still linger on, as it were, as subterranean bases of the current usage of the concept.

The better-known historic root of the concept of 'participation' goes back to the bourgeois emancipation in Europe in the eighteenth and nineteenth centuries. 'Participation' was here both the programme and the battle-cry of the political movement of the emerging bourgeoisie claiming its share in the economic and political sphere. The other genealogy of the term 'participation', the one in which we are interested here, reaches further back and is less obvious but equally important. Participation, in its early modern usage, meant primarily the participation of man in the infinite grace of God. To point this out is not just a matter of polemics but is also important in understanding the suggestive power of the term in current usage.

The concept of participation, in this context, is obviously endowed with a highly spiritual aroma, understandable only in the context of intricate theological attempts to explicate the relationship between God and the believers. Participation in the religious context, however, was not only an abstract theological concept. It had very concrete impacts on early modern society especially as it became a key issue in the Reformation movement. In the Reformation, the idea of 'participation' became salient on the level of theology and liturgical practice and as an overarching administrative principle. As is well known, the most important and far-reaching initial reforms of the Reformation were the shift from Latin as the language of religion and the claim that everybody should read the holy text themselves. Luther's translation of the bible from Latin into German in 1522 (and its further spread into other languages, first European and then beyond), made it possible to participate in the direct reading of the holy text.

This radical reform was accompanied by many other changes in theology and liturgy (for example, in the full participation of the congregation in the sacraments such as bread and wine). A major reform that is particularly interesting for us is the radical remaking of the bureaucratic structure of the Protestant Church. The (theoretically) strict – and indeed global – hierarchy of the Catholic Church was replaced by a far more decentralized administrative structure. One central aspect of this reform was the so-called 'subsidiarity principle', which states that all decisions that can be taken at subsidiary levels of the hierarchy should be taken at these levels, and that only those of overarching importance should be decided by the higher ranks. The Catholic Church, in contrast, championed, as it were, a strongly 'top-down' approach in its organization and minor and local issues were often decided in Rome. The theological background of this administrative reform is that while in the Catholic Church the lower ranks are representatives of the higher (and the Pope of God himself), in the Protestant Church the relationship between the believer and God is not mediated by the clerical hierarchy but is direct.

The legacy of these reforms can be felt today in surprising places. The subsidiarity principle, for example, has become prominent again in recent years as an administrative principle in the European Union to guarantee the highest possible degree of decentralization. Its origin in Protestant ecclesiastical law is seldom recognized. But to return to the theme of this chapter, the Protestant Reformation not only made the direct participation of the believer possible, but placed a moral imperative on participation. To be a good Christian required participation: in reading the scriptures, in participating in the liturgy, in governing the Church. Salvation was to be attained through individuals actively participating in the duties of the community.

In the British case we can trace this moral imperative through the nineteenth-century history of working-class non-conformity. Friendly societies, the cooperative movement, trade unions, the Labour Party, all to a greater or lesser extent grew out of non-conformist religious backgrounds. Active participation in the life of the chapel was paralleled by involvement in a series of more or less secular organizations. Throughout these organizations the dominant theme is of a moral imperative for individuals to participate actively in the creation of communities of believers. Not surprisingly many of the most prominent contemporary British development NGOs (Oxfam, SCF, Christian Aid) were founded by non-conformists or people with non-conformist roots.

We are tempted of course to explore further the relationship between religion and Enlightenment thinking but space (and competence) rule such a project out of court. However, there is one general point we think worth stressing. It is historical orthodoxy that the Enlightenment led eventually to the secularization of European society, that is to the confinement of religion to the private sphere while reason gained a privileged place in the public sphere (see Dumont 1971 among others). But it is also important to recognize the degree to which seemingly completely secularized concepts such as 'development', 'science', 'reason', and of course 'participation' bear marks of religiosity. They form elements in more or less closed systems of belief; systems of world-ordering knowledge. They thus become the objects of passionate belief and defence.

Thus the concept of 'participation' is rooted in a specific tradition and has distinct religious overtones, although it appears today in a completely secularized way. The concept of participation as it is used in contemporary development discourse is a culturally specific concept rather than a matter of universal common sense. Moreover, participation is not only – in some senses not even in the first place – a right, but also a duty. This is true not just for the Protestant reformers of the sixteeenth century, and the enlightenment social reformers of the eighteenth and nineteenth centuries, but also for the practitioners of the new orthodoxy in development.

Participation as Religious Experience

One of the common ways development workers have of characterizing themselves is in terms of the 'mercenaries, missionaries and misfits'. In actual practice these distinctions do not work too well: most people in the development world fit uneasily into these categories and at different times, even on the same day, fit different stereotypes. But if the proponents of the older orthodoxies of development are only too frequently dismissed as mercenaries (highly paid experts living in luxury hotels travelling in air-conditioned vehicles and taking home huge cheques in exchange for poor advice), the adherents of the new orthodoxy present themselves in a very different way. Not for them the luxury of international hotels nor the pleasures of development tourism; rather direct contact and indeed identification with the poor of the world.

Perhaps the best-known exponent of the 'new orthodoxy', at least in the UK, is Robert Chambers, who has published widely on the topic and has been extremely active in running seminars and workshops around the world. Not only has the quality of his work marked him out as a major figure in development thought and practice, but his charismatic personality has ensured that his message has had a wide and effective impact throughout the world.

Given the volume of his writings it is difficult to know where to start an analysis from, but most of the major themes in Chambers' work can be found in his recent volume, *Whose Reality Counts? Putting the Last First* (Chambers 1997). Reading this and his other works the first thing that strikes one is how Chambers' view of the world is structured in terms of binary oppositions: rich versus poor; powerful versus powerless; male versus female; urban versus rural, and so on. One recent example of this approach can be found in his essay, 'The primacy of the personal' (Chambers 1996). Here in a summary diagram he sums up how he appears to see the world: as a set of simple oppositions that can be diagrammed as two 'dimension/ context' columns, 'North Uppers' and 'South Lowers' (see Table 11.1). Furthermore, these oppositions are not value-free but heavily value-laden. Implicitly 'North Uppers' are morally bad; 'South Lowers' are morally good.

Given this way of seeing the world, the way forward is quite obvious. In order to change the world the existing series of oppositions has to be reversed – hence 'Putting the Last First'. Yet reversal, for Chambers, is not simply a matter of what he calls 'slot-rattling': the same structure but changed personnel. Rather, what he is calling for are 'reversals which neutralize forces of dominance and liberate, allowing freedom for relationships in all directions' (Chambers 1996: 243–4).

TABLE 11.1 North–south upper–lower relationships

Dimension/context	North Uppers	South Lowers
Spatial	Core (urban, industrial)	Periphery (rural, agricultural)
International and development	The North IMF, World Bank Donors Creditors	The South Poor countries Recipients Debtors
Personal ascriptive	Male White High ethnic or caste group	Female Black Low ethnic or caste group
Life cycle	Old person Parent Mother-in-law	Young person Child Daughter-in-law
Bureaucratic organization	Senior Manager Official Patron Officer Warden, guard	Junior Worker Supplicant Client 'Other rank' Inmate, prisoner
Social, Spiritual	Patron Priest Guru Doctor, psychiatrist	Client Lay person Disciple Patient
Teaching and learning	Master Lecturer Teacher	Apprentice Student Pupil

Source: Chambers (1996: 243)

Precisely what Chambers is advocating at this point is a little unclear, but for the moment let us stick with reversals. What we find particularly striking here is the way in which Chambers' call for 'reversals' as the means to attain development is remarkably reminiscent of many religious movements that seek to find salvation in the imminent future. Throughout the Christian tradition, 'The World Turned Upside Down' has been a continual theme of religious activism, reversals being both the means to attain the goal of salvation and a defining characteristic of salvation. So too with cargo cults in Melanesia, which are characterized through their attempts to gain salvation (a reversal of the present worldly order) through inversions of that order. What Chambers appears to be saying is that the tools to reverse the inequalities and power differentials that characterize 'underdevelopment' are themselves those reversals.

If Chambers' stress on reversals evokes a certain religious tradition, so too do his thoughts on how such reversals are to be attained. While not denying the weight of institutional and organizational inertia and the constraints they place on change, Chambers sees the way forward as being through personal conversion. What have to be changed, he claims, are personal attitudes: the self, which is 'ego, ambition, family-first motivation and the illusion of impotence' (Chambers 1995: 7). Once the self has been changed, he argues, so too can the practice of development and that somewhat shadowy salvation (the objective of development) be attained. What is required of practitioners is an experience akin to that St Paul underwent on the road to Damascus, and this, it is implied, is to be achieved through the correct practice of Participatory Rural Appraisal, which 'has often brought personal change for those who facilitate it' (Chambers 1995: 9). Indeed, personal salvation becomes synonymous with an identification of the self with what appears to be his implicit goal of development. And one could go further. If Chambers had read the work of Victor Turner then the latter's ideas of communitas (Turner 1974) would, we are sure, have found their place within Chambers' theology of development.

In sum, it seems to us that Chambers is advocating an approach to development that is remarkably akin to what is conventionally called 'religion'. One is continually reminded of Geertzian notions of religion as a model of and a model for behaviour; of the importance of morality and personal conversion (Geertz 1966). This is evident not only in Chambers' writings but also in the workshops he runs or is involved in. Attendance at these events is in many ways reminiscent of revivalist religious meetings. Participants are encouraged (one might say forced) to think in particular ways; control is exercised in such a way that participants appear to be controlling themselves; individuals attest to their conversion; sinners admit their faults before they saw the light.

Yet given the roots of the concept of participation that we have tried to outline earlier, the missionary habitus of Robert Chambers and his followers is both stunning and unsurprising: they are heirs to a long history of religious activism. The dualistic cosmos of good and evil, the importance of reversals, the significance of personal conversion and the role of the community of believers are no accidents but intrinsic attributes of an old and powerful heritage.

Of course, this is all somewhat unfair, and in many ways Chambers' work represents what we would agree is a major change for the better in development thinking. But then, we too share something of Chambers' religious outlook. And while Chambers is remarkably open about the provisional nature of his methods and the need for continual rethinking of concepts and methods, not so many of his followers, who have in effect 'routinized' the teachings of the prophet. This involves a stress on formulaic performance of particular methods and of arguments between those who can claim an immediate position in the apostolic succession and those whose relation to Chambers is less direct. Even mild questioning of Chambers' teaching can produce the most extreme reactions on the part of his followers and the damning of the heretic.

Empowerment

So far we have argued that 'participation' has its origins in the sphere of what is conventionally called 'religion', and that today's proponents of participation are, in some sense, heirs to a protestant tradition. We now want to turn to one of the major claims of the new orthodoxy: that its interventions will 'empower' the beneficiaries of development projects. Our intention here is not so much to dismiss these claims but rather to point to what we see as important implications of 'participatory' approaches. In a nutshell, our argument is that the empowerment the proponents of the new orthodoxy seek to secure through 'participation' might not be so straightforwardly liberating as it appears. Indeed, we suggest that what the new orthodoxy boldly calls 'empowerment' might be in effect very similar to what Michel Foucault calls 'subjection' (Foucault 1980).

Returning for a moment to the world of the Protestant Reformation, one of the continuing claims made by the reformers was that the forms of religiosity they were expounding were in some sense empowering: they freed the faithful from the 'slavery of Rome' and allowed them direct contact with God. In practice of course various other forms of religious authoritarianism were introduced, yet if we follow writers such as Weber or Marx, what the Reformation did was to empower people in very different ways from those envisaged by Luther, Calvin, Zwingli or other reformers. In the contemporary world, participation as an administrative or political principle eases authoritative force, in turn placing responsibility on the 'participants'. In the language of discourse theory, participatory approaches 'afford' certain subject positions to the participants, and thus, to some extent, presuppose and shape 'participants' from the very beginning. But this is done in ways not always foreseen by exponents of participation. It is in this sense that we suggest that participation, counter-intuitive though it may seem, is a form of governance – in fact the ultimate modern form.

Among the numerous participatory approaches to development, PRA (Participatory Rural Appraisal), closely associated with Robert Chambers, stands out as an archetype of the new orthodoxy. The basic features of PRA have become so widely known in recent years that it is hardly necessary to present them here again. Good summaries are available in Chambers' writings (Chambers 1994a, 1994b, 1994c) while other writers (e.g. Brown 1997; Leurs 1996; and Mosse 1994) provide useful critiques.

PRA is rather specific in that it is presented as a methodology that facilitates 'participation' and 'empowerment' not with reference to a specific development project, but rather as a universal methodology, applicable in any situation. The PRA approach centres around an institutionalized, communal construction of visual representations of reality, i.e. the construction of graphics such as maps, matrixes, diagrams and calendars. PRA, so its proponents often claim, leads to the 'empowerment' of local people by giving them both the means to analyse the problems of their communities on their own terms and a voice *vis-à-vis* external policy-makers such as politicians and development experts.

PRA displays a peculiar ambivalence about the role of the PRA graphics. On the one hand it is sometimes suggested that the construction of these graphics is a neutral technology that simply visualizes an already existent 'local reality'. This, however, does not mean that practitioners of PRA adopt a simple positivist approach involving the assumption that a 'true' version of reality exists that can be discovered and visualized in the graphics. On the contrary, the whole PRA approach is based on the assumption that there are different versions of 'reality' depending from which perspective one looks at it. How the graphics are drawn, PRA stresses over and over again, depends fundamentally on who is actually drawing them. PRA thus emphasizes that the teacher or the 'experts' have to step back and let the local people draw their own maps and diagrams. Only when everybody in the circle has had the possibility to contribute and a consensus is reached are the graphics transferred to paper and made permanent. But, and this is crucially important, the framework that is supplied by the PRA method is very clearly set by PRA documents. The participants are expected to draw their 'own' maps, matrices, etc. The framework of these representations, however, is never in question.

Proponents of PRA often argue that '[T]he process of map construction, discussion and literacy had given them [the participants] new insights into the progress of their lives and the problems they faced' and that these insights 'encompassed the different social roles they played as domestic, reproductive, productive and community players' (Archer and Cottingham 1996: 53). What is interesting in this statement and what is claimed again and again in the PRA literature is that the practice of constructing the graphics (within the institutional frame of the PRA circles) is a neutral technology. It simply helps to analyse reality and leads to a more rational attitude of people in a similar way in all the culturally divergent contexts PRA is applied to.

If we take, for example, the apparently most straightforward and unproblematic starting point of the PRA process, the community map, a critical perspective quickly makes clear the specificity of the PRA perspective. Mapping, as Nigel Penn points out, is an instrument of knowledge production and thus woven into the power structures of society. 'The mapper, in mapping, simultaneously exercises power over the charted terrain and gains enormous empowerment through having assimilated it as a field of knowledge' (Penn 1993: 22). Usually, as in Penn's case, the 'empowerment' that derives from the construction of maps is that of the European colonizer or the central administration mapping the social space to gain control over subaltern populations. In the case of PRA, as we have seen, this process is apparently inverted and it is the subaltern who gains 'power' through mapping the social space. But the sorts of knowledge involved and the types of empowerment generated are by no means all identical. The geographer John Brian Harley points out that maps are not just depictions of the morphological landscape, nor are they passive reflections of the world of objects:

> Instead they are 'refracted images contributing to dialogue in a socially constructed world … Both in the selectivity of their content and in their

styles of representation maps are a way of conceiving, articulating, and structuring the human world which is biased towards, promoted by, and exerts influence upon particular sets of social relations'. (Harley 1988: 278, quoted in Penn 1993)

In a historical perspective the map in its modern form began to emerge in the fifteenth century, not coincidentally in a period that is often seen as the beginning of modern history. Its predecessors, notably the itineraries of the Middle Ages, ordered space in a very different way. The modern map is the work of the cartographer, whose gaze comes from an abstract position outside the depicted landscape, while the itinerary depicts the experience of the traveller traversing the landscape. While the former depicts space as a structure, the latter visualizes space as a process. Both space itself and the position of the subject towards this space are represented in radically different ways in these two kinds of maps.

Another, contemporary, example of a different representation of space are the 'maps' made by Australian aboriginal artists (Cowan 1994). The most striking point here is that while the 'Western' map privileges the visual, the paintings of aboriginal 'cartographers' represent a mythical landscape where the visible and invisible become inseparable. In the aboriginal 'maps' what is thus made visible is what cannot otherwise be seen and the 'cartographer' figures as agent in this process. In the Western case, on the other hand, the cartographer acts as witness of what is already visible. In the case of the Western map, drawn for example in the PRA circles, consensus governs the achievement of the 'right' result. Its measure is thus the ability to represent a common view and it opens up the local to the global view. In the case of the aboriginal map its function lies essentially in its individuality. The secret knowledge of the artists inscribes in the map what cannot be common sense, hence the 'scandal' of exhibiting these 'maps'/paintings in international art galleries that render global what is inherently local.

What all of these 'maps' have in common is that they depict what seems important in the cultural context of their production, but what counts as important is radically different in all of them. What follows from this juxtaposition of different kinds of 'maps' is, we suggest, that different kinds of visual representations of space are crucially dependent on their cultural context, their institutional frame and their purpose. They are therefore culturally specific or 'ideological'.

The right of the participants to 'draw their own maps' in the PRA circles gives them indeed some kind of ownership. But as we have already pointed out, it is also crucial to recognize that to a large extent PRA already presupposes the frame of what can and cannot be done as it canonizes the kinds of visualizations acceptable. PRA does allow local variations of the Western version of the map to be drawn. But it prescribes, indeed presupposes, what kind of map is normal. The same thing applies in a similar way for all the matrices, diagrams and calendars of PRA. PRA, as it were, provides the grid: the local people can fill it in as they like. What PRA does through its various supposedly neutral visual techniques is to encourage a particular way of seeing, understanding and representing the world, which derives from the world of the PRA 'expert'.

Mapping, the dominant visual element in PRA practice, is only the most obvious aspect of the way in which PRA (and by extension other aspects of participatory approaches) encourages and generates a particular way of thinking and of organizing social life. The whole process of 'community mapping' is dependent, implicitly, on a concept of the social that is based on individuals entering into a form of social contract with each other and denies pre-existing forms of hierarchy, dependency or powerlessness. Upon this basis the whole apparatus of 'modern' society – committees, officials, elections, and so on – is constructed.

Seen in this light, the question that arises with regard to empowerment is not so much 'how much' are people empowered but rather 'for what' are they empowered. And in the case of many if not all participatory projects it seems evident that what people are 'empowered to do' is to take part in the modern sector of 'developing' societies. More generally, they are being empowered to be elements in the great project of 'the modern': as citizens of the institutions of the modern state; as consumers in the increasingly global market; as responsible patients in the health system; as rational farmers increasing GNP; as participants in the labour market, and so on. Empowerment in this sense is not just a matter of 'giving power' to formerly disempowered people. The currency in which this power is given is that of the project of modernity. In other words, the attempt to empower people through the projects envisaged and implemented by the practitioners of the new orthodoxy is always an attempt, however benevolent, to reshape the personhood of the participants. It is in this sense that we argue that 'empowerment' is tantamount to what Foucault calls subjection.

Conclusion

What we have tried to show here in a rather preliminary fashion is how participatory approaches to development, far from marking a radical shift away from an ethnocentric concept of modernity, are intimately part of the process of modernization itself. In fact, we argue, they might provide even more effective ways of incorporating people into the 'modern project' compared to those available to the 'old orthodoxy'.

Having important roots in the world of religion, contemporary participatory approaches to development display an ambivalence towards the 'beneficiaries' of their interventions strikingly similar to that of their Christian predecessors. Notwithstanding the fact that missionaries and Christian reformers of the past were often deeply concerned about the well-being of their flock, we know today how important their activities were in integrating populations into the fold of the nation-state and the system of colonial rule. In a strikingly similar way, we suggest, the projects of the new development orthodoxy tend to integrate the beneficiaries of their projects into national and international political, economic and ideological structures – incidentally, structures about which the people concerned generally have very little control.

In an important sense, what the new orthodoxy and older forms of development intervention are attempting to do is much the same as each other. Both are trying to change hearts and minds; both are trying to make people 'modern'. But while old-fashioned top-down modernizers were generally aware of what they were trying to do and open about their objectives, followers of the new orthodoxy are perhaps less aware of their objectives, or at least of the results of their activities. One of the attractions of the participatory approach to the development industry is that it shifts responsibility for the consequences of these projects away from the agencies and the development workers onto the participating people. By disowning the process they initiate, development agencies thus set themselves up as only 'facilitating'. In other words, the authors and practitioners of PRA tend to avoid the necessity for taking on responsibility for the outcomes of their interventions. But perhaps it is time that the often pervasive implications of even the most democratic and 'bottom-up' policy interventions were once again made central to the agenda of the development industry and its professionals. If this is so, however, what we urgently need is more knowledge and better tools of analysis not so much of the people 'out there' who are to be developed or empowered, but of the whole process of 'development': its discourses, institutions and practices; in other words, an Anthropology of Development.

Such an anthropological perspective on development might at times be at odds with 'development anthropology', which sees itself as part of the intervention. But more importantly, we think, the increasing involvement of anthropologists in the development industry can also constitute a real chance to address some of the problems discussed in this chapter. Given that practitioners of development often have important and singular insights into the development encounter it could be a crucial role for anthropologists working in development to make these insights available for a broader debate. In this way they could not only make development interventions more adequate and 'participatory', but could contribute to a greater level of self-reflexivity about development interventions. Such self-knowledge on the side of development agencies, it seems to us, is the precondition not only for taking greater responsibility for these interventions but ultimately also for ongoing conversations about the ends and means of development interventions between the development professionals and those whose lives are affected by them.

Acknowledgements

This chapter was originally presented as a paper at the University of Edinburgh in 1996. The authors wish to thank all those who have commented on the paper, and Stirrat would like to thank the ESRC, which supported some of the research on which it is based.

Bibliography

Acharya, B., Y. Kumar, V. Satyamurti and R. Tandon (1998) 'Reflections on Participatory Evaluation – the PVOH-II Experience', *Participation and Governance*, Vol. 5, No. 11, 11–16 March.

Adams, W., E. Watson and S. Mutiso (1997) 'Water Rules and Gender: Water Rights in an Indigenous Irrigation System, Marakwet, Kenya', *Development and Change*, Vol. 28, pp. 707–30.

Ahmad, A. (1994) *In Theory: Classes, Nations, Literatures*, Verso, London.

— (1995) 'The Politics of Literary Postcoloniality', *Race and Class*, Vol. 36, No. 3, pp. 1–20.

— (1997) 'Postcolonial Theory and the Post-Condition', in L. Panitch (ed.), *Socialist Register*, Merlin Press, London, pp. 353–81.

Allen, T. (1997) 'Housing Renewal – Doesn't it Make you Sick?', paper presented to HSA Conference, York University, 15–16 April.

Allen, V. L. (1971) *The Sociology of Industrial Relations*, Longman, London.

Allport, G. (1968) 'The Historical Background of Social Psychology', in G. Lindzey and E. Aronson (eds), *The Handbook of Social Psychology*, Random House, New York.

Alvesson, M. and H. Willmott (1996) *Critical Management Studies*, Sage, London.

Anthony, P. D. (1977) *The Ideology of Work*, Tavistock, London.

Apthorpe, R. (1997) 'Writing Development Policy and Policy Analysis Plain or Clear: On Language, Genre and Power', in C. Shore and S. Wright (eds), *Anthropology of Policy: Critical Perspectives on Governance and Power*, Routledge, London and New York.

Arce, A. and N. Long (1992) 'The Dynamics of Knowledge: Interfaces Between Bureaucrats and Peasants', in N. Long and A. Long (eds), *Battlefields of Knowledge: the Interlocking of Theory and Practice in Social Research and Development*, Routledge, London and New York.

Archer, D. and S. Cottingham (1996) 'Action Research Report on REFLECT: Regenerated Freirian Literacy Through Empowering Community Techniques: the Experiences of Three REFLECT Projects in Uganda, Bangladesh, El Salvador', *Overseas Development Administration Education Research Series*, No. 17, ODA, London.

Argyris, C. (1970) *Intervention Theory and Method, A Behavioural Science View*, Addison Wesley, Reading, MA.

Arkin, A. (1999) 'Return to Centre', *People Management*, 6 May, pp. 47–50.

Armstrong, M. (1999) *A Handbook of Human Resource Management*, Kogan Page, London.

Arnfred, S. (1995) 'Introduction', in S. Arnfred (ed.), *Issues of Methodology and Epistemology in Postcolonial Studies*, International Development Studies, Roskilde University, Occasional Paper No. 15, Roskilde University, Denmark, pp. 1–11.

Arora, D. (1994) 'From State Regulation to People's Participation: The Case of Forest Management in India', *Economic and Political Weekly*, Vol. XXIX, No. 12, pp. 691–8, 19 March.

Ashcroft, B., G. Griffiths and H. Tiffin (eds) (1995) *The Post-colonial Studies Reader*, Routledge, London.

Aycrigg, M. (1998) 'Participation and the World Bank: Successes, Constraints and Responses', Discussion Draft prepared for the International Conference on Upscaling and Mainstreaming Participation of Primary Stakeholders: Lessons Learned and Ways Forward, *World Bank Social Development Papers*, No. 29, Environmentally and Socially Sustainable Development Network, Washington, DC, November.

Bales, R. F. (1950) *Interaction Process Analysis: A Method for the Study of Small Groups*, Addison Wesley, Reading, MA.

Bastian, S. and N. Bastian (eds) (1996) *Assessing Participation: A Debate from South Asia*, Konark, Delhi.

Batliwala, S. (1994) 'The Meaning of Women's Empowerment: New Concepts Form Action' in G. Sen, A. Germain and L. Chen (eds), *Population Policies Reconsidered: Health, Empowerment and Rights*, Harvard University Press, Boston, MA.

Bebbington, A. (1994) 'Theory and Relevance in Indigenous Agriculture: Knowledge, Agency and Organisation', in D. Booth (ed.), *Rethinking Social Development: Theory, Research and Practice*, Longman Scientific and Technical, Harlow.

Bell, S. (1994) 'Methods and Mindsets: Towards an Understanding of the Tyranny of Methodology, *Public Administration*, Vol. 14, pp. 323–38.

Bezkorowajnyj, P. G., S. Jones, J. N. Khare and P. S. Sodhi (1994) 'A Participatory Approach to Developing Village Tree Programmes: The KRIBP Experience', *KRIBP Working Papers*, Centre for Development Studies, Swansea.

Bhabha, H. (1983) 'Difference, Discrimination, and the Discourse of Colonialism', in F. Barker (ed.), *The Politics of Theory*, University of Essex, Colchester, pp. 194–211.

— (1984) 'Of Mimicry and Man: The Ambivalence of Colonial Discourse', *October*, 28, Spring, pp. 125–33.

— (1995) [original 1985] 'Signs Taken for Wonders: Questions of Ambivalence and Authority Under a Tree Outside Delhi, May 1817', in B. Ashcroft et al. (eds), *The Post-Colonial Studies Reader*, Routledge, London, pp. 29–35.

Biggs, S. (1989) 'Resource-poor Farmer Participation in Research: a Synthesis of Experience from Nine National Agricultural Research Systems', *OFCOR Project Study*, No. 3, ISNAR, The Hague.

— (1995a) *Participatory Technology Development: A Critique of the New Orthodoxy*, Olive Information Service, AVOCADO series 06/95, Durban.

— (1995b) 'Participatory Technology Development: Reflections on Current Advocacy and Past Technology Development', paper prepared for the workshop 'Participatory Technology Development (PTD)', Institute of Education, London, March.

Biggs, S. and G. Smith (1998) 'Beyond Methodologies: Coalition-building for Participatory Technology Development', *World Development*, Vol. 26, No. 2, pp. 239–48.

Blackburn, J. and J. Holland (1998) 'General Introduction', in J. Blackburn with J. Holland (eds), *Who Changes? Institutionalizing Participation in Development*, IT Publications, London, pp. 1–8.

Blake, R. R. and J. S. Mouton (1964) *Managing Intergroup Conflict in Industry*, Gulf, Houston.

Blunt, P. (1995) 'The Cultural Limits of Process Consulting in Development Assistance', in R. D. Reineke and R. Sulzer (eds), *Management Consultancy in Developing Countries*, Gabler, Berlin.

Blyton, P. and P. Turnbull (1994) *The Dynamics of Employee Relations*, Macmillan, London.

Bond, R. and D. Hulme (1999) 'Process Approaches to Development: Theory and Sri Lankan Practice', *World Development*, Vol. 27, No. 8.

Boreham, P. (1992) 'The Myth of Post-Fordist Management: Work Organisations and Employee Discretion in Seven Countries', *Employee Relations*, Vol. 14, No. 2, pp. 13–24.

Bourai, V. A., S. R. Bahadur, K. M. Panwa and K. M. Mishra (1997) 'Props for Research', *PLA Notes*, No. 28, IIED, London, p. 91.

Bourdieu, P. (1977) *Outline of a Theory of Practice*, Cambridge University Press, Cambridge.

Bracewell, M. (1998) 'Be Small Again', *Guardian*, 22 August, pp. 26–7.

Brass, T. (1995) 'Old Conservatism in "New" Clothes', *Journal of Peasant Studies*, Vol. 22, No. 3, pp. 516–40.

Braverman, H. (1974) *Labour and Monopoly Capital: The Degradation of Work in the Twentieth Century*, Monthly Review Press, New York.

Brett, E. A. (1996) 'The Participatory Principle in Development Projects: The Costs and Benefits of Participation', *Public Administration and Development*, Vol. 16, pp. 5–19.

Brinkerhoff, D. W. and J. M. Coston (1999) 'International Development Management in a Globalized World', *Public Administration Review*, Vol. 59, No. 4, pp. 346–61.

British Institute of Management (1979) *Participation, Democracy and Control: Forms of Employee Involvement*, BIM Report No. 45, London.

Brown, D. (1994) 'Seeking the Consensus: Populist Tendencies at the Interface between Research and Consultancy', paper presented at the workshop *From Consultancy to Research*, University of Wales, Swansea.

— (1997) 'Professionalism, Participation and the Public Good: Issues of Arbitration in Development Management and the Critique of the Neo-populist Approach', paper presented at Public Sector Management for the Next Century conference, University of Manchester.

— (n.d.) 'Strategies of Social Development: Non-Government Organisation and the Limitations of the Frierean Approach', *The New Bulmershe Papers*, Department of Agricultural Extension and Rural Development, University of Reading.

Burke, W. W. (1987) *Organization Development – A Normative View*, Addison Wesley, Reading, MA.

Burke, W. W. and H. A. Hornstein (1971) *The Social Technology of Organization Development*, NTL, Fairfax, VA.

Burns, T. and R. M. Stalker (1961) *The Management of Innovation*, Tavistock, London.

Byrne, D. (1995) 'Radical Geography as Mere Political Economy: the Local Politics of Space', *Capital and Class*, Vol. 56, pp. 117–38.

Calás, M. and L. Smircich (1997) *Postmodern Management Theory*, Dartmouth, Aldershot.

Campbell, A. (1997) *Western Primitivism: African Ethnicity*, Cassell, London.

Campbell, J. (1968) *The Hero with the Thousand Faces*, Princeton University Press, Princeton, NJ.

Cernea, M. M. (ed.) (1991) *Putting People First: Sociological Variables in Rural Development*, 2nd edn, Oxford University Press for World Bank, New York.

Certeau, M. de (1985) 'Practices of Space', in M. Blonsky (ed.) *On Signs*, Blackwell, Oxford.

Chabal, P. (1996) 'The African Crisis: Context and Interpretation', in R. Werbner and T. Ranger (eds),*Postcolonial Identities in Africa*, Zed Books, London, pp. 29–54.

Chambers, R. (1983) *Rural Development: Putting the Last First*, Longman, London.

— (1992) 'Rural Appraisal: Rapid, Relaxed, and Participatory', *IDS Discussion Paper* 311, Institute of Development Studies, University of Sussex.

— (1993) *Challenging the Professions: Frontiers for Rural Development*, IT Publications, London.

— (1994a) 'The Origins and Practice of Participatory Rural Appraisal', *World Development*, Vol. 22, No. 7, pp. 953–69.

— (1994b) 'Participatory Rural Appraisal (PRA): Analysis and Experience', *World Development*, Vol. 22, No. 9, pp. 1253–68.

— (1994c) 'Participatory Rural Appraisal (PRA): Challenges, Potentials and Paradigm', *World Development*, Vol. 22, No. 10, pp. 1437–54.

— (1995) 'Paradigm Shifts and the Practice of Participatory Research and Development', in N. Nelson and S. Wright (eds), *Power and Participatory Development*, pp. 19–29.

— (1996) 'The Primacy of the Personal', in M. Edwards and D. Hulme (eds), *Beyond the Majic Ballet*, Kumarian Press, West Hartford.

— (1997) *Whose Reality Counts? Putting the First Last*, IT Publications, London.

Chang, J. (1991) *Wild Swans*, HarperCollins, London.

Christoplos, I. (1995) 'Representation, Poverty and PRA in the Mekong Delta', EPOS Environment Policy and Society, *Research Report*, No. 6, Linköping University, Sweden.

CIIR (1995) *Women and Aid in the Philippines: Management or Empowerment*, CIIR, London.

Clarke, M. (1999) 'Management Development as a Game of Meaningless Outcomes', *Human Resource Management Journal*, Vol. 9, No. 2, pp. 38–49.

Cleaver, F. (1995) 'Water as a Weapon: The History of Water Supply Development in Nkayi District, Zimbabwe', *Environment and History*, Vol. 1, pp. 313–33, White Horse Press, Cambridge.

— (1996) 'Community Management of Rural Water Supplies in Zimbabwe', unpublished PhD thesis, University of East Anglia, Norwich.

— (1998a) 'Gendered Incentives and Institutions: Women, Men and the Management of Water', *Journal of Agriculture and Human Values*, Vol. 15, No. 4, December.

— (1998b) 'There's a Right Way to Do it – Informal Arrangements for Local Resource Management', *WATERLINES*, Vol. 16, No. 4, April.

— (2000) 'Moral Ecological Rationality: Institutions and the Management of Common Property Resources', *Development and Change*, Vol. 31, No. 2, March.

Cleaver, F. and Kaare, B. (1998) *Social Embeddedness and Project Practice: A Gendered Analysis of Promotion and Participation in the Hesawa Programme, Tanzania*, University of Bradford for SIDA, June.

Cleaver, F. and I. Lomas (1996) 'The 5% '"Rule": Fact or Fiction?' *Development Policy Review*, Vol. 14, No. 2, June, pp. 173–84.

Clegg, H. A. and T. E. Chester (1954) 'Joint Consultation', in H. A. Clegg and A. Flanders (eds), *The System of Industrial Relations in Great Britain*, Blackwell, Oxford, pp. 28–51.

Cohen, R. (1991) *Contested Domains: Debates in International Labours Studies*, Zed Books, London.

Cohen, R., P. Gutkind and P. Brazier (eds) (1979) *Peasants as Proletarians: Struggles of Third World Workers*, Hutchinson, London.

Cohen, S. (1985) *Visions of Social Control*, Polity Press, Cambridge.

Cooke, B. (1997) 'From Process Consultation to a Clinical Model of Development Practice', *Public Administration and Development*, Vol. 17, pp. 325–40.

— (1998) 'Participation, "Process", and Management: Lessons for Development in the History of Organisation Development', *Journal of International Development*, Vol. 10, No. 1, pp. 35–55.

Cornwall, A. (1998) 'Gender, Participation and the Politics of Difference', in I. Guijt and M. Shah, *The Myth of Community: Gender Issues in Participatory Development*, IT Publications, London.

Correa, M. (1995) *Gender and Joint Forest Planning and Management: A Research Study in Uttara Kannada District, Karnataka*, India Development Service, New Delhi.

Cotton, J. L. (1993) *Employee Involvement: Methods for Improving Performance and Work Attitudes*, Sage, London.

Cowan, J. (1994) *Myths of the Dreaming: Interpreting Aboriginal Legends*, Prism Press, Bridport.

Craig, D. and D. Porter (1997) 'Framing Participation: Development Projects, Professionals and Organisations', *Development in Practice*, Vol. 7, No. 3, pp. 229–36.

Croft, S. and P. Beresford (1996) 'The Politics of Participation', in D. Taylor (ed.), *Critical Social Policy: A Reader*, Sage, London.

Crompton, R., D. Gallie and K. Purcell (eds) (1996) *Changing Forms of Employment: Organisations, Skills and Gender*, Routledge, London.

Crush, J. (ed.) (1995) *Power of Development*, Routledge, London.

Davis, N. and B. Anderson (1983) *Social Control: The Production of Deviance in the Modern State*, Irvington, NY.

Deere, C. and M. Leon (1998) 'Gender, Land and Water: From Reform to Counter Reform in Latin America', *Journal of Agriculture and Human Values*, Vol. 15, No. 4, December.

Dirlik, A. (1994) 'The Postcolonial Aura: Third World Criticism in the Age of Global Capitalism', *Critical Inquiry*, Vol. 20, pp. 328–56.

Dogbe, T. (1998) ' "The One Who Rides The Donkey Does Not Know The Ground is Hot": CEDEP's Involvement in the Ghana PPA', in J. Holland with J. Blackburn (eds), *Whose Voice? Participatory Research and Policy Change*, IT Publications, London, pp. 97–102.

Douglas, M. (1987) *How Institutions Think*, Routledge and Kegan Paul, London.

Drago, R. and M. Wooden (1991) 'The Determinants of Participative Management', *British Journal of Industrial Relations*, Vol. 29, No. 2, pp. 177–204.

Dumont, L. (1971) 'Religion, Politics and Society in the Individualistic Universe', *Proceedings of the Royal Anthropological Institute for 1970*, pp. 31–41.

Dwivedi, O. P. and J. Nef (1982) 'Crises and Continuities in Development Theory and Administration: First and Third World Perspectives', *Public Administration and Development*, Vol. 2, No. 1, pp. 59–77.

Dyer, W. G. (1987) *Team Building Issues and Alternatives*, Addison Wesley, Reading, MA.

Ecologist, The (1993), *Whose Common Future? Reclaiming the Commons*, Earthscan, London.

Edwards, M. (1999) 'NGO Performance: What Breeds Success? New Evidence from South Asia', *World Development*, Vol. 27, No. 2, pp. 361–74.

Escobar, A. (1995) *Encountering Development: the Making and Unmaking of the Third World*, Princeton University Press, Princeton, NJ.

Fals-Borda, O. (1998) *People's Participation: Challenges Ahead*, IT Publications, London.

Fals-Borda, O. and M. A. Rahman (1991) (eds) *Action and Knowledge: Breaking the Monopoly with Participatory Action Research*, IT Publications, London.

Farrington, J. and A. Bebbington with K. Wellard and D. J. Lewis (1993) *Reluctant Partners? Non-Governmental Organisations, the State and Sustainable Agricultural Development*, Routledge, London.

Feeney, P. (1998) 'Gender, Equity and Exclusion in the Western Ghats', in P. Feeney, *Accountable Aid: Local Participation in Major Projects*, Oxfam Publications, Oxford.

Ferguson, J. (1994) *The Anti-politics Machine: 'Development', Depoliticization and Bureaucratic Power in Lesotho*, University of Minnesota Press, Minneapolis.

Fine, M. (1994) 'Working the Hyphens: Reinventing Self and Other in Qualitative Research', in N. Denzin and Y. Lincoln (eds), *Handbook of Qualitative Research*, Sage, London, pp. 70–82.

Folbre, N. (1996) 'Engendering Economics: New Perspectives on Women, Work and Demographic Change' in M. Bruno and B. Pleskovic (eds), *Annual World Bank Conference on Development Economics*, World Bank, Washington, DC.

Foucault, M. (1973) *The Order of Things: The Archaeology of Human Sciences*, Vintage, New York.

— (1977) *Discipline and Punish: The Birth of the Prison*, Penguin, Harmondsworth.

— (1979) *The History of Sexuality: An Introduction*, Penguin, Harmondsworth.

— (1980) *Power/Knowledge: Selected Interviews and Other Writings*, Harvester Wheatsheaf, Brighton.

Fowler, A. (1997) *Striking a Balance: A Guide to Enhancing the Effectiveness of NGOs in International Development*, Earthscan, London.

Francis, P. and S. Jacobs (1999) 'Institutionalising Social Analysis at the World Bank', in C. Kirkpatrick and N. Lee (eds), *Integrated Appraisal and Decision Making*, Special issue of *Environmental Impact Assessment Review*, Vol. 19, pp. 341–57.

Freire, P. (1973) *Education for Critical Consciousness*, Seabury Press, New York.

Friedman, A. (1977) *Industry and Labour: Class Struggle at Work*, Macmillan, London.

Gates Jr., H. (1991) 'Critical Fanonism', *Critical Inquiry*, Vol. 17, pp. 457–70.

Gee, J. P., G. Hull and C. Lankshear (1996) *The New Work Order: Behind the Language of the New Capitalism*, Westview Press, Boulder, CO.

Geertz, C. (1966) 'Religion as a Cultural System', in M. Banton (ed.), *Anthropological Approaches to the Study of Religion*, Tavistock, London.

Giddens, A. (1982) *Profiles and Critiques in Social Theory*, University of California Press, Berkeley.

— (1984) *The Constitution of Society: Outline of the Theory of Stucturation*, Polity Press, Cambridge.

Gilroy, P. (1993) *The Black Atlantic: Modernity and the Double Consciousness*, Verso, London.

Goebel, A. (1998) 'Process, Perception and Power: Notes from "Participatory" Research in a Zimbabwean Resettlement Area', *Development and Change*, Vol. 29, pp. 277–305.

Goetz, A.-M. (1996) 'Local Heroes: Patterns of Field Worker Discretion in Implementing GAD Policy in Bangladesh', *IDS Discussion Paper*, No. 358, University of Sussex.

Goffman, E. (1997) 'The Presentation of Self in Everyday Life', in C. Lemert and A. Branaman (eds), *The Goffman Reader*, Blackwell, Oxford.

Goss, J. (1996) 'Postcolonialism: Subverting Whose Empire?', *Third World Quarterly*, Vol. 17, No. 1, pp. 239–50.

Granovetter, D. (1992) 'Economic Action and Social Structure: The Problem of Embeddedness', in M. Granovetter and R. Swedburg (eds), *The Sociology of Economic Life*, Westview Press, Oxford.

Gueye, B. (1995) 'Development of PRA in Francophone Africa', in IIED (ed.), *PLA Notes*, No. 24, pp. 70–3.

Guha, R. (1982) 'On Some Aspects of the Historiography of Colonial India', in R. Guha (ed.), *Subaltern Studies I: Writings on South Asian History and Society*, Oxford University Press, New Delhi, pp. 1–8.

Guijt, I. and A. Cornwall (1995) 'Critical Reflections on the Practice of PRA', in IIED (ed.), *PLA Notes*, No. 24, pp. 2–7.

Guijt, I. and M. Shah (1998) *The Myth of Community: Gender Issues in Participatory Development*, IT Publications, London.

Handy, C. (1985) *Understanding Organizations*, Penguin, London.

Harvey, J. B. (1979) 'The Abilene Paradox: the Management of Agreement', in J. L. Gibson, J. M. Ivancevich and J. H. Donelly, *Readings in Organizations*, Business Publications, Dallas.

Hirst, P. and G. Thompson (1992) 'The Problems of Globalisation: International Economic Relations, National Economic Management, and Trading Blocs', *Economy and Society*, Vol. 21, No. 4, pp. 359–95.

Hobart, M. (ed.) (1993) *An Anthropological Critique of Development: The Growth of Ignorance*, Routledge, London and New York.

Hoben, A. (1982) 'Anthropologists and Development', *Annual Review of Anthropology*, Vol. 11, pp. 349–75.

Hofstede, G. (1991) *Cultures and Organisations: Software of the Mind*, McGraw Hill, London.

Hyman, J. and R. Mason (1995) *Managing Employee Involvement and Participation*, Sage, London.

IASCP (1998) *Crossing Boundaries: Book of Abstracts*, Seventh Conference of the International Association for the Study of Common Property, 10–14 June, Simon Fraser University, Vancouver.

IIED (ed.) (1995) *PLA Notes*, No. 24, special issue on 'Critical Reflections from Practice', Sustainable Agriculture Programme, IIED, London.

— (1997) 'Methodological Complementarity', *Notes on Participatory Learning and Action*, No. 28.

IILS/UNDP (1997) *Social Exclusion and Anti-Poverty Strategies: Project on the Patterns and Cases of Social Exclusion and the Design of Policies to Promote Integration. A Synthesis of Findings*, International Institute for Labour Studies/United Nations Development Programme, Geneva.

Illich, I. (1990) *Tools for Conviviality*, Marion Boyars, London.

INTRAC (1998) *ONTRAC: The Newsletter of the International NGO Training and Research Centre*, No. 10, August.

IPA/IPM (1990) *Code of Practice on Employee Involvement and Participation*, London.

Jackson, C. (1998) 'Social Exclusion and Gender: Does One Size Fit All?', *European Journal of Development Research*, Vol. 11, No. 1, p. 125–46.

Jackson, C. and R. Pearson (eds) (1998) *Feminist Vision of Development: Gender Analysis and Policy*, Routledge, London.

Janis, I. L. (1982) *Groupthink: Psychological Studies of Policy Decisions and Fiascos*, revised and enlarged edn, Houghton Mifflin, Boston, MD.

— (1991) 'Groupthink', in D. Kolb, I. R. Rubin and J. S. Osland, *The Organisational Behaviour Reader*.

Jarman, J. and C. Johnson (1997) *WAMMA: Empowerment in Practice*, A WaterAid Report, WaterAid, London.

Jermier, J., D. Knights and W. R. Nord (1994) *Resistance and Power in Organisations*, Routledge, London.

Jobes, K. (1998) 'PME under the Spotlight: a Challenging Approach in St Vincent', *Waterlines*, Vol. 16, No. 4, pp. 23–5.

Jones, S., J. Witcombe and D. Mosse (1995) 'The Development Choice between High and Low Potential Areas', *KRIBP Working Paper*, No. 7, Centre for Development Studies, University of Wales, Swansea.

Jones, S., J. N. Khare, D. Mosse, P. Smith, P. S. Sodhi and J. Witcombe (1994) 'The Kribhco Indo-British Rainfed Farming Project: Issues in the Planning and Implementation of Participatory Natural Resource Development', *KRIBP Working Paper*, No. 1, Centre for Development Studies, University of Wales, Swansea.

Joy, L. and S. Bennett (n.d.) *Process Consultation for Systemic Improvement of Public Sector Management*, United Nations Development Programme, New York.

Kanneh, K. (1999) *African Indentities: Race, Nation and Culture in Ethnography, Pan-Africanism and Black Literatures*, Routledge, London.

Kaplan, R. (1994) 'The Coming Anarchy', *The Atlantic Monthly*, Vol. 273, No. 2, February, pp. 44–76.

Katz, C. (1992) 'All the World is Staged: Intellectuals and the Projects of Ethnography', *Environment and Planning D: Society and Space*, Vol. 10, pp. 495–510.

— (1993) 'Growing Girls/Closing Circles: Limits on the Spaces of Knowing in Rural Sudan and US cities', in C. Katz and J. Monk (eds), *Full Circles; Geographies of Women over the Life Course*, Routledge, London, pp. 88–106.

Khan, N. A. and S. A. Begum (1997) 'Participation in Social Forestry Re-examined: a Case Study from Bangladesh', *Development in Practice*, Vol. 7, No. 3, pp. 260–6, August.

Khare, A. (n.d.) 'Western Ghats Forest and Environment Project/Himachel Pradesh Forestry Project', *ODA Overview of Participatory Forest Management*, ODA, London.

Kolb, D., I. R. Rubin and J. S. Osland (1991) *The Organisational Behaviour Reader*, Prentice Hall, New Jersey.

Kothari, U. (1996) 'Development Studies and Post-colonial Theory', *IDPM Discussion Paper*, No. 46, IDPM, University of Manchester.

Lemert, C. and A. Branaman (eds) (1997) *The Goffman Reader*, Blackwell, Oxford.

Leurs, R. (1996) 'Current Challenges Facing Participatory Rural Appraisal', *Public Administration and Development*, Vol. 16, pp. 57–72.

Lewin, K. (1946) 'Action Research and Minority Problems', *Journal of Social Issues*, Vol. 2, pp. 34–46.

Lewis, I. M. (1971) *Ecstatic Religion: an Anthropological Study of Spirit Possession and Shamanism*, Penguin Books, Harmondsworth.

Li, T. M. (1996) 'Images of Community: Discourse and Strategy in Property Relations', *Development and Change*, Vol. 27, pp. 501–27.

Likert, R. (1961) *New Patterns of Management*, McGraw Hill, New York.

Lincoln, Y. S. and E. G. Guba (1985) *Naturalistic Inquiry*, Sage Publications, Newbury Park.

Lippitt, R. (1949) *Training in Community Relations*, Harper, New York.

Lohmann, L. (1991) 'Who Best Defends Biological Diversity: The Politics of Conservation', *The Ecologist*, Vol. 21, No. 1, January/February.

— (1994) 'Incentives and Disincentives for Bank Staff and Other Institutional Matters', Presentation at *Consultation on the World Bank Forest Policy Implementation Review*, London.

Long, N. (1992) 'From Paradigm Lost to Paradigm Regained?: The Case for an Actor Orientated Sociology of Development', in N. Long and A. Long (eds), *Battlefields of Knowledge*, pp. 16–43.

Long, N. and A. Long (eds) (1992) *Battlefields of Knowledge: The Interlocking of Theory and Practice in Social Research and Development*, Routledge, London.

Long, N. and M. Villareal (1994) 'The Interweaving of Knowledge and Power in Development Interfaces', in I. Scoones and J. Thompson (eds), *Beyond Farmer First: Rural People's Knowledge, Agricultural Research and Extension Practice*, IT Publications, London.

Loomba, A. (1998) *Colonialism/Post-colonialism*, Routledge, London.

McCourt, W. (1998) ' "The Bloody Horse": Indigenous and Donor Prescriptions for Civil Service Reform in Sri Lanka', *IDPM Discussion Paper*, No. 54, Institute for Development Policy and Management, University of Manchester.

MacFarquhar, R. and J. K. Fairbank (1987) *The Cambridge History of China: The People's Republic*, Part 1, Cambridge University Press, Cambridge.

McGee, R. (forthcoming) 'Participating in Development', in U. Kothari and M. Mingoue (eds), *Development Theory and Practice: Critical Perspectives*, Macmillan, London.

McNay, L. (1994) *Foucault: a Critical Introduction*, Polity, Cambridge.

Mair, L. (1984) *Anthropology and Development*, Macmillan, London.

Marchington, M. et al. (1992) *New Developments in Employee Involvement*, Education Dept, Research Series No. 2, Department of Employment, London.

Marx, K. (1959) *Capital. Vol. 1*, Lawrence and Wishart, London (first edn in English 1887).

Matthews, J. (1989) *The Age of Democracy: The Politics of Post-Fordism*, Oxford University Press, Melbourne.

Mayo, E. (1933) *The Human Problems of Industrial Civilization*, Macmillan, New York.

Mayoux, L. (1995) 'Beyond Naivety: Women, Gender Inequality and Participatory Development', *Development and Change*, Vol. 26, pp. 235–58.

Melhuus, M. (1995) 'The Role of Fieldwork and Construction of Anthropological Knowledge Today', in S. Arnfred (ed.), *Issues of Methodology and Epistemology in Postcolonial Studies*, International Development Studies, Roskilde University, Occasional Paper No. 15, Roskilde University, pp. 91–109.

M'Gonigle, R. M. (1997) 'Behind the Green Curtain', *Alternatives*, Vol. 24, No. 3, Fall.

Milimo, J., A. Norton and D. Owen (1998) 'The Impact of PRA Approaches and Methods on Policy and Practice: the Zambia PPA', in J. Holland with J. Blackburn (eds), *Whose Voice? Participatory Research and Policy Change*, IT Publications, London, pp. 103–11.

Mitchell, K. (1997) 'Different Diasporas and the Hype of Hybridity', *Environment and Planning D: Society and Space*, Vol. 15, pp. 533–53.

Mitra, A. (1997) *Oxfam JFPM Support Project Uttara Kannada: An Evaluation of First Phase Work*, Oxfam (India) Trust, New Delhi, February.

Mohan, G. (1999) 'Not so Distant, Not so Strange: the Personal and the Political in Participatory Research', *Ethics, Place and Environment*, Vol. 2, No. 1, pp. 41–54.

Mohanty, C. T., A. Russo and L. Torres (eds) (1991) *Third World Women and the Politics of Feminism*, Indiana University Press, Bloomington, ON.

Morgan, G. (1990) *Organisations in Society*, Macmillan, London.

Moser, C. and J. Holland (1998) 'Can Policy-focused Research be Participatory? Research on Violence and Poverty in Jamaica using PRA Methods', in J. Holland with J. Blackburn (eds) *Whose Voice? Participatory Research and Policy Change*, IT Publications, London, pp. 44–56.

Moser, C. and P. Sollis (1991) 'Did the Project Fail? A Community Perspective on a Participatory Primary Health Care Project in Ecuador', *Development in Practice*, Vol. 1, No. 1, pp. 19–33.

Mosse, D. (1994) 'Authority, Gender and Knowledge: Theoretical Reflections on the Practice of Participatory Rural Appraisal', *Development and Change*, Vol. 25, pp. 497–526.

— (1995) 'Social Analysis in Participatory Rural Development', in *PLA Notes*, No. 24, IIED, London.

— (1997) 'History, Ecology and Locality in Tank-Irrigated South India', *Development and Change*, Vol. 28, pp. 505–30.

Mosse, D., T. Ekande, P. Sodhi, S. Jones, M. Mehta and U. Moitra (1995) 'Approaches to Participatory Planning: a Review of the KRIBP Experience', *KRIBP Working Paper*, No. 5, Centre for Development Studies, University of Wales, Swansea.

Mosse, D. (with the KRIBP project team) (1996) 'Local Institutions and Farming Systems Development: Thoughts from a Project in Tribal Western India', *ODI Agren Network Paper*, No. 64.

Mosse, D., S. Gupta, M. Mehta, V. Shah, J. Rees and the KRIBP Project Team (forthcoming) 'Brokered Livelihoods: Debt, Labour Migration and Development in Tribal Western India', in A. de Haan and B. Rogaly (eds), *Migration and Sustainable Livelihoods.*

Mudimbe, V. (1988) *The Invention of Africa: Gnosis, Philosophy, and the Order of Knowledge*, Indiana University Press, Bloomington and James Currey, London.

Murphy, W. P. (1990) 'Creating the Appearance of Consensus in Mende Political Discourse', *American Anthropologist*, Vol. 92, No. 1, pp. 24–41.

Nelson, N. (1995) 'Recent Evolutionary Theorising about Economic Change', *Journal of Economic Literature*, No. XXXIII, pp. 48–90, March.

Nelson, N. and S. Wright (eds) (1995) *Power and Participatory Development: Theory and Practice*, IT Publications, London.

Norton, A. (1998) 'Analysing Participatory Research for Policy Change', in J. Holland with J. Blackburn (eds), *Whose Voice? Participatory Research and Policy Change*, IT Publications, London, pp. 179–91.

Norton, A. and T. Stevens (1995) *Participatory Poverty Assessments*, Environment Department Participation Series, Social Policy and Resettlement Division, World Bank, Washington, DC.

Nyamugasira, W. (1998) 'NGOs and Advocacy: How Well are the Poor Represented?', *Development in Practice*, Vol. 8, No. 3, pp. 297–308.

Oakley, P. et al. (1991) *Projects with People: The Practice of Participation in Rural Development*, ILO, Geneva.

Obeyesekere, G. (1992) '"British Cannibals": Contemplation of an Event in the Death and Resurrection of James Cook, Explorer', *Critical Inquiry*, Vol. 18, Summer, pp. 630–54.

ODA (1992) *Kribhco Indo-British Rainfed Farming Project – Project Document*, August, ODA, London.

Oliver, N. and B. Wilkinson (1988) *The Japanization of British Industry*, Blackwell, Oxford.

Ostrom, E. (1990) *Governing the Commons: The Evolution of Institutions for Collective Action*, Cambridge University Press, New York.

Parry, B. (1987) 'Problems in Current Theories of Colonial Discourse', *Oxford Literary Review*, Vol. 9, Winter, pp. 27–58.

Peet, R. and M. Watts (1996) 'Liberation Ecology: Development, Sustainability, and Environment in an Age of Market Triumphalism', in R. Peet and M. Watts (eds), *Liberation Ecologies: Environment, Development and Social Movements*, Routledge, London, pp. 1–45.

Penn, N. (1993) 'Mapping the Cape: John Barrow and the First British Occupation of the Colony, 1795–1803', *Pretexts*, Vol. 4, No. 2, pp. 20–43.

Peters, P. (1987) 'Embedded Systems and Rooted Models', in B. McCay and J. A. Acheson, *The Question of the Commons*, University of Arizona Press, Tucson.

— (1996) 'Who's Local Here? The Politics of Participation in Development', *Cultural Survival Quarterly*, Vol. 20, Issue No. 3, Fall.

Peters, T. (1992) *Liberation Management: Necessary Disorganization for the Nano-Second Nineties*, Macmillan, London.

Pickard, J. (1993) 'The Real Meaning of Empowerment', *People Management*, November.

Plunkett, L. C. and R. Fournier (1991) *Participative Management: Implementing Empowerment*, John Wiley, New York.

Poole, M. (1986) *Towards a New Industrial Democracy: Workers' Participation in Industry*, Routledge and Kegan Paul, London.

Porter, D. (1994) [originally 1983] 'Orientalism and Its Problems', in P. Williams and L. Chrisman (eds), *Colonial Discourse and Post-Colonial Theory*, Harvester Wheatsheaf, New York, pp. 150–61.

Pottier, J. (ed.) (1992) *Practising Development: Social Science Perspectives*, Routledge, London and New York.

Pottier, J. and P. Orone (1995) 'Consensus or Cover-up? The Limitations of Group Meetings', in IIED (ed.), *Critical Reflections from Practice*, PLA Notes, No. 24, IIED, London, pp. 38–42.

Power, M. (1998) 'The Dissemination of Development', *Environment and Planning D: Society and Space*, Vol. 16, pp. 577–98.

Pradesh Forestry Project (n.d.) *ODA Overview of Participatory Forest Management*, ODA, London.

Pretty, J. (1994) 'Alternative Systems of Enquiry for Sustainable Agriculture', *IDS Bulletin*, Vol. 25, No. 2, pp. 37–48.

Pretty, J. N., I. Guijt, J. Thompson and I. Scoones (1995) *Participatory Learning and Action: A Trainer's Guide*, IIED Participatory Methodology Series, IIED, London.

Putnam, R. D. (1993) *Making Democracy Work: Civic Traditions in Modern Italy*, Princeton University Press, Princeton, NJ.

Quarles van Ufford, P. (1993) 'Knowledge and Ignorance in the Practice of Development Policy', in Hobart, M. (ed.) *An Anthropological Critique of Development: the Growth of Ignorance*, Routledge, London.

Rabinow, P. (1984) *The Foucault Reader*, Pantheon, New York.

Rahman, M. A. (1991) 'The Theoretical Standpoint of PAR', in O. Fals-Borda and M. A. Rahman (eds), *Action and Knowledge*, IT Publications, London.

Rahnema, M. (1990) 'Participatory Action Research: The "Last Temptation of Saint" Development', *Alternatives*, No. XV, pp. 199–226.

— (1992) 'Participation', in W. Sachs (ed.), *The Development Dictionary: A Guide to Knowledge as Power*, Zed Books, London, pp. 116–31.

Ramsey, H. (1983) 'Evolution or Cycle? Worker Participation in the 1970s and 80s', in C. Crouch and F. Heller (eds), *Organisational Democracy and Political Processes*, Wiley, London, pp. 122–47.

Rew, A. (1985) 'The Organizational Connection: Multi-disciplinary Practice and Anthropological Theory', in R. Grillo and A. Rew (eds), *Social Anthropology and Development Policy*, ASA monograph No. 23, Tavistock, London, pp. 185–97.

Richards, P. (1993) 'Cultivation: Knowledge or Performance', in M. Hobart (ed.), *An Anthropological Critique of Development: The Growth of Ignorance*, Routledge, London and New York.

— (1995) 'Participatory Rural Appraisal: A Quick and Dirty Critique', in IIED (ed.), *PLA Notes*, No. 24, pp. 13–16.

Robbins, S. P. (1998) *Organisational Behaviour: Concepts, Controversies, Applications*, Prentice Hall, Englewood Cliffs, NJ.

Robinson-Pant, A. (1995) 'PRA: A New Literacy?', in IIED (ed.) *PLA Notes*, No. 24, pp. 78–82.

Roethlisberger, F. J. and W. J. Dickson (1939) *Management and the Worker*, Harvard University Press, Cambridge, MA.

Said, E. (1979) *Orientalism*, Vintage Books, New York.

Salmen, L. F. (1987) *Listen to the People*, Oxford University Press, London.

— (1995) 'Beneficiary Assessment: An Approach Described', *World Bank Environmental Department Papers*, Social Assessment Series, No. 23, Washington, DC.

— (1998) 'Towards a Listening Bank: A Review of Best Practices and the Efficacy of Beneficiary Assessment', *World Bank Social Development Paper*, No. 23, Environmentally and Socially Sustainable Development Network, Washington, DC, September.

Sartre, J.-P. (1972) *Being and Nothingness: A Phenomenological Essay on Ontology*, Pocket Books, New York.

Saxena, N. C., J. Sarin, R. V. Singh and T. Shah (1997) 'Western Ghats Forestry Project: Independent Study of Implementation Experience in Kanara Circle', May, ODA, London.

Sayer, A. and M. Storper (1997) 'Ethics Unbound: for a Normative Turn in Social Theory', *Environment and Planning D: Society and Space*, Vol. 15, pp. 1–17.

Schein, E. H. (1961) *Coercive Persuasion*, Norton, New York.

— (1980) *Organisational Psychology*, Prentice Hall, Englewood Cliffs, NJ.

— (1987) *The Clinical Perspective in Fieldwork*, Sage, Newbury Park, CA.

— (1987a) *Process Consultation. Volume 1: Its Role in Organization Development*, Addison Wesley, Reading, MA.

— (1987b) *Process Consultation. Volume 2: Lessons for Managers and Consultants*, Addison Wesley, Reading, MA.

— (1990) *Organisational Culture and Leadership*, Jossey Bass, San Francisco.

Schrijvers, J. (1995) 'Participation and Power: a Transformative Feminist Research Perspective', in N. Nelson and S. Wright (eds), *Power and Participatory Development: Theory and Practice*, IT Publications, London, pp. 19–29.

Scott, J. (1990) *Domination and the Arts of Resistance: Hidden Transcripts*, Yale University Press, New Haven, CT.

Scott, J. C. (1985) *Weapons of the Weak: Everyday Forms of Peasant Resistance,* Yale University Press, London.

— (1998) Address to the Seventh Annual Conference of the International Association for the Study of Common Property, Vancouver, 10–14 June.

Shaw, M. E. (1971) *Group Dynamics*, McGraw Hill, New York.

Sheehan, N. (1989) *A Bright Shining Lie*, Jonathan Cape, London.

Shohat, E. and R. Stam (1994) *Unthinking Eurocentrism: Multiculturalism and the Media*, Routledge, London.

Sibley, D. (1995) *Geographies of Exclusion*, Routledge, London.

Sjoblom, D. K. (1999) 'Land Matters: Social Relations and Livelihoods in a Bhil Community in Rajasthan, India', PhD Thesis, School of Development Studies, University of East Anglia.

Smith, L. (1999) *Decolonising Methodologies: Research and Indigenous Peoples*, Zed Books, London.

Spivak, G. (1987) *In Other Worlds: Essays in Cultural Politics*, Methuen, New York and London.

— (1988) 'Can the Subaltern Speak?', in C. Nelson and L. Grossberg (eds), *Marxism and the Interpretation of Culture*, University of Illinois Press, Urbana, pp. 271–313.

— (1990) *The Post-colonial Critic: Interviews, Strategies, Dialogues*, Routledge, New York.

Starkloff, R. (1997) 'Participatory Discourse and Practice in a Water Resource Crisis in Sri Lanka', in S. Bastian and N. Bastian (eds), *Assessing Participation.*

St Clair, C. (1995) 'Canadian Aid in the Philippines', in CIIR, *Women and Aid in the Philippines: Management or Empowerment*, CIIR, London.

Stewart, S. et al. (1995) *Participatory Rural Appraisal: Abstracts of Sources. An Annotated Bibliography*, Development Bibliography 11, Institute of Development Studies, University of Sussex.

Stiefel, M. and M. Wolfe (1994) *A Voice for the Excluded: Popular Participation in Development*, Zed Books, London.

Stirrat, R. (1997) 'The New Orthodoxy and Old Truths: Participation, Empowerment and other Buzzwords', in S. Bastian and N. Bastian (eds), *Assessing Participation.*

Stoner, J. A. F. A. (1968) 'Risky and Cautious Shifts in Group Decisions: the Influence of Widely Held Values', *Journal of Experimental Social Psychology*, Vol. 4, pp. 442–59.

Storey, J. (1987) 'Developments in the Management of Human Resources: An Interim Report', *Warwick Papers in Industrial Relations*, IRRU, University of Warwick, November.

— (1995) 'Human Resource Management: Still Marching On, or Marching Out?' in J. Storey (ed), *Human Resource Management: A Critical Text*, Routledge, London, pp. 3–32.

Theis, J. and H. Grady (1991) *Participatory Rapid Appraisal for Community Development: a Training Manual Based on Experiences in the Middle East and North Africa*, IIED and Save the Children, London.

Thompson, J. (1995) 'Participatory Approaches in Government Bureaucracies: Facilitating the Process of Institutional Change', *World Development*, Vol. 23, No. 9, pp. 1521–54.

Thompson, R. (1966) *Defeating Communist Insurgency: Experiences from Malaysia and Vietnam*, Chatto and Windus, London.

Thrift, N. (1997) 'The Still Point: Resistance, Expressive Embodiment and Dance', in S. Pile and M. Keith (eds), *Geographies of Resistance*, Routledge, London.

— (1998) 'The Rise of Soft Capitalism', in A. Herod, G. O. Tuathail and S. Roberts (eds), *Unruly World: Globalization, Governance and Geography*, Routledge, London, pp. 25–71.

Tichy, N. (1983) *Managing Strategic Change: Technical, Political, and Cultural Dynamics*, Wiley-Interscience, New York.

Tiffin, C. and A. Lawson (eds) (1994) *De-scribing Empire: Post-colonialism and Textuality*, Routledge, London.

Townley, B. (1989) 'Selection and Appraisal: Reconstituting Social Relations', in J. Storey (ed.), *New Perspectives on Human Resource Management*, Routledge, London, pp. 92–108.

— (1994) *Reframing Human Resource Management: Power, Ethics and the Subject at Work*, Sage, London.

Trompenaars, F. (1993) *Riding the Waves of Culture*, Brearley, London.

Turner, V. (1974) *Dramas, Fields and Metaphors: Symbolic Action in Human Society*, Cornell University Press, Ithaca, NY.

Uphoff, N. (1992a) *Local Institutions and Participation for Sustainable Development*, Gatekeeper Series No. 3, IIED, London.

— (1992b) 'Monitoring and Evaluating Popular Participation in World Bank Assisted Projects', in B. Bhatnagar and A. Williams (eds), *Participatory Development and the World Bank*, Discussion Papers Series No. 183, Washington, DC.

Uphoff, N., M. Esman and A. Krishna (1998) *Reasons for Success: Learning from Instructive Experiences in Rural Development*, Kumarian Press, West Hartford, CT.

Valentin, C. (1999) 'Developing Critical Managers for Public and Voluntary Organisations', paper presented at University of Manchester conference 'People and Performance', June.

Village AiD (1996) 'Beyond PRA: A New Approach to Village-led Development', unpublished Business Plan, Village AiD.

— (1997) *Application Summary: Growing from Within*, Programme Documents, Village AiD.

— (1998) *Application Summary: Empowering Dagomba Women Through Social and Cultural Change*, Programme Documents, Village AiD.

Watson, T. J. (1994) *In Search of Management: Chaos and Control in Managerial Work*, Routledge, London.

Watts, M. (1995) ' "A New Deal in Emotions": Theory and Practice and the Crisis of Development', in J. Crush (ed.), *Power of Development*, pp. 44–62.

WERS (1998) *Workplace Employee Relations Survey*, DfEE/ESRC/PSI/ACAS Survey, Dartmouth Publishing, Aldershot.

Weston, W. (1999) 'The Brand's the Thing', *People Management*, 28 October.

Whaites, A. (1998) 'NGOs, Civil Society and the State: Avoiding Theoretical Extremes in Real World Issues', *Development in Practice*, Vol. 8, No. 3, pp. 343–53.

White, S. C. (1996) 'Depoliticising Development: the Uses and Abuses of Participation', *Development in Practice*, Vol. 6, No. 1, pp. 6–15.

Williams, R. (1976) *Keywords: A Vocabulary of Culture and Society*, Fontana, London.

Willis, P. (1977) *Learning to Labour: How Working Class Kids Get Working Class Jobs*, Saxon House, Farnborough.

Wood, G. (1999) 'Concepts and Themes: Landscaping Social Development', *DFID*, London.

Wood, G. D. (1981) 'The Social and Scientific Context of Rapid Rural Appraisal', *IDS Bulletin*, Vol. 12, No. 4, pp. 3–7.

— (1998) 'Consultant Behaviour: Projects as Communities: Consultants' Knowledge and Power', *Project Appraisal*, Vol. 16, No. 1, pp. 54–64.

Woodhouse, P. (1998) 'Thinking with People and Organizations: People as Informants', in A. Thomas, J. Chataway and M. Wuyts (eds), *Finding Out Fast: Investigative Skills for Policy and Development*, Open University Press, Milton Keynes.

World Bank (1994) *Internal Implementation Review*, World Bank, Washington, DC.

— (1995a) *Social Assessment*, Environment Department Dissemination Note 36, Washington, DC.

— (1995b) *Social Assessment Structured Learning: Preliminary Findings*, Environment Department Dissemination Note 37, September 1995, Washington, DC.

— (1996) *The World Bank Participation Sourcebook*, ESD (Environmentally Sustainable Development), World Bank, Washington, DC.

— (1997) *World Development Report*, World Bank, Washington, DC.

— (1998) *Social Development Update: Making Development More Inclusive and Effective*, Social Development Paper, 27, Social Development Department, World Bank, Washington, DC.

— (1999) *QAG Review Report: Social Development*, Quality Assessment Group, World Bank, Washington, DC.

Wright, S. and N. Nelson (1995) 'Participatory Research and Participant Observation: Two Incompatible Approaches', in N. Nelson and S. Wright (eds), *Power and Participatory Development*, pp. 43–59.

Yang, D. L. (1998) *Calamity and Reform in China: State, Rural Society and Institutional Change Since the Great Leap Famine*, Stanford University Press, Stanford, CA.

Young, C. (1988) 'The African Colonial State and its Political Legacy', in D. Rothchild and N. Chazan (eds), *The Precarious Balance: State and Society in Africa*, Westview Press, Boulder, CO, pp. 25–66.

Young, R. (1990) *White Mythologies: Writing History and the West*, Routledge, London.

Ziller, R. C. (1957) 'Four Techniques of Group Decision Making under Certainty', *Journal of Applied Psychology*, Vol. 41, pp. 384–8.

Zwarteveen, M. and N. Neupane (1996) *Free Riders or Victims: Women's Non-participation in Irrigation Management in Nepal's Chhattis Mauja Irrigation Scheme*, Research Report No. 7, International Irrigation Management Institute, Colombo.

Index

Development Studies Titles from Zed Books

Samir Amin, *Capitalism in the Age of Globalization: The Management of Contemporary Society*

Walden Bello, Nicola Bullard and Kamal Malhotra (eds), *Global Finance: New Thinking on Regulating Speculative Capital Markets*

Robert Biel, *The New Imperialism: Crisis and Contradictions in North/South Relations*

C. M. Correa, *Intellectual Property Rights, the WTO and Developing Countries: The TRIPS Agreement and Policy Options*

Emma Crewe and Elizabeth Harrison, *Whose Development? An Ethnography of Aid*

Bhagirath Lal Das, *An Introduction to the WTO Agreements*

Bhagirath Lal Das, *The WTO Agreements: Deficiencies, Imbalances and Required Changes*

Bhagirath Lal Das, *The World Trade Organization: A Guide to the New Framework for International Trade*

Diplab Dasgupta, *Structural Adjustment, Global Trade and the New Political Economy of Development*

Oswaldo de Rivero, *The Myth of Development: An Emergency Agenda for the Survival of Nations*

Wim Dierckxsens, *The Limits of Capitalism: An Approach to Globalization Without Neoliberalism*

Mark Duffield, *Global Governance and the New Wars: The Merging of Development and Security*

Graham Dunkley, *The Free Trade Adventure: The WTO, GATT and Globalism: A Critique*

Terence Hopkins and Immanuel Wallerstein et al., *The Age of Transition: Trajectory of the World-System, 1945-2025*

Arthur MacEwan, *Neo-liberalism or Democracy: Economic Strategy, Markets and Alternatives for the 21st Century*

John Madeley, *Big Business, Poor Peoples: The Impact of Transnational Corporations on the World's Poor*

Hans-Peter Martin and Harald Schumann, *The Global Trap: Globalization and the Assault on Prosperity and Democracy*

James Petras and Henry Veltmeyer, *Globalization: The New Face of Imperialism*

Harry Shutt, *The Trouble with Capitalism: An Enquiry into the Causes of Global Economic Failure*

Kavaljit Singh, *The Globalisation of Finance: A Citizen's Guide*

Kavaljit Singh, *Taming Global Financial Flows: Challenges and Alternatives in the Era of Financial Globalization*

Bob Sutcliffe, *A 100 Ways of Seeing an Unequal World*

Oscar Ugarteche, *The False Dilemma: Globalization: Opportunity or Threat?*

David Woodward, *The Next Crisis? Foreign Direct and Equity Investment in Developing Countries*

For full details of this list and Zed's other subject and general catalogues, please write to: The Marketing Department, Zed Books, 7 Cynthia Street, London N1 9JF, UK or e-mail: sales@zedbooks.demon.co.uk

Visit our website at: http://www.zedbooks.demon.co.uk

Printed in the United States
125823LV00002B/2/A

9 781856 497947